This book is a must-read if…

- you are interested in gaining insight into public services;

- you are interested in the history of policing and law enforcement over the last 50 years in the UK and beyond;

- you like finding out how people overcome adversity;

- you enjoy reading gritty memoirs;

- you are curious to know what it takes to step outside your comfort zone;

- you enjoy the dynamics of relationships;

- you are a baby boomer and you like reminiscing about your life;

- you are a man who is on an emotional journey;

- you are a man looking for inspiration to voice your story.

What people are saying about Colin Tansley...

I was delighted to be able to secure an advance copy of this book by the very interesting and insightful Colin Tansley.

Experience can be shared and in business and life a good fact-based book is a way of gaining insights into how others dealt with difficult situations successfully, avoided failures, and made the most of opportunity. It helps if the reference topic is interesting such as the army, the police, and the financial crime private sector. Mastering the Wolf covers the experiences of one man who has covered all three, both as an individual as well as within teams, and leading people.

Colin's memories and storytelling made me wish I'd kept meticulous records of events or had as good a memory. A young soldier, then a good copper, and then working to combat fraud and cyber risks. Iraq, Yorkshire and the Isle of Man are rarely in the same book!

As much as I enjoyed the compelling stories, I found it also helped me find and remember events in my own life that I may have forgotten and that were important learning points. Whether you are a civilian, a veteran, or a former police officer you will enjoy this book. I am sure you will find incidents and problem-solving that will resonate with what you are doing today and what you have ahead of you.

Peter Taylor
Fraud Consultant
Peter Taylor Consultants Ltd
Cheshire, UK

Colin Tansley was an outstanding Police Officer. His quiet and unassuming manner belies a smart, committed and caring individual. *Mastering the Wolf* is a courageously open book on his decades of service to his country, in both the military and the police. It provides more than an eyewitness insight into the challenges of day-to-day policing in modern history; the book reveals some the consequences of commitment to such a profession.

Those consequences are frequently underestimated and subsequently under-reported. Colin's frank self-portrayal illustrates the impact of 'the job,' on family, friends and relationships. As is his way, he never shies away from taking personal responsibility for his actions and is honest about his own weaknesses.

Policing can be addictive, not just for Police Officers performing the special privilege of the office of Constable; our television screens are littered with policing documentaries and factionary adventures every day. Whilst it can be an exciting, adrenaline fuelled experience, officers face some of the worst aspects of humanity and it would be incomprehensible to believe that does not impact upon them and their loved ones.

The caring and compassionate side of policing is well represented by Colin's writing. The calling to help others is a significant motivation for people entering the Service. That and dedication keeps special people turning up for duty whatever the weather!

Mastering the Wolf has it all, nothing is left out.

Adam Briggs
Deputy Chief Constable (Retired)

I've always said that if you want to get to know a person, read their memoirs.

Colin Tansley does not hold back in his book, *Mastering the Wolf*. From sharing his raw and inexperience as a young 16-year-old who joins the army, to stepping into manhood and the rising of his position in the police and beyond his career, to touching on the most intimate details in his private life, this is a book that I found hard to put down.

Kudos to Colin for finding the courage to share such a moving, funny and insightful story.

Mike Roberts
Managing Director
Making Digital Real (MDR)
North Yorkshire, UK

◊◊◊

This is undoubtedly one of the truest and most candid accounts of what it means to provide service. If you strip back modern technology and our fast-paced lives, what you get is our innate desire to protect our interests and provide a better future for our families. Colin demonstrates to us, how hard work and goal-setting helps you develop skills and experience that allow you to rise the ranks regardless of your background.

Chris Ashford
Former Captain, Royal Artillery
Director, Ashford Fitness Consultancy
Hampshire, UK

I was asked if I would review Colin Tansley's book. As soon as I saw the cover and read about his background and the context, I could not wait to get started. When I began to read, I could not stop. This is not another story of someone's life – this is Colin's story about Colin's life. From his early years, I was seamlessly led through his life journey, from joining the army as a 16-year-old, through to a full career with the police and beyond.

Those in the services, in particular the Police, will be intrigued to compare the changes or be reminded of their own experiences (or not) after all these years. For the rest of us, it is a reminder of a police officer's lot. Colin found his purpose from a young age; he didn't need the qualifications to get started, but certainly earned many on his journey to fulfil his career dream. Despite the knuckle ride he encountered on his way to the top, his passion never waned.

Balancing personal and family life which had its challenges, yet staying focussed on the job, took tenacity, courage, grit and dedication. I found myself sitting on the edge of my seat as if I was on the set of an action thriller. It reinforced my knowledge about people and the impact they can have on the physical, mental, and emotional health of others and not even be aware of it. That we, like Colin, never know what is around the corner. It was evident how those in our service sector step up and face danger, sometimes on a daily basis; something we may well at times be oblivious to. Gratitude to Colin for his service to the communities in which he served.

Caroline Purvey
Founder & CEO of TRE UK ®
Kent, UK

Mastering the Wolf is a searingly honest account of a challenging journey through life whilst charting a career in Public Service, from a youth joining the Armed Forces through to a full and varied career in the Police Service.

Colin shines a light on the safeguarding of children and adults, both in a professional capacity and in his own personal life.

The book will provide the reader with a great insight into a fantastic career, and outlines how Colin achieved his ambitions despite some significant adversity.

Lisa Atkinson
Retired Detective Chief Superintendent

◊◊◊

Mastering the Wolf opens the door on the world of law enforcement from training, to probation, to the hierarchy in the force, to undercover policing. It also charts the change in policing and police attitudes towards women, ethnic minorities, domestic violence, child protection issues and generally what is 'expected' of a Police Officer.

The narrator is engaging, completely open and honest about his time as a public servant, warts and all. Despite the many traumas and difficulties the narrator has encountered, he remains resilient and unbowed. *Mastering the Wolf* is a thought-provoking and raw, unsettling memoir that leaves us with plenty to savour.

Olivia Eisinger
Editor
Surrey, UK

One man's story of emotional enlightenment

Mastering the Wolf

Colin Tansley

First published in Great Britain in 2022
by Book Brilliance Publishing
265A Fir Tree Road, Epsom, Surrey, KT17 3LF
+44 (0)20 8641 5090
www.bookbrilliancepublishing.com
admin@bookbrilliancepublishing.com

A CIP catalogue record for this book is available
at the British Library.

ISBN 978-1-913770-38-9

Typeset in Garamond.
Printed by 4edge Ltd.

Some names and identifying details have been changed
to protect the privacy of individuals.

For Frankie

CONTENTS

Foreword

Gripping and searing. Words that might be used in a commentary on a novel or crime thriller. It would be rare to find them referring to an autobiography. This is a compelling read and hard to put down. I read it in two sessions.

Colin tells us a story that will gel with many of us. Not just those who have spent time in the military or in policing.

He takes us on the journey of a small boy coming from a poor, single parent family in East London, combining a life in the army and police with a journey through the many trials and tribulations that some of us have with our relatives, spouses or partners.

Colin opens his heart and shares with us his feelings, hopes and fears. The disappointments and the successes. He places us with him at the heart of an abusive relationship; where this big, strong ex-soldier, Northern Ireland veteran and an undercover cop, who worked at senior level in the Iraq War, is the victim.

At times, my heart was in my mouth as I rushed to turn the next page.

His life as a junior soldier and then on operations in Northern Ireland will take you right into the barrack room and then on to South Armagh.

Colin's reflections on life as a police officer in West Yorkshire during and after the miners' strike tells a little known story of community tensions and dealing with trouble as a police officer in areas with a heritage of dislike and distrust of the police. There, the local officers were left to pick up the pieces left by the officers from the Metropolitan Police, Merseyside and Greater Manchester, who had been drafted in to back up the local force.

His life with the CID and as an undercover officer infiltrating animal rights activists will raise some eyebrows, as will his stories of the drinking culture of detectives.

His insights into investigating child abuse are moving as they are disturbing.

All whilst dealing with a torrid personal life and continual domestic assaults upon himself.

Colin takes us to the heart of Baghdad and the Green Zone as a police officer, daily dodging mortars and managing the politics of being junior partners to the Americans.

A fascinating and enthralling read.

Kevin Hurley

Former Senior Police, Army Officer and
International Policing Consultant to governments
in conflict zones

Introduction

The wolf is a much-maligned animal, maybe because of fairy tales, such as Red Riding Hood, where the wolf is portrayed as cunning and conniving. There is no doubt a wolf can be aggressive; as a pack animal, they hunt, fight, and defend each other without question. But there are lesser-known characteristics, including intelligence, a lover of family and friendliness that don't get quite the same attention. I was asked during the preparation of this book by my publisher what animal I would liken myself to. Without any knowledge of the aforementioned information, I instantly said a wolf, mostly because of the connotations with a 'lone wolf', maybe because I don't fear solitude and often work alone.

Looking back at my life, I can see now that all those qualities resonate with me. The difference now is that I have become better equipped to understand and control my emotions. As a man, that is not something that is easy to say or acknowledge. *Mastering the Wolf* is an apt description of my life journey and is by far the most appropriate title for this book.

Since I was a small boy, I have always wanted to write a book. I think my love of books and virtually any reading material came from my parents. They both read avidly; Mum had a lovely habit of writing something on the inside cover of the many books she bought for me. I still have them stored away safely. Growing up, I would immerse myself in books or comics, often under the bedcovers with a torch. I doubtless picked up a sense of adventure and thirst for information whilst reading stories about 'Biggles', scouring through war comics or even trying to understand what *The Wind in the Willows* was all about. I never anticipated writing a book of any kind. The idea was formulated initially only to act as a manuscript to leave for my grandchildren as a permanent memory of me, just in case I lost my marbles as I got older. As I emptied my head onto these pages, I formed the opinion that it may also be of interest to a wider audience. I will let you be the judge of that.

Spending my formative years in the Armed Forces and a large chunk of my adult life in the police service has provided me with self-discipline and a wide array of life skills. Amongst those many competencies are resilience, tenacity, and determination coupled with a not insignificant sprinkling of intolerance, impatience, and stubbornness. It is inevitable in the course of public service that you encounter things that will have a lasting impact on your personality, as well as those close to you. Writing this book has been a difficult task at times. More than once I have had to put it down and come back to it some weeks later. It is a brutally honest account of my own experiences, recalled to the best of my memory, at times aided by search engines and any official records I could lay my hands on. I could not possibly detail or document every single incident. With the passage of time and onset of age, your recall can be clouded. I have doubtless forgotten certain things; some I would prefer not to remember. There are memories buried away in a deep inner consciousness though. Every so often something happens; it could be a smell, a noise, a TV programme, a film, and before you know it, the memories come flooding back. They tap you on your shoulder to remind you they are still lurking in the caverns of your mind. Sometimes I laugh as I remember the good times: on other occasions, I get sad, and occasionally I shed a tear.

I consider myself extremely lucky to have worked with some very colourful, talented, helpful, and humorous people. They have supported me as I navigated my way through life, some of whom feature in this book, but unfortunately there is not enough room for them all. Thankfully they vastly outweigh the weirdos and small number of individuals who have brought me grief. To protect some of them, I have not identified everyone and have changed certain people's names. I am also not proud of everything I have done. This is a story about a person. My experiences are not unique, for many in a similar position they will have experienced the same, if not worse. I've shared mine in the hope that if you are suffering or questioning yourself, you are not alone. There is hope and a bright future, you just have to find it. For me it took a while, but I now understand that my journey was just as important. It was part of a huge learning experience and so worth it. Perhaps this book will make you sad at times. I truly hope it makes you laugh as well, because my life has also been a lot of fun and it isn't over yet – not by a long chalk.

1. Growing up

I don't remember too much about my early childhood. I was born in the late fifties at Hackney Hospital in the East End of London. I qualify as a Cockney by virtue of the hospital being within the sound of Bow Bells. Both my mum and dad came from huge families, with lots of brothers, half-brothers, sisters and half-sisters. They had grown up as neighbours close to the old Arsenal ground in Highbury, both being huge supporters of that very popular North London club. The respective families knew each other well. What I do remember is a closeness amongst my parents with their siblings. We often spent time visiting my aunties', uncles' and cousins' houses in London. Unfortunately, most of that ended abruptly because my parents' ill-fated marriage didn't last long. It was much later in life that I learnt what led to the break-up. Dad just didn't love my mum. He disclosed to me many years later that he only married her because they had an illegitimate child. A brother whom I never met, who died some months after he was born. It was quite apparent that from the conversation with my dad that he felt that sad occurrence had made the marriage a complete waste of his life. I couldn't help but conclude that he must have felt the same way about me, my sister and brother.

Mum loved her music and was always singing around the house. We had what was known at the time as a radiogram. It worked with valves and had to be 'warmed up' before you could use it. That was the first job in the morning before the kettle went on. She was always considerate of others, thoughtful, loving and caring. I like to think some of her traits rubbed off on me. She did tend to worry too much though, at times being a little over-protective. I recall she didn't want me to play rugby just in case I had my ears pulled off; she also worried about cricket in case the ball hit me in the face. My dad's view of boys was a little different; you had to be tough, stick up for yourself and never, **ever** shed tears. It was a case of 'big boys don't cry' as far as he was concerned. Woe betide you if you fell over and cried in front of him.

Dad left us all when I was around eight or nine years old. Mum was devastated but in the spirit of the times, got her head down and raised the three of us virtually single-handedly. Dad had left her for a younger woman he had met in one of the banks he visited as a messenger. With our new stepmother, he moved away to a much nicer place on the other side of town. Her parents were, to us anyway, well off, her father being a picture editor at a prestigious newspaper. I remember visiting their house and marvelling at the furniture and garden.

At home, things for us were much more basic. Dad and Mum had originally purchased the house to renovate. Once he left, it was obvious that some of the work was never going to be completed. We had no running hot water, the toilet was outside, the bath in the kitchen downstairs was out of commission and remained permanently covered with a wooden board. We stood in a bowl of water from a saucepan heated on the cooker in order to get washed. I shared a bed with my brother and we only had carpets on some of the floors. I wouldn't say we were poverty-stricken but it was close. On Sunday afternoons we all huddled around the black and white television in the living room to watch movies, drink sugary tea and eat biscuits. As children growing up in the mid sixties, Mum always made us feel safe. We didn't have much in the way of possessions, but we were loved and happy.

Like most boys, when I was growing up, I wanted to be like my dad. As the years have gone by, I have come to realise that whilst I love and respect him dearly, it's more important to be yourself. From an early age, I think I always tried to impress him. I think we all like to make our parents proud. I know that I achieved that with Mum. I'm not sure I have ever fully realised that with Dad. At least, I have no recall of him telling me so. It seems to be in his nature to find fault with most things. Nothing was ever quite 'good enough'; it always seemed impossible to please him. There was always that little 'something' that you could have done better. Perhaps that is a good quality to have as it can make you strive to be better. That trait has rubbed off on me somewhat, as I know at times I tend to be overly critical. When bringing up children I'm no longer so sure it is the best approach, in most cases being completely counterproductive. I know now that gentle encouragement and praise gets far better results.

After Dad left home, all three of us got to see him relatively frequently. As I recall, he was certainly present and influential in our upbringing as children. We had some good times at his large flat above a bank in Limehouse. There was a massive empty room, which we inventively called 'The Big Room'. We played football in there together, occasionally broke the windows and bashed the hell out of the keys of a piano in the corner. We had bags of fun at that place; for me and my siblings, this was when Dad was at his best. Despite his negativity, he was quick-witted, good-humoured and he made us laugh a lot. Whilst bitter, I don't think Mum ever really stopped loving him, which reared its head from time to time. I have a few memories of the arguments that followed when we returned home after spending time with him. The pair of them would frequently end up shouting at each other. We saw and heard it all, including some minor physical stuff, slapping each other around the face and that sort of thing. On one occasion I split my head open during a weekend visit to his flat. When I arrived home after a short visit to the hospital, Mum saw I had stitches on my head and all hell broke loose. In my dad's view it was a scratch, but as far as Mum was concerned, he hadn't taken good enough care of me. They were both quite opinionated and wouldn't give each other an inch.

Both were also very strict: the phrase 'children should be seen and not heard' was used frequently to remind us of our position in life. We were brought up to be respectful to adults, say please and thank you, and had to ask to leave the table after meals. We had jobs to do in the house and were expected to help. Mum didn't stand for any shit either, for when my siblings and I played up at home, a bamboo cane came out and you knew you were for it. This was a standard method of disciplining children at the time and something she was also well-accustomed to whilst growing up. It was tough for her on her own. I recall her going to the doctors with what was probably depression and being told by her GP that I had to behave myself at home to help her.

Shortly after that, I was despatched to a children's home to give her some rest. The little I can recall was horrendous. As a young child, I felt that I was being punished for something, as it was just me that was sent away, not my brother and sister. I don't remember how long I was there for. I certainly didn't enjoy it. I vividly recall getting shouted at and having my legs smacked by a member of staff for mistakenly opening a toilet door when a girl was in there.

I think it is fair to say that in the sixties there was an element of shame heaped upon on any woman who was divorced. They were perceived to be the ones at fault, not able to fulfil the duties of a wife and mother in the way that society expected them to. Nothing could have been further from the truth in Mum's case. I'm biased, of course, but she did a fantastic job in raising all three of us. Growing up where we lived in London and to a single mother, it could have so easily been a different story.

As small children, both my parents were evacuated from London during the war years because of the Blitz. That must have had an impact on them, growing up amongst strangers and apart from their own family. They both seemed to come away with contrasting experiences. Mum talked about it often. She had spent time in Wales and Cornwall, seemingly enjoying the extended holidays. Dad rarely spoke of his time as an evacuee. Only once did he relate a story of his experiences to me. It was the only time I have ever seen him visibly upset and close to tears. He was the last of an evacuated group of children to be taken in by a family in Wales. He told me that no one seemed to want him. A lady had to take him from house to house begging for him to be taken care of. From the little he said, it seemed to be the case that he was physically abused by the people that provided him with what must have been a miserable existence.

In my humble opinion, I think it is those experiences that have made him quite cold and emotionally detached at times. Not once in my life can I ever recall him hugging me, my sister or brother, or even saying he loved us. He went on to have two other children with his second wife. From what I saw, their experience was very different. To this day I have never understood why that was the case. I'm not saying he didn't love the three of us, he just never really showed it with any overt displays of affection. Maybe he had been conditioned that way. I believe some of that has rubbed off on me and my siblings.

I was introverted as a child with only a small circle of friends. I spent a lot of time with my brother and sister when we were younger. I was quite content in my own company. You could often find me reading books, comics, drawing or doing puzzles. Once I knew people well enough, I tended to open up more, yet you would rarely ever find me starting a conversation. I don't think I ever liked school for that reason. I didn't like being amongst lots of other children. I found it difficult to concentrate unless I found things stimulating. My mind would wander off frequently, reliving comic book adventures or just daydreaming. When selected to answer questions, I had no clue what the teacher was referring to and ended up in trouble. I have vivid memories of being the recipient of free meals at school. Entitlement to them was signified by tickets which were purple in colour. Even now, I can picture them; they resembled raffle tickets, but there were no prizes. I would be summoned out of the class to go and collect them on a Monday morning. This immediately identified me as a recipient of a handout. I was the only kid in my class to get free meals. As a result, I was singled out as being 'poor'. Kids can be cruel and once they found out that my dad had left us, that became yet another stick to beat me with. I think it was those experiences that forged a closeness to my brother and sister as we looked out for one another.

As the eldest, Mum made sure I took care of my siblings. She had to find work to supplement her income, even cutting leather at home for handbags made at a nearby factory. I was invariably the one put in charge of childcare as babysitters were expensive. One evening my sister and I were playing a game designed with the sole intention of running our younger brother ragged. It involved shining a torch beam on the walls whilst we encouraged him to touch it. We were having a fine old time watching him run around the house, until I shone the torch onto a pane of glass in the bedroom window which he banged with his hand. This resulted in the glass falling to the ground below with an almighty crash. I still remember telephoning Mum desperately trying to explain what had happened. All this was long before anyone really paid attention to age limits for children being left alone. I really don't think it did me, or my siblings, any harm at all. It certainly gave me a sense of responsibility. It's something I think I carry to this day, it maybe even influenced my choice of careers.

2. New beginnings

After the divorce was finalised, Mum had one or two relationships, one with a man called Charlie, a Metropolitan Police officer. He was a large, cheerful type and heavily involved in the St John Ambulance Brigade. I got on well with him and to this day, I think he was a significant factor in me eventually joining the police. I went camping in Ireland with the Brigade and spent time on a canal barge trip. It was great fun and it kindled a love of the outdoors in me.

There was another guy who came to stay with us at the house. He was from Cornwall. He wanted to join the police; I remember him taking me to 10 Downing Street, where he spoke to the officer stationed outside the door. This was at a time when you could stroll right up to the entrance. The husband of my mum's friend and next-door neighbour was also in the police. At school I remember being asked to draw what I wanted to be when I grew up. I drew a picture of a policeman. You can see a pattern emerging…!

Mum loved Cornwall; she had made friends there as an evacuee and remained in contact with many of them. In the summer of 1971, we were all packed off to my dad's to go on holiday with him and my stepmother to Devon. Mum had arranged for some time away for herself in Cornwall. We had a great time at a bungalow in Brixham, where Dad was very attentive. We went to the beach a lot and had some memorable times.

As I recall, he was teaching my stepmother to drive, but these impromptu lessons didn't always go so well. The three of us were party to some fairly heated arguments in the car. Dad has always had a terrible temper. If something went wrong, he was prone to shouting at the top of his voice. He was always right; the bawling was his way of forcefully getting his point across. We knew best to stay quiet when it happened. He was never physically violent to us, but I feared him when he was angry and so did my brother and sister. I wouldn't say we ever got used to it, but it did become the norm. It was best to keep out of the way when things weren't going well for him.

At first, I didn't understand why Mum had returned from Cornwall with such a spring in her step. Eventually she told us that someone would be coming to stay for a while. Sometime later, a man arrived. Unbeknown to the three of us, her trip to Cornwall had been engineered by one of her friends to introduce the pair of them to each other. Their relationship had advanced at lightning speed. Morecambe and Wise were popular on the television at the time and the man reminded me of Eric Morecambe. It soon became apparent he didn't share his humour or comedy though. Having a stranger in the house was unsettling for all of us. Even though I was only 12 years old, I had become accustomed to being the 'man of the house'. Initially, things were good whilst he spent time getting to know the three of us, but that seemed to wear off quickly. He was even more strict than Mum, wasn't used to having children about the house and was very set in his ways.

They married on Christmas Eve of 1971. There were only a few people at the registry office. After the official stuff had concluded, we all headed off to a restaurant for a slap-up meal. It seemed that within a few days of the marriage, we were packing up and heading to Cornwall to live! Prior to our departure, I remember seeing my dad. He had been made aware of the plans for us to move away. He sat me down and said something along the lines of, "Do you want to live with us, or would you prefer to go to Cornwall with your brother and sister?". This was a no-brainer for me. Whilst I felt a strong sense of loyalty to him, I certainly did not want to be parted from my siblings. Perhaps it was because I felt very protective of them all. It wasn't until some years later that I fully appreciated what I had been asked that day. What he meant was, "**You** can stay with us but we have no room or place for the other two". I have never once regretted my decision to go to Cornwall to be with Mum, my brother and sister.

Whilst I had been to Cornwall on holiday, I had little knowledge about the place other than the beaches were quite nice. One evening I was bundled into a removal van with my stepfather and Dennis the removal man, a friend of a friend, who had badly miscalculated the capacity of his truck. Much to my stepfather's displeasure, certain items of furniture and other belongings were left behind as a result. Dennis became 'Dennis the Menace' as far as my stepfather was concerned. Mum, my brother and sister all travelled by train. By contrast, my seat for the journey was the engine cover located in the cab of the truck. Clearly not designed as a seat or bed for the night, this cover was very uncomfortable.

We arrived in the early hours of the following morning. As the sun came up, I caught sight of our new home. It was one of four council houses at the top of a hill, in the middle of nowhere. Literally, the middle of nowhere! We were surrounded by open countryside, cows and sheep; this was rural. Nowadays, I would probably view that setting as idyllic. As a 12-year-old kid who had become accustomed to London and the ease with which you could access transport, see your friends and even go into the city, this was horrific.

The next thing I really remember was queueing for a bus to take me to a secondary school. My stepfather had called in a favour from one of his friends, for his son to escort me to the school that day. Having spent my first year at an inner-city secondary school in London, I mistakenly thought I was ready for anything. How wrong I was! This was a complete culture shock. The journey to the school on the bus itself was frankly terrifying. There was a group of rowdy lads on the back of the bus who took the piss out of everyone, including the elderly bus driver, Mr Sawle. Mr Sawle was an old guy with a donkey jacket and flat cap who endured the verbal onslaught every single day and rarely said a word to anyone. Maybe he was scared to do so. I sported a skinhead haircut and big brogue shoes with white and black laces; they were all the rage in London. Not so in Cornwall. My crew cut made my big ears stand out. The fashion trends in London had not reached this remote outpost of UK. I was called a 'poof' for wearing my chosen footwear. This, along with my London accent, ensured that I was singled out for extra special treatment from the school bullies. I was a stranger, and as far as they were concerned, a foreigner.

My classroom experiences at school were not much better. It would be easy to blame the upheaval at home for my own behaviour, maybe that played its part. I was an awful student, spending much of my time outside the classroom rather than in it, which was mostly because I was so bloody disruptive. In one of my school reports, the form teacher commented, "With a small group of other boys he frequently finds himself involved in minor mischief". That was very true, me and my little gang excelled at doing just enough to get noticed, but not quite enough to get the cane. French, geography and maths were without a doubt my most hated subjects. Whether this was due to the dire way the subjects were presented by the teachers, or my inability to listen, is now only a matter for conjecture. From what I know about kids now, this was a means of me trying to get attention. Something I probably felt I was getting little of at home.

3. Escape

It didn't take long for the relationship with my stepfather to break down. Me, my brother and sister used to fight quite a bit. At times we were noisy and boisterous. No doubt accustomed to peace and quiet, this I am sure, irritated him no end. Ultimately, it ended up with conflict. We were shouted at frequently and told to go out and play. I don't think he ever really understood what taking three relatively young children on meant in terms of the financial or emotional commitment. It caused some friction in the marriage and I know that Mum felt caught in the middle of it all.

It didn't seem that long before they were expecting a child and we had a half-sister. From our perspective as children, it seemed to be the case that she got a lot of attention and we were sidelined. This was not her fault, of course, but this went on for many years and I believe was partly responsible for driving a deep division into the family. I do remember that our stepsister seemed to get brand new things, yet the three of us had to make do with second-hand bikes and hand-me-downs.

At around the age of 13, I took a job in the evenings and weekends to get out of the house. One evening I arrived home from work and a minor argument blew up between me and my stepfather. I must have been rude to him or Mum, so as a result, he pinned me up against a wall. I was subsequently sent to my room. I'd had enough and decided I was leaving home. Being the adventurer that I thought I was, I packed my rather dapper tartan duffle bag with a spare set of underwear, socks, a torch, and a few other essentials. I climbed onto the porch roof from my bedroom, jumped over a hedge, through a field and off I went. I had no plan and no idea where I was going. About 15 minutes later I was found on a nearby country lane by my employer, George, who promptly took me home to face the music.

George was the owner of the local filling station and grocery store where I worked. A larger-than-life character, rotund and jolly, he and his wife Jean were always good to me. They paid me the not so grand sum of 10 pence per hour, but I was always fed and watered when working. Whilst working there I made a host of new friends, mostly adults. They provided me with a different perspective on life and were quite influential for me as a teenager. One man, who also worked at the filling station, wasn't keen on me. He was officious and thought I was too cocky and cheeky. He tried to tell me what to do and I didn't take too kindly to that. Being a typically mouthy teenager, I told him where to go. He pushed me one day because I answered him back and I walked out. Later, George's wife came out to see me, apologised for the way he had behaved and begged me to come back, which I did a couple of days later. Looking back, I must have been a proper little shit. Awful in the classroom, disruptive at home and rebellious when it came to authority. Not exactly fitting for my later choices in life.

My seven Certificates of Secondary Education (CSE) results were as anticipated: bland. Whilst I knew I wasn't stupid and had the brains, I left my revision far too late. I was also at work after school each night and at the weekends. One result surprised everyone though. I achieved a Grade 1 in Rural Studies. This translates as gardening, farming and animal husbandry. My grade mostly related to the effort I put in to transforming a garden for one of my adult friends, with a rockery and flower beds. Presented in a book with accompanying Polaroid photographs, my creative flair must have done the trick. The handheld 'vegetable digger' that I built as part of my Physics project at around the same time didn't attract quite the same level of adulation. I remember describing that piece of mechanical genius to police colleagues later in life, much to their amusement.

Based upon my one significant exam result, Mum and my stepfather took it upon themselves to steer me towards a career in horticulture or farming. In all honesty I didn't fancy the prospect of either. The sole reason I had undertaken the project in the first place was because I got on so well with the couple who owned the plot of land; they provided me with cakes, refreshments and adult conversation. Unless I did something to alter my career path myself, then I was to be heading for an apprenticeship at a nearby experimental garden. The mere thought of it was servitude as far as I was concerned.

Growing up watching Trooping the Colour on television, plus a diet of war movies and magazines, meant the idea of joining the military had always appealed. I distinctly remember watching a programme as a teenager called *World at War*. I was fascinated by it. I think this partly shaped my decision about joining the forces. What I also remember is the images of what the Nazis did to the Jews during the war. To this day, I still remember the grainy black and white footage of bodies being bulldozed into mass graves. Even at that young age I simply could not comprehend why other human beings could do that to each other. Based on some of my experiences in Cornwall, I had already developed an inherent dislike of bullies; this though was on a different level. Perhaps even back then I had developed a sense of needing to help or protect people.

I also got into outdoor pursuits in Cornwall. With money earnt from my job, I saved for a school skiing holiday in Austria. I completed the Bronze Duke of Edinburgh's Award which involved kayaking and camping which I really took to. As a result, I decided to myself that I was joining the Royal Marines so I could ski and climb mountains for a living. Never mind the soldiering, that never even occurred to me. I took myself along to the recruiting office in Truro and passed the written examination with flying colours, only to be told that there were to be no Junior Marine vacancies for some time due to budget cuts. They advised me to wait until I was 17 and a half, when I could apply to join as an adult.

I was devastated. I wanted to get away from home, away from my parents and do my own thing. It seemed my mum and stepfather were equally as keen. They both persuaded me to go to the Army Recruitment Office to find out more. Soon after, I was asked to attend an army assessment centre in Sutton Coldfield where I underwent a series of tests to see whether I was suitable material. The army was on a big recruitment drive. If you were halfway right with your test results, you were matched with any vacancies it had.

During one of the many interviews, I proudly announced that I had built a radio in my Physics class at school. The Recruiting Sergeant nodded and said something like, "That's interesting," yet there may well have been a hint of sarcasm in his voice. Anyway, it seemed to be enough to qualify me as a candidate for the Royal Signals. I had been given advice by a neighbour, and a former Master at Arms in the Royal

Navy that it was an imperative to get an appointment with a trade. Under no circumstances should I accept a position as an infantryman, so this job seemed to fit the bill.

There was a minor interruption in my application as I failed the first medical. I suffered from sporadic eczema at the time. The view was that it would be irritated still further by the types of woollen-based shirts worn at the time in the army.

On 9th September 1975, at the tender age of 16, after a successful medical appeal, I said goodbye to Mum and got onto a train to 'join up'. I disembarked in Plymouth briefly to be sworn in. I then headed north to Harrogate in Yorkshire. I had no idea where I was going or how long it would take me. I had enlisted as an Army Apprentice, colloquially known as a 'brat' soldier. We were often referred to as 'college brats' by regular soldiers. The Army Apprentice College in Harrogate was then the training centre for 'boys' joining the Royal Corps of Signals. The motto for the Corps is 'Certa Cito' (Swift and Sure). It signifies that messages of whatever type always reach their target quickly and efficiently.

My introduction to army discipline was equally 'swift and sure'. I was one of the last to arrive and was hurriedly pushed into a briefing session which seemed to end as soon as I got there. We were dismissed to our rooms to unpack. My bed was closest to the door of the barrack room, shared with seven strangers. I was unpacking my gear into a wardrobe when the next thing I knew I was being shouted at.

"What the fucking hell did I tell you not more than half an hour ago, you snivelling little twat?" I jumped. The Sergeant was so close to my face, I could smell his breath. I honestly had no idea what he was making such a fuss over. "Get down and give me ten."

"Ten what?" I asked innocently.

"Ten fucking press-ups and it's fucking SERGEANT!! In fact, make it fucking twenty!!" My new life had begun in earnest. I was skinny, had no muscle mass and ended up in a heap, much to the amusement of my new roommates.

The blokes in my room included our nominated Lance Corporal, Taffy. He was an Army Apprentice as well, but several terms in front of us. He had a very strong Welsh accent, which I often found difficult to understand. We had to call him Corporal. If we didn't then there were a variety of punishments, ranging from more press-ups, being sent to the NAAFI canteen or some errand or other. There was an Apprentice Sergeant on each floor. He was to be obeyed, no matter what. Above our floor, there were more apprentices at differing levels of their training. Senior term resided on the top floor. They were deemed godlike. It was imperative not to upset them or visit their quarters without invitation. There was a clear hierarchy, probably designed to instil a form of self-policing within the blocks. We were without a shadow of doubt, the lowest of the low.

The next morning, we were awoken early. None of us had been issued with any kit and today was when we were to begin the transformation. To sum it up, we were about to get beaten down to get rebuilt. For some, it would take much longer than others. For others, they simply would not succeed and leave of their own accord. If you were a non-conformist like me, the transition was going to be a difficult one. I took an early decision to be semi-compliant and certainly with the Permanent Staff. They were regular soldiers – adults – and I was shit scared of them. Haircuts, uniform smelling of mothballs, boots and webbing were the order of the day. Later we were further indoctrinated, with instructions on personal hygiene, how to shave properly, how to iron our uniform, fold our clothes, construct bed packs and bull our boots. There was a lot to take in.

On the second morning, the intensity of it all went into overdrive. It was dark outside, around 5am. I heard the shouting and banging down the corridor, well before the lights in our room were switched on. We were about to get introduced to our morning physical training. One of the favourite terms used by the duty officer would be: "Feet on the floor, hands off cocks, on socks!" The duty officers were regular soldiers, mostly sergeants, and they were fearsome. We had to dress quickly in a very fetching PE kit which consisted of a red V-neck t-shirt, blue (to the knee) cotton shorts, green army socks and black plimsolls. A short time later we were being run and beasted around the barracks in three ranks.

The weather in Yorkshire over those autumn and winter months was always awful; it was either raining, cold or windy. It didn't matter what the weather was, you wore T-shirts and shorts. Standing there in a body of three ranks trying to keep warm in the bitter cold is a lingering memory for me. Other than two blokes in our room who had been in the army cadets, it was a rude awakening for all of us. Being in shock might be a more apt way to describe it. You arrived back in your room, did your ablutions (new word to me) and had to get to breakfast. There was never enough time.

Parade in uniform was next and held at 0745hrs sharp. I arrived early and was immediately set upon by the legendary Sergeant Hails. He was your stereotypical drill sergeant. He would shout in your face, talk quickly and generally make you feel about two foot tall. Everyone knew Ron Hails. He was able to pick you out from 200 yards away; if you weren't swinging your arms and marching, you were for it. My questions from him on this, my first formal parade, related to my morning shave, or lack of it: "Why haven't you shaved, lad?!"

My lacklustre response of, "Er, I don't need to yet, Sergeant," didn't hold any water. I had, in fairness, only a modicum of bum fluff present on my face.

With his wooden pace stick placed firmly in my chest, he said, "Everybody here shaves, lad, so get yourself a razor and sort yourself out!!" I had to telephone Mum and ask her to send me one straight away, for I had little money at that time and it was nowhere near pay day. Thankfully my Gillette shaving razor arrived the next day!

To put this all into context: this was the mid seventies, there were no mobile phones and there was no such thing as email. If you wanted to contact your loved ones, you wrote a letter, or joined the queue outside of the few telephone kiosks dotted around the camp. It is difficult to describe just how different things were then compared to nowadays. For example, all the recruits and Permanent Staff were male. There were no females other than the ones that worked in the NAAFI. Homosexuality was strictly illegal in the Armed Forces. It was actually an offence for two soldiers to be on one bed with their feet off the floor. By contrast with 21st century values, it was markedly different. As very young boys we were continually reminded about how the army expected you to behave. If you dared to question anything, you were in for the high jump. It was simple: you either conformed, or you were not for the organisation. I didn't see it as a bad thing then and to be fair, I still don't – it did me a world of good. It was a form of conditioning, and at such a young age becomes embedded into your psyche.

Drill was another way of instilling discipline and was our next lesson. We were told this was to get us to operate as a team. Anyone who has ever watched the spectacle of Armed Forces recruits trying to march together will know how ridiculous it looks if not done properly. Arms swinging out of sync, legs not in tune with the rest of the squad and people turning the wrong way. Being part of that and watching it all fall apart, it's very difficult not to laugh. If you didn't get it right, were discovered to be giggling or not taking things seriously, you would find yourself running around the parade square. All of us suffered insults screamed at us from the drill sergeants in equal measure. We had to stand up straight; the slouching of shoulders was strictly forbidden. There was a way to march, to turn left, to turn right, to turn about, to come to attention, to stand at ease and to fallout. We were all remodelled, our deportment was important and we had to stand up straight, "Chin out, shoulders back," was another drill sergeant favourite.

All of this was designed to get you to understand the true meaning of self-discipline, have personal hygiene, function individually where necessary, but be part of a team with the highest standards. I didn't realise it at the time, but the training was also about leadership, instilling within you a morality and sense of duty.

It has served me well throughout my life. I am eternally grateful for those early lessons in the army. I discovered a lot about myself, had amazing experiences and forged lifelong friendships. However, there are times when you realise that your approach to certain things can make you quite rigid with an expectation of the same high standards from others. The early services conditioning to discipline has provided me with an unshakeable intolerance to things like a lack of punctuality.

If people are late without what I believe to be a reasonable excuse, then I find it to be disrespectful. From my perspective, I must be at least five minutes early for appointments or meetings. I still polish my shoes and must have creases in my trousers and formal shirts. Old habits die hard.

4. In the Army now

Recruit, or 'Rook' troop as it was better known, occupied the bottom floor of every Squadron block. My Squadron was Bradley; the others – Penney, Philips, Scott and Rawson – were close by. As mentioned earlier, the senior term were top dogs. At night they would send regular raiding parties to terrorise us, give us a beating or 'tip' us out of our beds. You would hear them in other rooms creating havoc, often whilst drunk. You just had to lay in your bed and wait for the inevitable. The Permanent Staff knew it went on but did little to stop it. There was the odd occasion where things went a bit too far and guys got injured. At one point I was hung out of a window by a member of senior term holding my ankles. Apparently, I had been 'gobby' and had to be sorted out!

This was all routine stuff and most of us took it in our stride. It was a rite of passage; you had to suck it up and get on with it. Deep down though, I knew I would never do this sort of thing to fellow soldiers. It was bullying, pure and simple. If you have ever been bullied yourself, I don't think you are disposed to do it to others.

I adapted to service life relatively quickly. I desperately needed structure and the army helped me enormously. Everything had to be done properly and with a sense of urgency; you either ran or marched everywhere on the camp. There was a schedule each day and woe betide you if you were late for anything. Even when getting breakfast, lunch or dinner, there was never enough time. This led to you bolting your food before getting onto the next task. I still eat too quickly and often blame service life for that. There was good humour, minor antics, a bit of fighting and a lot of physical exercise. Most ex-service personnel will tell you that the feelings of camaraderie in the Armed Forces are unequalled in civilian life. You share clothes, borrow money from each other, have peculiar and sometimes harrowing experiences together. I found all that to be true; finally, I felt a sense of belonging. My troop mates were like brothers and were mostly really good friends; something that had been absent when I was growing up. It wasn't for everyone though and there were some early dropouts.

One lad in our room lasted no more than two days. He was homesick and spent his nights crying because he had never been away from his family. Little sympathy was available, as anyone displaying this sort of perceived weakness got unwarranted attention from the PS and fellow apprentices. 'Grow up, shape up and get on with it' was the attitude. I was determined not to show any signs of being feeble. The intolerance with people who in my opinion, lack motivation, or appear to be lazy, is probably borne out of these early experiences.

It was made perfectly plain to every single one of us that, first and foremost, we were soldiers; our trade would always come second. We were trained in weapons drills (safe handling): for pistols, rifles, sub-machine guns, light machine guns, and grenade launchers. We crawled in mud, applied camouflage cream, underwent frequent visits to the assault course, climbed ropes and were exposed to CS gas. Regardless of what mess we got into, we had to take care of our equipment and ensure it was always clean and tidy. It was drummed into us that the

Russians were a huge threat. Despite our young age, we knew there may even come a time when we would be fighting in Germany and be expected to defend our country; to dispense with any and all enemies.

I hadn't fully appreciated the intensity of the trade training. It was like going to school during normal hours with soldiering sandwiched into the timetable. Wednesday afternoon was always devoted to sports. I found myself getting involved in all manner of activities such as kayaking, gliding, horse riding, skiing, rock climbing, and pretty much anything other than the more traditional sports, such as rugby or football; much to the disappointment of my dad. He has always been a lover of football. His family was so large that his brothers and half-brothers formed their own football team and played regularly at Hackney Marshes. I often watched them as a young child.

I continued to struggle with most of the classroom work and I found it difficult and tiring when coupled with all the physical activity. Unless lessons had a practical element to them, I found it almost impossible to concentrate. Some of the instructors were Senior NCOs (Non-Commissioned Officers) and they did not tolerate any nonsense or failure. Anything to do with numbers or mathematical calculations caused me problems. I hadn't done well at school in maths, it didn't interest me, and I always felt as though I was behind everyone else and gave up. My attitude to some of the classes wasn't great either. Down to my own stupidity, I later lost out on a promotion because I was continually disrespectful to one of the civilian lecturers.

However, some of the lessons really appealed to me. I loved sending and receiving Morse code. We had to sit in rows with tatty old headphones and listen to hours of Morse cipher and clear text. To this day, I think that continual exposure to what was known in the trade as the 'dits' and 'dahs', is partly to blame for the tinnitus I suffer. I also learned to type, which was something I never thought I would be doing. This was an essential skill if you wanted to progress as a telegraphist and was certainly useful later in life.

5. Trouble

Like my days at school, it seemed that I couldn't resist getting into trouble. One evening, two of my roommates and I decided we would be cheeky to 'Taffy', our room corporal. We'd got far too familiar with him and had started to be disrespectful. We were imitating him with our pretty poor attempts at the Welsh accent. Exacerbated by being unable to control us, we were told to report to the duty officer, who was the member of Permanent Staff stationed downstairs at night in the Squadron Office to ensure good order. The three of us decided we weren't going to present ourselves to him. As required, we did go downstairs, but merely hung about in the stairwell for five minutes and then returned to report that we had been suitably admonished.

We assumed that was the end of it, but how wrong we were! I turned up early for the next morning's parade. Unfortunately, my punctuality was not going to do me any favours on this occasion. Sergeant Hails spotted me out of the Squadron office window. He beckoned me in an animated manner to report to the office. He did not look happy and I had a sense that trouble was afoot. I marched into his office and came to a snappy halt. He launched into me straight away with a variety of expletives about the behaviour we had displayed the previous evening. Foolishly, the three of us had assumed that Taffy wouldn't make his own enquiries. Shortly after, my two partners in crime were wheeled in. We received a massive bollocking and were told to return at lunchtime to see the Sergeant Major. Now we knew we were in the shit.

Lunchtime came... we reported to the office, lining up to attention in the corridor. The Sergeant Major came out of his office. He was a giant of a man, a member of the Scots Guards with a very broad Glaswegian accent.

"You little fuckers think you're funny? You can come back and see me at 5pm, don't be fucking late!" he barked.

At the allotted time we returned, only to be told that we were going to be formally charged with insubordination. Our case had been elevated to the Officer Commanding (OC) of the Squadron. I don't think any of us had expected that. Thoughts of spending time in the camp's jail or being dismissed from the army were uppermost in our minds. We were marched into his office in double quick time, Sergeant Hails shouting out, "Left, right, left, right, left, right left!" I momentarily saw the OC's dog was sprawled out on the floor directly in front of the desk. It was too late. As I drove my foot into the floor to come to a snappy halt, I accidentally stamped on the dog's tail. It yelped loudly; not the greatest of starts. Taffy came in to give his evidence; we were not in a position to dispute any of it. I don't think we dared to do so.

Duly convicted, we were sentenced to seven days' Restriction of Privileges, or ROPs. ROPs involved reporting to the guardroom at the end of the working day. You were assigned additional duties, not allowed to leave the camp and had a nightly parade in best uniform. If you didn't show up with your uniform and boots gleaming, you would return every hour on the hour until you satisfied the Regimental Police. Our extra work included peeling potatoes in the cookhouse, polishing floors, sweeping stuff up, picking up litter; all menial tasks, which had to be performed to a high standard. On the Saturday night of our punishment detail, we were informed that we were going to be working in the sergeants' mess. This involved waiting on tables for the Permanent Staff and bringing them their drinks from the bar. We soon noticed that they were all so drunk that as long as we kept them topped up, we could pretty much do what we liked. It allowed us to get as much food and alcohol as we wanted, which we consumed greedily in the kitchen. We had a fantastic night and turned up a little worse for wear for our parade. Thankfully our happy demeanour went unnoticed.

Military exercises were frequent. One of our first was in Scarborough, North Yorkshire. It rained so much we were all pulled off to a village hall to dry out. It was miserable and smelly but memorable. On another exercise we had to set up communications in a wood, man the radio systems, feed ourselves with compo rations and do 'stags' of duty. When your stag was complete, you climbed fully clothed into your green maggot (sleeping bag) to grab some rest. This was our first 'tactical' exercise where we were expected to perform like real soldiers. It felt like I had just got to sleep when there were loud bangs, flares going off and the firing of weapons. Even though I knew they were blanks, they still made a whole lot of noise. I jumped out of my sleeping bag, got my rifle and headed to a trench: not before tripping over a guy rope and going head first into a puddle of very deep mud. The Permanent Staff were attacking our position and as you would expect we were overrun, totally useless and received an almighty bollocking.

At first light, all of our rifles were 'up ended' barrel first into the mud, our tents were kicked over, and we were left in no doubt that we had to improve. I later came to understand that this was all part of the process. It didn't matter what you did, it was never, ever going to be good enough. During those early months at the college, we would and could never be allowed to win.

Swearing, cursing and a plethora of special army terminology also became part of everyday parlance. This is partly what makes soldiers so unique and sets them apart from others. Prior to joining up, 'bloody' and 'bugger' were the only swear words I had ever heard. I do remember my mum asking me shortly after I joined, if there was a lot of swearing at the barracks. I think she was concerned I might be making use of this new language. I denied any suggestion of cursing being used, but by now I had amassed a whole new vocabulary. None of that sort of behaviour was evident to visitors, such as during passing out parades, because we always acted professionally. These were held to denote the elevation from snotty-nosed civilian to young soldier and then onwards to the next stage of apprentice training. On my very first passing out parade, Mum travelled up from Cornwall on her own and my dad and stepmother also attended. Dressed in our best uniform, we performed a display of drill, complete with rifles, and were accompanied by a band of pipes and drums. We all marched past the Camp Commandant who took our salute. The initial training had done me a world of good. Every one of us that had got through that stage had become physically stronger, leaner, fitter and had learnt how to operate as a team. I felt a sense of achievement. I was growing up, becoming a man and was able to fend for myself. What perhaps was less evident was that we had all been trained to kill, and when required to, became aggressive at the flick of a switch.

6. New term

After returning from our first spell of leave, we were moved onto the next floor of the accommodation block and dispersed amongst the wider squadron. There was a natural flow each term as lads graduated and others moved into senior troop. We were also allowed out of the camp at the weekends and evenings.

Most of the guys in my troop were a little older than me. It really wasn't that long before I was introduced to the sport of consuming alcohol, often to excess. Despite being under 18, it was relatively easy to get served in the local bars. It was also usual practice to be able to borrow driving licences from some of the older guys as your 'proof of age'. At that time, driving licences were just green slips of paper. They didn't have photographs so provided you could memorise the details and had a bit of confidence about you, then you would get served. You had to learn to navigate your way through the 'civvies' who didn't like us 'squaddies'. As far as they were concerned, we stole all the women. There were numerous reports of large fights and a general air of hostility when we went into the town. Other than being chased through the streets once or twice by a couple of gangs (they always tried to single out soldiers when they were alone), I never witnessed any massive problems. I have no doubt that some of it was urban myth, blown up out of all proportion, and used by my colleagues to add to their repertoire of 'war stories'.

My roommates and I preferred to travel to the nearby city of Leeds at the weekend. It was bigger, better, had many more pubs, less trouble and was only around half an hour away on the train. Quite how we found the Hofbräuhaus in Leeds is anyone's guess. For a 17-year-old who had spent most of his teenage years in Cornwall, this place was like an adult theme park! Bavarian-costumed girls with low cut tops waited on long bench tables. There were wall to wall women, a band playing on stage and upon instruction from them, we were required to clamber onto the wooden benches and sing oompah songs. The beer came in one litre steins; it was strong, the atmosphere was great, and everything was very good hearted. On my first visit, after drinking far too much I ended up throwing up into the road outside, only to be approached by a police officer who was concerned for my welfare. I realised I had only ten minutes to get to the railway station and catch the last train back to Harrogate. I assured him I was OK, found my mates and we all ran to the station, me desperately holding back the urge to be sick again. On arrival back at camp, the challenge was then to get past the guardroom as quietly as possible without being noticed as being drunk, and of course underage.

On another weekend soiree into Leeds and visit to the Hofbräuhaus, I met my first real girlfriend. Whilst I'd had one or two in my time at school, it never got beyond 'walking around' with each other. I was a late developer, painfully shy around the opposite sex and it was only when alcohol greased the wheels that I loosened up enough to make conversation. Before I left to head back to camp, she passed me a telephone number scribbled onto a piece of paper. I remember that I kept checking it on the journey home, to make sure I didn't lose it. It turned out it was the number for a telephone box on a patch of grass close to her home. The process was simple;

call the number in the hope that someone would pick up the phone! Then explain that they had to go and fetch her from number seven, the house opposite.

We saw a lot of each other during my time at Harrogate. On one occasion I had arranged to meet her in Leeds, but the whole of our Squadron was 'gated'. Gated meant that we were not allowed out of barracks, a punishment for not performing well enough on the drill square or something similar. This tended to be a relatively frequent event. I decided that it wasn't going to stop me. I paid Monty, a mate of mine, to take me into Leeds on his motorbike. I got back just in time for the nightly 'bed check', clambering under the blankets fully clothed, narrowly avoiding the duty officer doing his rounds. Beating the system and getting away with things was a bit of an adrenaline rush for me. It is something I have continued to do at various times in my life, for better and for worse. If I can see the rationale or sense in something, I'll comply, but if I don't, I often resist and buck the system.

During my periods of leave I always tried to get home to Cornwall, even though it was a long journey. I caught up with mates and even called in at school to show some of my former teachers that I had achieved something. Mum and my stepfather had moved to a different house in another village and financially things were much better for them. My stepfather had secured a good job at the Clay Works, a large local employer. My relationship with him also improved massively. I was no longer the cheeky little shit, having grown up and matured. Other than him disapproving of me coming home in a bit of a state after various drinking bouts with my old school friends, we got on well. My sister was shortly to leave home and join the army too. My brother was several years younger and still at school. I think he still harbours a deep-seated resentment that I left him behind and has often recounted what he perceives to be ill-treatment at the hands of our stepfather. I have always remained neutral on that point because I was not there to witness anything. Other than my stepsister, all three of us joined the services, mostly because job prospects in the area were limited. However, as it turned out, my stepsister married an RAF policeman. So, we all ended up with experiences of service life and I remain of the opinion that it was the making of us all.

During my progression through the college, I was selected to attend an outward-bound course in Wales. I had shown a continued interest in rock climbing and the outdoors. Captain Kemp, who ran this activity, was rumoured to be a former Special Forces Operator. Whether that was true or not was never fully established, but he was a tough, intimidating character and you didn't mess with him. He was the man who put me forward for the training; somewhere along the line it seems I had impressed him. This course was extremely hard work; you were swimming in the early morning sea, carrying and then throwing massive logs around, mountaineering, and navigating all sorts of terrain. It was both physically and mentally challenging but immensely enjoyable and gave me the confidence I had lacked before. It was pure adventure and the stuff I had joined the army for.

On one day, we were taken rock climbing at a popular spot. There were several groups of us. We were roped up, had our helmets on and were ready to ascend. The face was sheer; I had not climbed anything like it before. This was not going to be easy for any of us. It was very high. Initially I really struggled with the fear of falling and not feeling physically strong enough. At times my whole body was shaking, with what I know now to be adrenaline. I completed the first climb and felt elated. We were all well-acquainted with climbing protocols and what the verbal signal of 'below' meant. It was generally reserved for instances where a rock, or rocks, were dislodged by climbers. To avoid injury, it was a warning shouted to those beneath you.

As we were about to start our second climb of the day, I heard panicked shouts of, "Below! Below!" As you do under these circumstances, you naturally look up. I saw a man with his legs and arms outstretched, facing towards the sky, and plummeting towards us. Everything seemed to be in slow motion. He bounced off a large outcrop of rock on the way down and I saw one of his arms being severed and flying off to one side. I recall noticing he had no helmet and was not secured with a safety rope. The next thing I knew the ground close to us shook with a loud thud where he came to rest. He was lifeless, there was blood and guts everywhere. This was the first, but not the last time, I would see a dead body. We were ushered away, the police attended and some of the Permanent Staff from the outward-bound school helped to recover pieces of the man's body. There was no further discussion about it and to the best of my memory, none of us who were present and witnessed what had happened were ever asked anything further about it.

In July 1977 I graduated from the Army Apprentice College as a fully-fledged Radio Telegraphist. The passing out parade was resplendent, a huge affair with family and friends invited. It was a massing of all the Squadrons and hugely significant for every one of us. Ron Hails had drilled us for weeks, and at all hours of the day and night so that we would deliver a highly polished performance. We wore our best uniform, carried rifles, this time with fixed bayonets, and were again accompanied by a band of pipes and drums. Even today thinking about it sends tingles down my spine. It was one of my proudest moments. After two years of hard work, I felt like I had reached a milestone in my life. Mum travelled all the way up from Cornwall to see me graduate. My girlfriend came along. I introduced them to each other. I don't think Mum was overly impressed. In her eyes, this had all become too serious, too quickly. My girlfriend went on to become my first wife and the two of them became great friends. To my eternal shame, I left Mum in town and went off to celebrate in Leeds with my girlfriend, something which she never let me live down…

7. Regular soldier

In the final weeks of my apprenticeship, I had applied to be part of a secret and elite team of signallers. The Morse code instructor at Harrogate, who had persuaded me and a few others to join, had served with them previously. He regaled us with stories of the selection course. It involved going out into the wilderness alone, fending for yourself and avoiding capture. It was all the stuff from the war movies I had grown up with as a young boy. I had attained a degree of proficiency in Morse and was subsequently accepted for assessment with 602 Signal Troop.

The location for the intense four-week course was at the then home of 22 Special Air Service (SAS) regiment in Hereford. There were about 20 of us, I knew one or two of the guys from Harrogate. It was made quite clear that under no circumstances were we to pretend to be members of the SAS. Previous attendees of this course had done that in town to try and impress the ladies and ended up being dealt with by the real deal. This unit was so secret that I didn't really find out what they did until some years later. They were intelligence gatherers and worked closely with Special Forces. I only lasted a couple of weeks. The day was broken up with two periods of continual Morse lessons: morning receiving, afternoon sending. It was mind-numbingly boring. To this day, I regret giving up and throwing in the towel. Another factor in my premature decision and perhaps not entirely evident to me at the time, was being away from my new girlfriend. Desperate to be spending more time with her, my mind was elsewhere. On reflection I think my head had been turned far too early in my army career.

One thing that did work out for me quite well during my time at Hereford, was my regular forces sign up. At Harrogate it was well-known that you would be 'persuaded' to enrol for a minimum nine years of adult service, when you attained the age of 18 years. This was an unspoken directive from on high and designed to get maximum return on the investment in apprentices after their trade training. I reached the age of 18 during my short spell at 602. I was summoned into the office to 'sign on the dotted line' where a Corporal gave me the papers. I recall saying to him, "Do I have to sign for the full nine years?"

He shrugged his shoulders and replied, "Do what you want, no skin off my nose". I signed for the minimum three years; something that worked out quite well for me in the end. After asking to leave 602, I was sent to Catterick Garrison for a short time before being re-deployed to a regular unit. My time was spent on guard duty or making teas and coffees for more senior members of the unit. This was also extremely boring. It soon became apparent to me that once you were in the regular army, unless you were on exercise, travelling overseas or on active duty in places such as Northern Ireland, there were mostly menial tasks to perform. This was not really what I expected.

After what seemed like an eternity, probably only a few days, the Manning and Records Office got their arse in gear and I received my new posting. I had absolutely no idea what they had in store for me. The letter I received told me I was told to report to an infantry battalion in Kent. I was joining a Rear Link Detachment (RLD), a small team of signallers who were responsible for the provision of secure communications to

Brigade HQ. This sounded interesting, at first. The fact that it was in the UK also made it a little easier to travel to Leeds, where I was now spending most of my time off.

I hadn't had much to do with infantry soldiers previously. We were told somewhat unfairly by our peers that they were 'tick tocks', army barmy and gravel bellies. This is not unusual in the Armed Forces. Each unit has their own identity and mostly look down on others who aren't part of their tribe. Their camp in Gillingham, Kent was awful. It was made up of ancient, galvanised huts. The rooms had been partly modernised so you had your own space, but the washrooms were spartan and freezing in the wintertime. The food wasn't much better either.

The battalion I was assigned to work with sported a fawn-coloured beret. Our own berets were black, but we were made to wear their hats and insert our cap badges into them. It didn't feel right. I felt we were being stripped of our identity. Our sergeant was called 'Chic'. Another larger-than-life Scotsman, his bark was worse than his bite and he had a heart of gold. He oversaw our little outpost. In total there were five of us, a corporal and three signallers including me. I soon made friends with Steve. We were of a similar age. He was a Brummie who was friendly, charming and seemed to enjoy a lot of success with the local girls. We were opposites in some respects. He smoked – I hated it; I was still quite reserved – he would talk to anyone and everyone. I had only one relationship with a girl to my name, but I lost count of the number he had on the go at any one time. Despite our differences, we really got on and had some fine times over the two years we were together on this detachment.

I got the feeling that the battalion didn't really want us there. Their history was with the East of England where they recruited most of their men from. None of us were from that area and were classed as outsiders. We were embedded with their signals troop and got on reasonably well with them, the remainder just about tolerated us.

The daily routine continued to be mundane. It consisted of attending a morning parade, having a NAAFI break for half an hour at around 1030hrs, having lunch, going for a short sleep, reporting to signal troop, checking equipment and finishing at around 1600hrs, then repeating. The two years of hard work and apprenticeship training at Harrogate was, in my opinion, now of little use. I had begun to get quite resentful of the army. It was all my doing though; I had squandered a great opportunity at Hereford by not applying myself to the task in hand.

Around this time, the UK was in the midst of industrial turmoil and unrest. The Fire Service were threatening to strike, and as a result, all service personnel were to be mobilised to provide cover. The Green Goddesses, as they were known, were the military fire engines. Shortly after my arrival, we all received training in how to extinguish fires using these archaic machines at a nearby naval base. As it happened, we were never used, as we went onto what was known as 'Spearhead' rotation. In other words, we were the first in line in the event of war, a military conflict or other emergency, and expected to respond quickly.

In December of 1977, I went to Leeds to visit my girlfriend's house for the short Christmas break that some of us were allowed. It was on the proviso that you could get back to base within 24 hours. I enjoyed my visit so much that I reached the conclusion I wasn't going to return. I hated being with this battalion. I had already come to the attention of the Officer Commanding of Headquarters Company because I asked his permission to get engaged, something which you had to do at the time. 'The Frog', as he was affectionately known, told me I was a stupid boy for even thinking about getting married at such a young age. He was, of course, absolutely right. However, my youthful exuberance and arrogance couldn't see that. I decided that he was a dickhead, that the whole battalion was against me and embarked on a 'go slow', doing as little as I possibly could. In my view, there wasn't enough to do or keep me occupied. So, to extend my Christmas leave, I pretended I had food poisoning. I got my girlfriend to call the camp for me. There was nothing at all wrong with me; I just wanted another day or two in Leeds. When I finally returned 48 hours later, I was hauled before 'The Frog' and interrogated as to the seriousness of my illness. It landed me a stint of guard duty for my troubles. This was me trying to fight a system that just couldn't be beaten. I was drawing undue attention to myself and decided I just had to knuckle down and get on with it. The battalion then received notice that they were to be redeployed to Germany. We were informed that we would not be accompanying them. Our services for some reason were no longer required. We were then told that we would be staying in Kent and travelling a bit further down the coast to join another infantry battalion in Dover.

Thankfully, this next unit was much more welcoming. I have no idea why that was the case; they mostly hailed from the south of England, and perhaps my accent struck a chord. We got on straight away with the guys in the signal troop and soon joined them on the many drinking trips into the nearby town of Dover. We were also given a schedule of upcoming exercises and deployments. In the next year, we were going to be attending a huge exercise in Germany, travelling to Canada for a battle camp and then preparing for an emergency tour in Northern Ireland. Northern Ireland in the seventies was dangerous, and murders and attacks on the military were routine. We also learnt that we were heading to bandit country, South Armagh. The reality of what we had trained for began to sink in.

8. Travelling soldier

I cannot say the day-to-day work at the new camp improved very much. We continued to do menial tasks, such as maintenance, making sure vehicles were in order and general tidying up. I think this was just a way of keeping us occupied. As part of wider signals troop duties, we did get to do other things around the camp. This included on occasion manning the battalion telephone exchange. Well before automation, this old-fashioned system involved receiving calls, asking in a very formal manner who the caller wanted to be connected to and then inserting a plug from a cable into a board. It was all very low-tech. We were also briefed that, for security reasons, we were expected to monitor some of the calls. During one of my stints, a woman rang up in a very panicked state and asked to speak to her husband, one of the sergeants. I chose to listen to the call, and it went something like this: "John, John, are you there? Brian has a nail stuck in his ear!" I burst out laughing and had to rapidly disconnect the cable when I realised I'd left the line open and heard the caller accuse her husband of not taking their son's mishap seriously...

It wasn't long before we travelled to the Schleswig-Holstein area of Germany to take part in a very large NATO exercise called 'Bold Guard'. This was an annual show of strength by the British Army of the Rhine (BAOR) that was designed primarily to deter the Russians from encroaching into Europe. The night prior to the big exercise, Steve and I sneaked off into a nearby town and got absolutely steaming drunk. We got back around 3am and had to be on parade ready to go at 5am. Thankfully I couldn't drive so Steve did – how he stayed awake was anyone's guess.

We arrived in a large forest, where excavators had dug vehicle pits which our vehicles reversed into, making a complete mess of the woodland. This was all about camouflage and reducing the visibility of our communications hub. It was customary for us to either sleep in the cab of the Land Rovers or occasionally on the roof. This was mostly to avoid the cold or damp ground. In the morning, for some reason the two of us walked out of the vehicle pit momentarily to grab a cup of tea. We heard a loud creak and then a crash as a large pine tree collapsed onto the roof of our vehicle, where we would otherwise have been sleeping and working. The roots of the tree had become weakened because of the excavation. This shook the pair of us for a little while when we realised that we were minutes from being crushed to death.

I did plenty of travelling during my time with this battalion, but Canada stands out head and shoulders as the best. It was also the furthest I had travelled overseas so far. We set off from RAF Brize Norton in Oxfordshire on military flights. On arrival in Canada, we were driven out to a vast expanse of land containing a military base operated by the Canadian army. The sheer size of the surrounds made it ideal for exercising artillery and tanks. The things I remember were the size of the civilian trucks and motor cars, how the sky was so blue and how the landscape stretched for miles; it was stunning. It remains to this day one of my favourite travel destinations. We were assigned American-style Jeeps and with our jungle hats and bandanas, we really hammed it up when posing for photographs.

My mishaps continued though. On one occasion after a long night in the Communications Centre, one of the sergeants collared me before I got into my sleeping bag. He ordered me to top up the primitive water heaters. This was a simple means of having a ready supply of hot water for tea and coffee. It was two or three used compo ration cans with holes in the side, filled with sand soaked in petrol. It maintained a steady flame for the pan of hot water perched above it on a grill. The cans looked to me as if they had extinguished. Without thinking, I got a nearby jerrycan of petrol and poured it directly into the cans. There was a loud whoosh as the jerrycan I was pouring from caught alight. I tried to shut the lid, panicked and threw the jerrycan towards a bush which then also caught fire. Unbeknown to me, a few of my colleagues were sleeping behind it and frantically scrambled out of the way. The fire was eventually brought under control but could have been so much worse. The Sergeant came running towards me, punched me in the chest and shouted, "You fucking idiot, you could have killed them!" He was right, and I could have done myself serious injury as well, but thankfully everyone escaped unscathed.

Steve and I always wanted to push the boundaries and do different things. On one of our weekends off, we decided to hitchhike into Vancouver. We got picked up by a very attractive young Canadian girl who didn't seem to care that she had two strangers in her car. Everyone we met there had a carefree nature about them; it was great. We were also offered a job on the oil rigs by a trucker. It was tempting but would have meant deserting the army; I admit it did enter both of our heads for a while. We were eventually dropped off in the city which was absolutely buzzing. We spent two nights in Vancouver, visiting all manner of drinking establishments.

One night we were in a bar and the DJ shouted out, "Is anyone here from England?" Steve and I stood up and shouted at the top of our voices, "YES!!!" The place went mad, everyone was clapping and whistling. We didn't pay for a single drink there all night. After getting completely wasted, we stumbled into the street. I piled Steve into a shopping trolley and pushed him into the middle of the road, failing to notice a police patrol car with two armed officers watching us. Thankfully, it only resulted in a stern warning for the pair of us.

On another night off, we decided to slip out of camp without permission. We hitchhiked again and wound up in a remote bar full of locals. English people seemed to be a bit of a rarity in this part of Canada and once again we were very well looked after. Somehow, we ended up talking to a cowboy-type called Wayne. He was dressed in the traditional hat, Levis and boots. Towards the end of the night, he offered to drive us back to the base. Unbeknown to us, it was illegal to have alcohol in a motor vehicle in the state of British Columbia, unless it was in the boot of the car. Our trip back to the base was interspersed with Wayne asking us if we wanted a drink, to which we always replied in the affirmative. Time after time he proceeded to stop the car, open the boot and return with bottle after bottle of spirits, which we guzzled from as we passed it around. To this day I have no recollection of getting through the security barrier and onto the base. I do remember Steve and I taking turns at driving Wayne's car around the parade square though. How we did not get caught is anyone's guess!

The next morning, Steve and I woke up with monster headaches. We both slept on the top of two opposite bunk beds. We squinted to look at each other as we woke from our slumbers. I then looked down and saw Wayne with his cowboy hat perched on his face, fast asleep and snoring on the bed below me. It was one of those moments, that went from being hilarious to deadly serious in nanoseconds. Our roommates were now rousing, making their way to the showers, and looking at the interloper quizzically. One of the Corporals passing by on his way to the showers looked at us both and said, "Who the fuck is that?!" Without admitting to anything, we told him to leave it with us. Steve and I realised we had to get Cowboy Wayne off the base before our bosses became aware, and quickly. To make things worse, we looked out of the window and saw his car was parked at an angle on the grass directly outside the block! This was sacrilege of the highest order at any military establishment and would soon attract attention. We woke Wayne up hurriedly. He was still in a drunken stupor. We knew we had limited time to get him off the camp. We shoved him out of the door, told him to go, thanked him for a great evening and spent the day waiting to be visited by the military police. Nothing came of it and whether Wayne escaped that day without a problem remains a mystery.

Canada was a blast and it still has a special place in my heart. I often describe it as a country that has all the great things about America and the UK rolled into one.

9. Northern Ireland and beyond

Not long after returning from Canada, our training for deployment to Northern Ireland commenced in earnest. Regardless of role or position, every soldier had to attend NITAT (Northern Ireland Training and Tactics) training before arrival 'in country'. We were all despatched to Hythe in Kent to complete most of it. The location was an old army base consisting of unoccupied married quarters that had been adapted for urban combat scenarios. However, we already knew we were to be deployed to the bandit country of South Armagh, which was, for the most part, rural.

South Armagh had a fearsome reputation. The paramilitary wing of the IRA, PIRA (Provisional IRA), operated like professional military units in this area. They would frequently mount Vehicle Check Points (VCPs) and their tactics of targeting the army and police with roadside bombs and ambushes were highly effective. It was known as 'bandit country' for good reason. During the training, we were shown photographs and films depicting the types of devices that PIRA were using to devastating effect. Bombs disguised in milk churns, car bombs, water bottles designed to attract inquisitive soldiers. We were told that they saw themselves as a guerrilla force, wearing camouflage, sinister black hoods, and were equipped with M16 rifles (or Armalites, as they were known at the time); it sounded more like a war zone than a peacekeeping mission.

We arrived at night into Belfast in March 1979 in full uniform and webbing, after being flown from England complete with 7.62 SLRs (Self Loading Rifles). We were all loaded onto four-ton military trucks to be driven to South Armagh. Our convoy of vehicles could hardly have gone unnoticed. We hadn't been issued with any ammunition. I wasn't alone in thinking, what would happen if we were to be ambushed by the professionals we had been briefed about? Thankfully, nothing happened. For the most part, that summed up Northern Ireland. There was a constant threat in the air with occasional bursts of activity but for most of the time it was a case of "hurry up and wait".

The changeover was, to the best of my recollection, with 42 Commando Royal Marines, and uneventful. Like any unit leaving the area at that time, it had been a tough four months for them; they had suffered losses and casualties. Few units escaped unscathed. Bessbrook Mill, or The 'Mill' as it was known to all who served in her, was a sprawling building and former linen factory. The area surrounding it was rural and strikingly beautiful. It reminded me of Cornwall. The border was porous and exploited by the terrorists who mostly conducted their operations from the town of Dundalk, a PIRA stronghold in the Republic of Ireland located some 20 miles away.

In The Mill there was no privacy; rooms were shared and mostly blocks of four to eight blokes in each. You slept after your shifts in a sleeping bag and were often woken up by mice crawling across you. There was a bar and you were allowed two cans of beer each day if you were not working. The shop within the base was called 'The Choggie'. This was a somewhat less than complimentary term for the Asian chaps who ran it. They were the only civilians brave enough to work for the army. Unsung heroes they most certainly were, not least for the abuse they had to put up with from certain individuals at the base. In the seventies it is not unfair to say that racism was fairly standard.

At the time, Bessbrook Mill was the busiest heliport in Europe. By all accounts it had been requisitioned in the seventies by the army as the headquarters to cover Newton Hamilton, Forkhill and the infamous Crossmaglen. Road movement south of Bessbrook was heavily restricted due to the prevalence of roadside bombs and ambushes. However, the army was fighting back. Bessbrook had its own resident SAS troopers. These guys, with their long hair, plain clothes and droopy moustaches, drifted in and out at all hours of the day and night. When I worked night shifts, I would often see them getting food from the canteen at odd hours. It was rumoured that on occasion they would bring paramilitaries back to their wing, located upstairs, to 'have a chat'. The operatives concerned kept themselves to themselves and didn't engage in small talk. Working in the Communications Centre, it was routine to receive a package regularly after midnight from 'upstairs'. There would be a knock on the hatch, you would open it, always to nobody there and a brown envelope addressed RUCLO, KNOCK and marked 'SECRET' would be lying there. For a while, the meaning of the address eluded me until I found out that it meant RUC (Royal Ulster Constabulary) KNOCK, being a place where the police Special Branch operated from. The envelopes contained cassette tapes and I can (of course) only speculate how the information had been obtained and what was contained in those tapes.

Days dwindled into weeks and monotony set in for most of us. But this, as we had been told many times during our training, was when PIRA could be at their deadliest. In a very short period, I recall the following incidents taking place. One of our smaller helicopters was shot at with a heavy machine gun whilst out on patrol, completely shattering the glass bubble canopy. Amazingly, the pilots survived and landed safely. One of the bases was mortared after a lorry pulled up close-by, unleashing five home-made mortar bombs on the compound. During that attack, a colleague known to many of us was sadly killed, with several other soldiers injured. The ante was on the up; we were being tested. In the Communications Centre (ComCen), intelligence was always incoming about suspects, events and what informants were saying.

Seeing all of this only served to remind me just how treacherous the place was. One morning in April whilst on duty, there was a huge boom from outside the perimeter. I had heard nothing like it before. The ground shook, all hell broke loose inside, and the QRF (Quick Reaction Force) were mobilised, alarms were going off, people were shouting and running about. An explosion close to the main gate had killed four police officers whilst inside their armoured Land Rover. It was a tragic loss of life. I later discovered that a 1,000-pound van bomb had been remotely detonated. At the time, this was believed to be the largest bomb ever used by the IRA. It was difficult not to let these things prey on your mind, but you had to get on with your job.

It certainly didn't deter me and one of my mates, Les, from leaving to get some air. Les was also Royal Signals, a brash, opinionated Mancunian. He didn't give a shit about very much, had a quick wit and we got on well. He discovered that there was a post run every day which always required a plain clothes and armed escort. Without consulting me, Les volunteered the pair of us and told me he had a plan. We presented ourselves in civilian clothes, booked out a Browning 9mm pistol and a full magazine each, which we proceeded to tuck into the back of our jeans. We were in the back of the van for the whole journey, but persuaded the battalion postman, an older private soldier, to drop us off in Lisburn. We then proceeded to go for a few drinks in a couple of bars. Thinking back, it was idiotic and a completely foolhardy, stupid thing to do. Lisburn was a relatively peaceful town, but we were found out straight away by a group of youths from the minute we arrived. By the grace of God, the pair of us, the postie and the mail made it back in one piece to Bessbrook, albeit the armed escort being a tad intoxicated.

On another uniformed escort into Belfast, there were four of us in a Land Rover. We were in traffic when a loud bang rang out. Our Corporal instantly thought we were under attack and had us all exit rapidly from the vehicle. I have to say that on this occasion I was scared, really scared, my heart was pounding. I remember thinking, "I've been trained but am I up to it if this is for real?" What was I supposed to do? I stood in the middle of the road like a plonker and had to be reminded to take cover. As it turned out, there had been a road traffic accident near to our vehicle which had caused the noise. We were told to get back into the Land Rover; the training kicked in, walk backwards, look around, turn around, look around, be alert. However, I fell into a traffic bollard behind me and tripped over, much to the amusement of some local youths on a bus.

During the four-month tour you were entitled to four days off, titled R&R (Rest and Recuperation). Clearly spending time locally was out of the question. You were told what days you would take and were duly transported to RAF Aldergrove for a flight home. Transport was invariably very early in the morning. It was dark and there were possibly around 20 of us to be driven to the airport, all in plain clothes. As I was about to jump onto the four-ton wagon, one of the sergeants shouted over and said, "Can you fire an SMG soldier?"

I said, "Of course!" I was then presented with a loaded sub-machine gun and told that I was doing the escort in the Q Car (plain vehicle).

As I got in, he said, "Lay the weapon across your lap pointing at the door. If you get stopped by those bastards, fire through it, no questions asked." This certainly had the effect of keeping me alert and awake for the whole journey...

Our tour lasted four months in all. Northern Ireland was a rite of passage for most soldiers at the time, but far too many gave their lives or received life-changing injuries over there. Had I remained in the army, then I would almost certainly have been returned there several times on rotation. As a 19-year-old I don't think I fully understood or appreciated the threats, or the situation we were in. It certainly gave me a grounding for my future career. I visited Northern Ireland again much later in the course of other work when 'The Troubles' had subsided somewhat. It brought back many memories and I thank my lucky stars I got out of there safely.

10. Leaving

Not long after returning from Northern Ireland, I received word that I was to be posted away to a regular signals regiment. I have no real recollection as to the reasoning behind it. It may have been because there were regular moves brought about by the powers that be.

After a short period of leave, in August of 1979 I arrived in Blandford, Dorset, the home of 30 Sigs. Shortly after arriving, news came in of many soldiers being killed by the IRA in Warrenpoint, an area well known to those of us who had served in South Armagh. They had murdered 18 soldiers from one of the most elite regiments in the British Army, the Parachute Regiment. This was a major coup for the IRA. For whatever reason, hearing the news hit me quite hard. I have no idea why, because I wasn't there, nor did I know anyone who had been killed. I remember calling Mum and telling her that I had only been there a few weeks ago and how lucky I had been. It was sad to hear so many men had lost their lives in such a cowardly attack.

The regiment I had been posted to were renowned globetrotters and I was told on arrival to expect to be travelling regularly. The base was huge and included the Royal Signals Museum. The barrack blocks had been built by John Poulson who had been imprisoned for bribery. I had no complaints as they were the most modern I had yet to encounter in all my military service. After the buzz of my time in Northern Ireland and being kept relatively busy, the place was initially dull. Once again, we seemed to spend an inordinate amount of time performing basic maintenance tasks and painting vehicles over and over again. I often found myself slipping away from work, going back to the block, going into town or generally not doing much.

I now had the added complication of getting from a remote part of Dorset to Leeds to see my girlfriend when I had time off at the weekend. By this time, I had asked her to marry me. I didn't see a future for either of us on a military base, so I began to make plans to leave the army.

My problems getting to Leeds were solved when I was introduced to Brian, a fellow soldier whose brother was also known to me. By sheer coincidence, his girlfriend lived in Leeds as well. He had a motorbike and offered me a lift if I could cope with the rigours of being a pillion rider. I had never done this before but the idea of riding on the back of his Honda 750 Four motorcycle was quite exciting. Brian could really ride his bike and we would fly along the country roads and motorways after sneaking off early on a Friday afternoon. The expectation on a Friday was that you would present yourself in the bar for a drinking session. Failure to do so would leave you singled out as not being 'a team player'. When it was unavoidable to attend, we would both turn up, speak to a few people, and leave as soon as we could.

Drinking was firmly embedded in services culture. You were definitely not 'one of the lads' if you couldn't or wouldn't down several beers. It certainly seemed to be the case that promotion was off the agenda if you failed that test. The drinking culture reared its head time and time again when I was in the services. It was commonplace, a way of relaxing and letting off steam. At times it got completely out of hand with some very outlandish bar games, such as running along with a lighted newspaper between your arse cheeks, also known as the Zulu warrior, but that's another story...

Blandford to Leeds was about 270 miles and we would often get there just before 6pm when the pubs opened, long before all-day opening. Brian and I would spend most weekends in Leeds. We would head back to Blandford when the pubs had shut, most often after both of us had been drinking. One night, very tired and completely bored, I dropped off asleep on the back of the motorbike. I was jolted upwards just in time as my body began to fall backwards. Brian, feeling that the balance was being lost on the bike, thankfully slowed down and pulled over for a breath of fresh air. All night motorway services were not the norm at the time. We would often arrive at the camp around 4am absolutely knackered. I would lay down on my bed for an hour or two, get showered, have breakfast, go to morning parade, and then go back to the block to sleep.

My motivation for soldiering was slipping away. I had my heart set on setting up home in Leeds. In October 1979, we were notified that our Colonel in Chief, Her Royal Highness (HRH) Princess Anne was to be inspecting the Regiment. The powers that be decided for some reason, that rather than wear ceremonial dress for the parade, we would wear 'combats' (our camouflage uniform). We were all issued with a brand-new set which then had to be ironed to have creases put into them. For the more professional soldiers this was violation, for the purpose of camouflage was having to an unbroken and random pattern, making it easier to blend into terrain so you could not be seen. This wasn't something you could achieve with razor sharp creases. We practised drill for what seemed like weeks. Rather than marching in three ranks, we were to be jogging to the parade square. It resembled the sort of ceremony you would see in an African nation. It seemed bizarre to all of us, but no one could question it.

The day arrived, and we were told that Princess Anne would inspect us and may choose to converse with one or two of us. No one instructed us on what we should say if that was to be the case. We trotted onto the square, some of us trying to keep it together after the many hilarious comments from jokers within our ranks. We knew if we were caught laughing, or even smiling, then we would be heading to the camp jail but it didn't deter us. The inspection began. Being relatively tall, I was in the front row and on the far left. When this type of inspection takes place, it is often the case that those in the front get the most attention from the reviewer. I could see Princess Anne out of the corner of my eye, accompanied by three senior officers including the Camp Commandant. I was silently praying to myself that she wouldn't bother to talk to me, and my heart was pounding. I realised that she hadn't stopped for a little while and before I knew it, royalty was stood directly in front of me. The conversation was short and went something like this.

"How is 30 Signal Regiment?"

All I managed to utter was, "Nice, Ma'am." I could see the Camp Commandant's face grimace and glare back at me. Completely star-struck, I couldn't think of anything remotely coherent to say. My colleagues, thinking it was hilarious, ribbed me about it for weeks on end. Thankfully I never heard anything from the Commandant.

I made some really good friends in Blandford and my interest in forces life was rekindled for a time, when I discovered that a small number of us were to be heading to Norway with the Royal Marine Commando Logistic Regiment. We were to undergo the rigours of Arctic Warfare training, something I had wanted to do since I attended the Royal Marines recruiting office in 1975. Preparation for the course would involve a lot of fitness training. On arrival in Norway, we were to be taught how to ski Langlauf-style and survive in a variety of snow and ice shelters. This was the type of thing that I joined up for.

In October of 1979, I undertook some of the most intensive training that I ever encountered during my time in the forces. In all, it took three months to get us to the required standard. It involved numerous route marches with weapons and full kit in readiness for deployment in arctic conditions. Distances ranged from nine miles to 30 miles. It also entailed trips to places like Mount Snowdon in Wales to test map-reading skills and our resilience to inclement weather. It was well understood that there was an expectation that we would have to 'keep up' with the Green Berets. Our officers did not want us to be found wanting when working with the Commandos. We also had two guys from the Royal Air Force join us and one of them, 'DB', became one of my best drinking buddies. Undoubtedly, this was a time when I was at my fittest.

To the best of my recollection, our small team joined the Royal Marines at their Plymouth base in January 1980 to travel overseas early the next morning. This annual exercise was titled 'Pendulum 80', another event designed to demonstrate to the Soviets that the British Military were able to operate in the harshest of winter conditions. Norway has a border with Russia and over the years there had been a source of tension between the two countries.

Each of the three services has its own way of doing things with accompanying unique slang. We were quickly familiarised in the language used by our Royal Marine hosts: 'the heads' for example, meant the washrooms and toilets, whereas 'nutty' translated as sweets, and 'trapping' signified a level of success with the opposite sex.

We left that morning in a huge convoy of 'Arctic ready' military transport. For some of our vehicles, this merely meant studs in the tyres and thick rubber matting on the floors of the Land Rovers used to transport our radio equipment. We were told to expect it to be very cold. Frostbite was a distinct possibility if we did not take precautions. On our way, we drove past villages in Cornwall that I knew well. Whilst I didn't see them, my mum and stepfather came to wave me off at Falmouth, where we embarked onto military shipping.

Arriving in Norway, I realised just how cold it was going to be. It was a dry sort of cold, and I had never experienced anything like it. We drove in convoy to a Norwegian holiday park which was closed for the winter. The whole complex had been taken over by the military, including a large bar area, which, of course, was considered essential. We were quite lucky to be allocated a small pine lodge where four of us shared the accommodation. It was warm, cosy and only a short walk through very thick snow to all the necessary facilities.

We received instructions to head to the stores and sign out our skis and poles. Across the road from the camp, a slope had been commandeered by our colleagues who were all practising their skiing skills. These skis were not of the type I was familiar with. They were painted white, made of wood and had to be waxed regularly. The heavy Arctic boots we now wore had to be clipped into the skis via a part of the sole which protruded from the front. The heel of the boot lifted off the ski so you could propel yourself along. This was known as 'Langlaufing', a hybrid of cross-country and downhill skiing. It was used by the Norwegian army who were renowned for their expertise in Arctic Warfare. I signed out my new equipment, along with a few other lads, and headed over the road to the slope, eager to break the kit in.

Because of the volume of troops on the slope, the snow had become compressed quickly and looked ideal for a speedy descent. Our little team positioned ourselves at the top, deciding we were to have a race to the bottom. As young men generally do, we all launched ourselves at the slope with gusto, shouting obscenities at each other as we pelted along. It wasn't long before I completely misjudged my speed and several obstacles. I lost control quickly, tripped and embedded my right ski into some thick snow. The speed I was travelling, coupled with the sudden impact of the snow, launched me head over heels. I landed on my back and heard a loud crack but thankfully no pain. When I picked myself up, much to the amusement of my friends, my right ski was in two pieces. You could say I had done a great job of 'breaking them in'… I gathered myself up, picked up what was left of my dignity and headed back to the store to get another pair of skis. The Royal Marine Quartermaster was not at all happy. Questioning my parentage in a tirade of abuse, I thought better of answering back. It was in fairness, only a matter of about 20 minutes earlier that I had signed out the kit from his store.

Six of us had been selected for the three-week Arctic Warfare Training course which we already knew was going to gruelling. It involved skiing long distances in full kit with a very heavy Bergen rucksack and the 7.62 standard issue SLR rifle. These rifles were long, cumbersome and heavy. When you fell off your skis, which happened frequently, the rifle butt would hammer into your face. Getting up off the ground after falling off skis and regaining your balance is difficult enough at the best of times. With a heavy Bergen and rifle, it was ten times as hard. Once you had fallen on the deck, you had to remove your rucksack and rifle and carefully lay it in the floor. You then got to your feet gingerly before leaning down to put your equipment back on. Invariably it meant falling over several times. It was tiring and the process drained you of energy. You had to take in food regularly and drink copious amounts of water to stand a chance of surviving each day. Failure was not an option for us; we had to keep up.

During this training, we were deep in Norwegian countryside in their winter. It was extremely cold and from our training we knew that removing our gloves for longer than a few seconds, we would get frostbite, possibly leading to amputation of our fingers. We had two layers of gloves, the top cover being mittens and the second layer contact gloves. The contact gloves had plastic pimples on them and were essential when touching the metal surfaces found on radio masts and the like.

Sleeping out in the Norwegian wilderness in a variety of snow shelters was also part of the course. There were two that stick in my mind, the first of which was a snow hole. This involved burrowing a tunnel directly into the layer of snow on the mountain you were on. On this particular evening, the snow was falling heavily, and the driving wind upped the chill factor. To keep warm, we took it in turns to dig. Once a full body length could comfortably lay in the tunnel, you then had to dig upwards so as to create an upper shelf for four men to sleep in. Once you had burrowed in, the snow became much firmer. Ski poles were then driven through the snow from the inside to allow air into the sleeping area. We were then informed by the instructors that it was going to be an exceptionally cold night. They told us to position candles in the tunnel to warm the air up sufficiently to allow it to rise upwards into our makeshift bedroom. I think we all thought we would be found dead in the morning. Somehow, I won the position closest to the tunnel to sleep on. It won't surprise you to learn that I didn't get much sleep that night. I was continually making sure our candles didn't expire and us with them.

On another night, we were tasked with digging a large circular hole in the snow. All of us carried a diamond shaped waterproof canvas. These canvases could be laid side by side and secured together to make a large circular cover. It was then used to act as a roof covering for an underground shelter. About twelve of us clambered inside. Everyone's feet had to point to the centre; we were positioned like hands of a clock. After another tough day of cross-country skiing, we were dog-tired and after eating our rations, got into our sleeping bags and rested. You couldn't really call it sleep. Unbeknown to us, there was a massive dump of snow overnight. I remember waking up with something heavy on my face: it was the roof that had collapsed because of the sheer volume of snow. No one could move and we had to be dug out by our colleagues. No one panicked, as I think we had all been conditioned to just get on with it.

As we were rescued, I remember looking over to one of my new mates, a black sailor. All I could see was a pair of white eyes. I told him so and we laughed continually. It was a very nervous type of laughter though, a coping mechanism. Thankfully, everyone escaped unhurt. There was no fuss, no chatter; we made breakfast, got back on our skis and all left the area. For service personnel this sort of thing is entirely normal, drama is not welcome or necessary. You didn't have time to sit and think for too long about what might have been. You took it in your stride and got on with it.

I was in Norway for three months, training for Arctic Warfare, providing communications and wherever possible getting much needed rest and recuperation. This at times involved lots of drinking. The Norwegian people were very friendly and we caused them no trouble, as far as I am aware. The girls were friendly and attractive, wearing what were affectionately known at the time as 'spray-on' trousers. Beer was extremely expensive. A half pint of lager was the equivalent of £1.50, probably three times as much as what we were accustomed to paying for a pint. Not to be put off, our little gang of miscreants came up with a solution. The Royal Marines had a duty-free bar on the camp. You could get every type of drink you could possibly need for a fraction of the local prices. First, we approached a couple of friendly nurses we had got to know on the camp for some small plastic bottles. These were then filled from bottles of duty-free rum, whisky or vodka purchased from the bar. We then fashioned a sort of strap with what was known as 'para cord', so that we could smuggle the booze into the nightclubs between our legs. It had the effect of making the bottles and the drink contained within them very warm. This meant we were saving money and getting drunk without paying silly prices. We even shared our drinks with some of our new-found Norwegian friends who often commented on the temperature, but we didn't disclose to them the reasons why.

11. The last few months

The final exercise was held in the mountain ranges of Narvik in Northern Norway, close to the Arctic Circle. It was a full-blown military deployment for which we provided the communications. It culminated in an attack on a simulated enemy base on a frozen lake in the early hours of the morning. My mates and I discovered that, if you spat at minus 30 degrees, it would solidify into a tiny pellet. This distracted us endlessly as we fired them at each other and was an indication of just how cold it was. So cold in fact that my rifle froze completely that morning, leaving me unable to discharge any blank rounds during the attack.

Norway was a fantastic experience on so many levels, not least because of the many physical challenges. Importantly though, I had achieved my childhood dream by completing the Mountain and Arctic Warfare course. I departed on a high, but I also knew that I was going to be leaving the army soon and getting married that year. My fiancée had been working hard on the preparations for the wedding whilst I was away. Somewhat naively, I hadn't given a great deal of thought about what I wanted to do for a job when I left. However, I do remember watching news clips about the Special Patrol Group or SPG in the Metropolitan Police, who were dealing with riots in London. Their direct, uncompromising style struck a chord with me for some reason.

It was around this time that I decided I would begin to explore joining the police service. I went to Leeds to check in with my wife-to-be. We had some early discussions about where we were going to live. Something else I had not given enough consideration to. Service life is such that most things get sorted out for you. At the time most soldiers lived on camp. Even the married guys had quarters within the bounds of the barracks. As a single soldier, from a domestic perspective you had little to concern yourself with. Food, bedding and uniform was provided. You obviously had to take care of your own washing, ironing and civilian clothes, but other than that, life was easy. Most of us spent our recreational time with each other and viewed 'civvies' as a different race altogether. My frequent trips to Leeds had given me different perspectives though and I was quite looking forward to becoming a civvy once more.

Somewhere around this time, I managed to get myself enrolled on an army driving course and pass my test, which was a bit of a coup. I didn't think the army would train me to drive in the knowledge that I was due to leave in a matter of months. I passed my test the first time around. Whilst I had been having some driving lessons with civilian instructors, they had been expensive and, because of various deployments, sporadic. Having a full driving licence for when I finally left the forces was immensely helpful.

After returning from Norway and a short period of leave, I found myself on the move again. This time to Cyprus for a six-week-long battle camp and exercise. We flew in and were despatched to a bleak looking barracks in the middle of nowhere called 'Bloodhound Camp', just outside a place called Episkopi. The Cypriot and Turkish dispute over land in the country was still quite raw. At the time of writing, the country remains divided into two territories: Northern and Southern Cyprus.

On the day we arrived, there was a rumour that EOKA, a Greek Cypriot nationalist paramilitary organisation that fought a campaign for the end of British rule in Cyprus, had placed a bomb on a water pipe leading into our camp. I never found out whether that was true or not. It was a reminder that not everyone in the country was happy with the considerable military presence on the Island.

In sharp contrast to Norway, it was extremely hot. It called for a slightly different period of acclimatisation. During our working days, this meant a gradual but increased exposure to physical exercise in preparation for the more serious military manoeuvres that lay ahead.

As you would expect, our recreational time there involved drinking copious amounts of alcohol when we had time off. A small group of us had discovered that local bars served a drink called 'brandy sour'. This national cocktail was mostly brandy mixed with a hint of lemon and cane sugar spread around the rim of the glass. We became very partial to them. The hangovers were something else. Education around the subject of hydration was not as readily available as it is today. I am sure lots of those banging headaches could have been avoided if we had consumed more water.

Since returning from Norway, a new second in command had been appointed. Captain Vasper was a hard taskmaster. He made it plain from the outset that we were all going to be tested. No one really appreciated what he meant. The rumour was that he had been previously associated with the Special Forces. In other words, he could come up with all sorts of excruciatingly painful tests to push us hard. Unfortunately for me, he had learnt that I was planning to leave the army. Because of this, I seemed to come under additional scrutiny. One of our first tasks was a route march across a mountainous and barren area of Cyprus. It was to be held over the course of a day and we were broken up into teams of three or four. We had a series of checkpoints that we had to arrive at by a certain time. Allocated only one water bottle each, we were informed that there would be a water bowser at each checkpoint location. Here we could top up and be told where we would be heading next. None of us had a clue as to when and where we would be finishing. The heat was searing. It was apparent we had to carefully manage our individual water consumption. Drink too much and too often and you were going to struggle, but drink too little and you would collapse with dehydration.

My team and I arrived at our first checkpoint well within time. We topped up our water and were then presented with a donkey. The latest addition to the team, we were informed, was now to be taken with us everywhere. We had no equipment to speak of, so it was not going to help us with anything. The donkey proved to be both stubborn and burdensome. It had a rope around its nose. If it didn't want to move, you had a tug of war on your hands. It was tiring, it slowed us down, the sole purpose being psychological. None of us had any previous experience of handling donkeys! There were a significant number of checkpoints. Almost all were several miles apart and most involved going back up, or down, the hill we had just come from. We had minimal rations and despite all the promises, there was no food at the checkpoints. The kindly Captain Vasper, as we later discovered, was trying to replicate aspects of Special Forces training. The sort designed to test your resolve and determination when pushed. His expectations were that we would sit down and give up. I wouldn't say we didn't eff and blind, but we didn't give up. It was hard work and we kept going until finally we turned a corner in the dark to find our transport ready to take us back to camp. We handed back our allocated donkey and headed off for a much-needed meal and rest.

There was much more in store for us over the next few days. Exercise 'Lions Sun' was a battle camp. We got to fire all manner of weapons and take part in 'live fire' exercises. It also involved being broken up into smaller groups to experience other aspects of military capability.

At one point, we visited a Military Police Dog Handling unit stationed nearby. We gathered around an enclosure to watch how a trainee attack dog deals with aggressors. One of the dog handling team was present in a padded suit. It covered all his body, his hands completely concealed and out of view. To ensure that his head was safe, he had a metal cover attached to the top of the suit. It resembled a hanging basket, but had more of a bulbous shape to it. Once kitted out, he went to hide behind a wooden barrier. We were told to watch for the dog and his handler as it entered the enclosure. The German Shepherd was quite young and bouncy, but very alert and was tugging on the lead already. It was being pulled back regularly by its handler to the command of 'heel'. Both got to about a quarter of the way across the compound when the handler in the padded suit broke from cover. The dog handler shouted several times for his suspect to stop before releasing his dog. When he did, it was like watching the launch of a guided missile. The dog literally flew across the enclosure, looking at nothing but the guy in the padded suit. Launching upwards within a few feet of the 'suspect', it grounded him instantly, taking hold of his arm and violently shaking it in his mouth, until the handler casually walked up and made his arrest. I looked around; jaws had dropped as we were all in awe of the power of the dog.

Still talking about what we had witnessed, one of the dog handlers announced that they wanted a volunteer for the next phase. As you can probably imagine, after seeing what had happened, no one came forward. However, Captain Vasper was present and he promptly identified me as someone who was due to leave the army very soon. This was to be his parting gift to me. I wasn't a fan of dogs at the time, we hadn't had one as kids, and I didn't relish the thought of being savaged. To a few cheers from my colleagues, I gingerly stepped forward.

The padded suit and head cage were quickly fitted before I was told to go to the side of the enclosure. The instructions I was given were, that on seeing the dog, I was to run across the compound as had been demonstrated earlier. Some minutes later, I saw the handler and dog arrive in the compound. Something was different though. This was a much larger German Shepherd. My so-called friends cheered me on as I ran for my life, which was impossible in a padded suit. The next thing I knew was that I had been struck from behind with what felt like a sledgehammer. This dog was on a mission, and he meant business; he was growling, barking and extremely aggressive. I laid face down in the dirt, but it somehow managed to pick me up, roll me over and go for my throat! I was being pulled about like a rag doll, much to the amusement of my friends. This was not a pleasant place to be. After what seemed like an eternity, the dog was placed back on its lead. It was then announced that the first dog we had seen was in training. The dog they had set on me was a veteran and the fiercest they owned! As ever, Captain Vasper found that highly amusing...

Next, we were all told that we were taking part in an Escape and Evasion exercise. This involved being stripped down to the most basic of equipment, being driven into the middle of the Cypriot wilderness, and making our own way back to camp. The overall objective was 'not' to be captured by a Hunter Force who we were informed had attack dogs with them.

We were in small groups, captured quickly and shepherded into a barn. It was all a set-up; one of the umpires told us that if an opportunity arose, we should attempt an escape. A short time later, a door was found to be insecure. We all burst out en masse and set off again. I was on my own and took the decision to lay low for a while, my rationale being that I would allow others to get caught first.

A couple of hours later, I set off and began to make my way through a corn field. I was strolling at a leisurely pace, confident that no one was about. Then I heard dogs barking in the distance accompanied by shouts of "There's one of them!" I hit the deck and crawled along the ground hoping for the best. I could hear their voices; I couldn't see anyone and was pretty sure they couldn't see me. Then I heard dogs barking quite close to where I was. One of the voices shouted, "Come on out or we'll let the dogs off!" The same voice shouted, "Last chance!"

At that point I stood up, arms in the air. I'd assumed that the barking dogs would be the standard German Shepherd I had encountered a few days earlier. Imagine my surprise when I saw that the two dogs stood there on leads were both Labradors, or in other words, sniffer dogs. Had they been set on me, they would probably have licked me to death! I'd been well and truly conned but in my defence the reaction was hardly surprising, given my earlier experience with attack dogs.

I was blindfolded by the 'enemy' and transported face down in their vehicle to the camp, a boot firmly in my back throughout the journey. On arrival, most of my mates were now in a metal cage. I was one of the last to be caught because I had laid up for a while. It was about 5pm but still quite hot. We were not provided with any water and were regularly ordered to perform press-ups or sit-ups. There were about 20 of us in this makeshift prison. Before I had the chance to settle down and have a chat with anyone, I was pulled out and dragged into a darkened room. There was a bright light shining in my direction, making the figures behind it shadowy. I was then forced to look directly at the light and kneel on a broom handle laid across the floor. This, I can tell you, is very painful. The figures behind the light demanded to know who I was. We had all been briefed before the exercise started that if an interrogation situation arose, we were only to provide 'Name, Rank and Number', nothing more. I recognised the voices behind the light as our troop sergeants. Nonetheless the fact that I was tired, thirsty and hungry made it at times feel quite real. I was shouted at, threatened and called all manner of names but found it relatively easy to stick to the script. Ultimately, nothing bad was going to happen; this, after all, was designed to provide some exposure to the process if we were ever captured by a **real** enemy. I couldn't help but ponder that the chances of this happening to me prior to leaving the army, were extremely limited.

After about 10 minutes or so, I was taken out of the room and back into the cage. A short time later I was pulled out again, a hood placed on my head and taken to an area of the camp I had not been to before. It was a comfortable office with soft furnishings and was a welcome interlude from the heat outside. The Sergeant, whom I knew, offered me a glass of water and a biscuit. I took it without hesitation as I was so hungry and thirsty. He went on to ask how I was, what sort of day I had experienced so far and slipped in a few questions about where I lived and what I did at the weekends. I relaxed and entered into a conversation with him. I was at the receiving end of a bit of psychology. I came to realise some years later that I had been on the receiving end of a system known as 'good cop, bad cop', often used to unsettle interviewees. During the debrief, we were congratulated on how well we had performed. But of course, Captain Vasper couldn't possibly resist making a point of telling all and sundry about my reaction to the Labrador search dogs.

Cyprus was my last military outing. Upon arriving back at Blandford, the leaving celebrations took place and I departed with discharge papers in hand. I headed to Leeds to start the next chapter in my life.

For a while, I stayed in touch with many of my service friends. I knew I would miss them much more than the army. The comradeship you receive in the forces is unequalled. It is difficult to describe and only those who have served will understand what I mean. The Army provided me with a wide range of skills including self-discipline, motivation and tenacity. It didn't prepare me for everything I was to experience in my next career. I'm not sure anything can do that.

12. Green to Blue

Imarried the mother of my children in a small town on the outskirts of Leeds in August of 1980. Because I was still officially in service and on leave, I was permitted to wear military best dress on the day. At the tender age of 20, we were both young and naïve, yet in love nonetheless. The reception was a very low-key, family affair. In keeping with the times, it consisted of a buffet at a local public house. My mum was there, proud as punch. My dad attended with my stepmother and two stepsisters. However, they came only to the church service and then made their excuses and left. I've never fully understood why they felt they couldn't stay for a short time. Our honeymoon in Great Yarmouth was equally low-key. To this day, I have no idea why we chose that place. I have little, if any, memory of what we did, where we went or stayed, but it was for only a few days as I recall. Our savings had been swallowed up by the wedding.

We both knew we had to find somewhere to live, and quickly. At the time we were living with my mother-in-law, but that was only going to be a short-term solution. We had been unable to resolve the small matter of a place to set up home. Finally, via a family contact we found a small ground floor flat and settled on it. The property was in a rather insalubrious part of Leeds.

The next step was to get myself mobile. I purchased my first ever car from the neighbour upstairs. It was a white

L-registered Ford Cortina and reasonably reliable. Cars back then suffered from terrible rust and holes in the bodywork quite early on in their life, and mine was no exception. They were also easy to break into. Within weeks of moving into the flat, my toolbox was stolen from the boot. I was soon to become accustomed to dealing with thefts from vehicles.

I knew I also had to find a steady job. I had often thought about joining the police. It seemed like a natural progression from the army. For some reason, the first application I made to join the police was as a civilian in a communications role. I went along to the interview in Bradford where I met two senior officers. They both promptly talked me out of the position, telling me I would be wasted in a control room, that I would be much better applying for the 'real' police and that I would only be frustrated listening to what was going on at the other end of the radio. It was good advice, and I am glad I took it. I submitted more forms and waited for the response.

The next stage was an invitation for a written exam in Leeds which I passed. However, I was told that it may be several months before I would hear more. I had to find myself a job in the interim and applied for several via an agency. They all involved manual work in factories and the wages were awful. By chance, the neighbour I had purchased the car from needed a labourer to work away with him during the week. The money was very good. During the months prior to hearing back about my application to join the police, I lived in Scarborough, North Yorkshire, from Monday to Thursday, in a bed and breakfast, spending most evenings in the pub with the guys I worked with. The job was unskilled, but it kept me busy. I was well looked after by the boss. We even disappeared together for long lunch breaks playing Space Invaders and suchlike at the various amusement arcades on the seafront.

About the time I applied to join the police, a long overdue report into their pay and conditions had been released. Police salaries had been on the decline for years. Married officers were reported to be taking second jobs and in receipt of benefits to make ends meet. Lord Edmund-Davies had published his report calling for an immediate increase in wages. This triggered a huge rise in recruitment, and as a result I was swept along with an influx of applicants, which only served to slow things down still further.

As part of the process, a local police inspector came to our flat. I still remember his name and his demeanour. An indication of police managers at the time, he was very stern and officious. During my 'home interview', he related a scenario to me. It went something like this:

"OK, son, you're in the police, you're on patrol in Leeds at night and three drunken guys come up to you and start giving you some hassle, what are you going to do?"

I thought about this for a short time and said, "I would tell them to calm down and if things didn't improve, I would get on my radio and call for back up."

He shook his head and replied, "No, this is what you would do. You would hit the biggest one as hard as you possibly could. The others would just fuck off!" He went on to tell me that the police had to win every time; they always had to be harder, be faster and not take any shit whatsoever. That was the way to uphold the law and I wasn't about to question it. Not quite the message I had read in the recruitment brochure, but the police at that time held a tremendous amount of respect; quite possibly because of this approach.

A medical and another interview held on the same day at the police headquarters in Wakefield followed shortly after. The examination was nothing to speak of – deep breaths, cough and so on – and didn't seem to last too long at all. I passed and was taken to sit outside a room with two small lights, red and green mounted on the door frame. I was told that when the green light came on, I was to knock and enter the room.

On came the green light and I walked through the door. There were three Superintendents behind a long oak table, one of whom was a female. This was the first time I had seen a woman in a senior position. I certainly didn't recall it from my time in the military. The chair of the board said they were impressed with my exam results and the fact that I had an exemplary service record. If the truth be known, unless you did something bad in the army everybody was marked as exemplary on their discharge papers. I was asked if I had witnessed or had been involved in anything risky or scary whilst in the army. I related some of the incidents in Northern Ireland, choosing to leave out any mention of the recreational trip to Lisburn.

After a very short time, they told me to wait outside. At that point, I thought I had blown it. I sat down only briefly, because the green light came back on almost immediately. I went back in and the chair of the board said, "Congratulations, you have been successful." I was over the moon and thanked them profusely. I had a job and the one I wanted!

There were no mobile phones at the time and we didn't even have a landline at the flat, so I had to wait until I arrived home to tell my wife, who was pleased but concerned in equal measure. I hadn't really thought much about the risks associated with the job, nor had I considered how she felt about it, if I am honest. I was just happy to have secured a position.

I received my acceptance letter a few days later. It confirmed that I would be joining West Yorkshire Metropolitan Police in February of the following year.

13. Training school

In February 1981, I reported for duty at what was then known as the West Yorkshire Police Academy. The lecture theatre was packed with men and women of all ages, shapes and sizes. All of us were told that this was the largest intake of recruits the Force had experienced for many years. I did not know a soul. Whilst I had been living and travelling to and from Yorkshire for many years, I was not a native and my Southern accent was noticeable. I didn't have many friends and already felt out of place. I was only 21 years of age; a lot of the people were much older and seemed to have much in common, not least the fact they were relatively local.

An inspector and a sergeant entered the room, and we were ordered to stand up. This was nothing new to me; I had been used to it and stood bolt upright. Others looked puzzled and clearly had no idea what they were being asked to do. Both men stood on the stage at the front and introduced themselves. They were to be responsible for us before we were despatched to our training schools.

The Sergeant went through what we should expect in the coming weeks. He also made it plain that if were married, our partners would have to be very special because the career we were about to embark upon was going to test them as well as our relationships. He told all the men present that we should never leave our homes unshaven or be scruffy in public whether off or on duty. We were not to take on debt and permission was required for a whole range of things, including buying a house. Female officers were in the minority in the police at that time and our intake was no different. At some point during the proceedings, all the ladies were taken away by a female sergeant to be briefed on how they were to behave and dress.

As the events of the morning unfolded, the Inspector announced that we were to be called individually to the stage. A subject of conversation was to be provided to us and we would be expected to tell everyone present about it. This was one of my biggest fears. I absolutely hated the thought of speaking in front of a group of people whom I did not know. I watched as different people clambered onto the stage, some of them natural speakers who had us howling with laughter. Even now I remember one or two of them very well. Others, like me, were incredibly nervous. The whole purpose of this exercise was to get us accustomed to going to court and giving evidence. Or at least that is what they told us. It felt more like ritual humiliation to me. As my time came nearer, my heart was pounding and when called forward, my legs were like jelly. I climbed reluctantly onto the stage, to be presented with my allocated topic of conversation: 'The inside of a ping pong ball'. I stammered, erred and ummed throughout with little to say other than, "These balls are white and used for table tennis". I was awful but many of my colleagues were in the same boat. It did serve to break the ice as a few of us compared notes after the ordeal had finished.

We were then issued with uniforms, handcuffs and truncheon (or staff, as it was known locally). It was a very traditional form of dress: a serge tunic with belt and thick trousers, blue shirts and a clip-on woollen tie. The helmet was large and cumbersome, designed so you were visible when on patrol but hardly practical. It was a very *Dixon of Dock Green* image which over the years has evolved and thankfully made way for more functional clothing. West Yorkshire had a completely different coloured uniform for police 'women', as they were referred to at the time. Their uniform was light blue in colour, collar numbers prefixed with the number '5', and they also had a truncheon which was half the size of their male counterparts, the reason being it was designed to fit into their handbag. For the jokers amongst us, the size and shape of this cylindrical lump of wood meant it was often compared to a very different type of device...

Our intake was so large, we were to be spread between two regional training centres: Dishforth in North Yorkshire and Bruche in Cheshire. I was to be heading to Bruche. Typically, the few friends I had made were destined for Dishforth. I had no idea where Bruche even was! I found out it was twice as far as the journey to Dishforth. I had real concerns whether my trusty Ford Cortina would be able to make it there and back each week. I drove to Bruche the following Sunday evening, the longest journey I had made in the car. Incredibly, it made it there and back every week without issue.

As a former military camp, the surroundings were familiar. To my surprise, I discovered every recruit had a room of their own. Compared to my time in the military, this was sheer luxury. My immediate neighbours were from the surrounding area, Greater Manchester Police (GMP) and Merseyside. We found out that the next morning we were to present ourselves in uniform on the parade square, where we would be meeting our Directing Staff (DS). Boots were expected to be bulled and shiny, uniforms pressed. Again, this all came easy. I was well versed in sharp creases and gleaming boots. My tunic sported a medal ribbon as I had served in Northern Ireland. There were a few of us around and it made for a talking point. What I wasn't so quick to notice was that each of the classes had at least one ex-service member sporting the same ribbon.

The DS arrived and introduced themselves. Both were sergeants from Merseyside Police and had that rich Scouse accent. I was called forward and told that due to my time in the services, I would be 'drill commander' for my squad. Furthermore, I was told that it would be my responsibility to ensure that all the class could march properly and be immaculately turned out each and every day for inspection. That proved to be an ongoing problem because there were one or two members of our class who just didn't polish up too well at all and were not motivated to improve. It gave me an additional burden as I spent extra hours showing people how to press uniform and bull their boots.

Initial police training at the time totalled around 12 weeks. It was residential, Monday to Thursday; you were not allowed off the premises until Friday afternoon when you travelled home. You had to return on Sunday evening without fail. There was a lot of classroom work; we had to have a thorough understanding of the law and the legal responsibilities when depriving members of the public of their liberty by making an arrest. I was back in the classroom again and struggled. Every morning there was a test of some sort. Accompanied by a series of progressive written examinations, you had to pass each one, otherwise you were out of a job.

The practical elements were what I enjoyed the most. You would be taught an aspect of the law in the class, say traffic legislation, and would then go outside to partake in a scenario. Another member of staff would be dressed in civilian clothes acting as the criminal or member of the public. As the unsuspecting, hapless, wet-behind-the-ears copper, you then had to deal with the situation as it unfolded. They were managed in such a way that meant you could never come out on top. It ranged from being presented with a motorist driving a car, to an abusive, fighting drunk or domestic dispute. It was a good way of learning, and on at least one occasion I had my helmet knocked off my head.

One morning, whilst being taught about dangerous parts on motor cars, we were taken to the student car park. Much to my dismay, the sergeant stopped alongside my patched-up vehicle! He looked at it for a short time, uttered something about hoping it didn't belong to any of us, and said, "Take this heap of shit… what offences do you see on here?" My colleagues, none of them realising it was mine, took great delight in pulling it apart, pointing to a near-illegal tyre with patches of rust around the wings and wheel arches. At one point, so as not to give the game away, I drew attention to the broken radio aerial I had been meaning to fix for weeks on end. I spent the following weekend rectifying the faults, purchasing a reconditioned tyre, and plugging holes in the bodywork with ISOPON filler, the answer to a poor motorist's problems.

The rigours of classroom training increased week on week. We learnt about all sorts of offences and were expected to recite them verbatim. We were told that by knowing the offence, it would help us to identify the 'points to prove' in evidence. There was so much to take in: vagrancy, dangerous dogs, motor vehicles, public order, damage, theft, burglary, deception, fraud, assaults, and murder. There was a clear divide in the class from those with an intellectual background who were able to swiftly assimilate information, and those not so great with memory and the academic side but had the ability to apply themselves in a practical fashion. I most certainly put myself in the latter category. There was a phrase I heard later in my career from seasoned officers which summed it up: "If you're not sure, but it looks wrong, lock 'em up and look it up." Most of us had a fair understanding of what was right and what was wrong. The challenge was always going to be remembering everything.

We were inspected once a week on the parade square by the Camp Commandant. There was a prize at stake for the best turned-out class. We had one guy in the class, 'Ivan', who consistently let us down. Every single week we presented ourselves, and every single week we came nowhere. I always got the blame, as I was the 'drill commander'. For our passing out parade, I was determined that for the big day and our last chance, I was going all out to win. I'd learnt a trick in the army about boots. You could apply a type of liquid floor polish known as 'Seal' to make them gleam. There was a risk because if the boots got wet, the glossy shine would turn to a shade of blue. So, as long as it didn't rain, everything would be good. I got hold of Ivan's uniform, pressed it and applied the polish to his boots. I made sure everyone was in the best order and we marched out onto the parade square. To my astonishment, we won 'best turned-out class', for the one that really mattered! One of our class sergeants came to my room as I was packing to leave. He shook my hand and said, "That, was down to you, Colin! Well done, I'm so proud of you."

I didn't disclose to him what I had done with Ivan's boots... Some might see it as cheating, I see it as problem-solving, which is something I think I have become pretty good at over the years. Going through initial police training was, in many ways, quite different to what I had experienced in the army. As recruits, we were never shouted at. We were all treated like adults being addressed formally as Mr, Mrs or Miss and not, in services fashion, by just your surname. However, we were still being conditioned and prepared for our role in society. We were continually reminded that our job was a serious, and at times dangerous, one. Our primary role was to maintain the Queen's peace and prevent crime and disorder. We were to police by consent and had discretion at our disposal. This is something I still believe to be the greatest strength of British policing. Using your discretion is a skill which takes many, many years to learn and only comes from experience. That experience only comes from being out there doing what is affectionately known as the 'job'.

14. Probationer

As my initial course came to an end, I learnt that we were expecting our first child. Our small one-bedroom flat would no longer be suitable. At that time, the Force carried some housing stock or paid you a rent allowance if you had a mortgage. Police houses could be provided upon request, subject to availability. My first posting was originally intended to be South Leeds. There were no available houses in that area though. Some hasty changes had to be made to my very first posting.

April of 1981 saw a snowstorm of epic proportions in Yorkshire, falling on the very day I had to report to my first police station. I struggled through the snow in my clapped-out Ford Cortina to a mining town in a place I knew nothing about. My allocated shift, or rota as it was then known, meant that I was on duty that day. I was taken to see my sergeant, also a former serviceman. As a probationer fresh out of the training school, you were not allowed on the streets on your own until the sergeant was happy with your performance. He introduced me to my tutor 'Dave' who proved to be a level-headed, very experienced and practical copper. He had been disciplined some weeks previously and demoted from Detective Sergeant. To his credit, he made it back up the ladder to inspector several years later and attained a law degree on the way.

I owe a lot to Dave, not least for his patience and the way he freely shared knowledge and experiences. In that very Yorkshire way, he could at times be direct and extremely blunt, but he also had enormous compassion. He set a great example to me and as a young 21-year-old in a very new and demanding job, he was a supportive role model that I aspired to.

I learnt that for the first few days, I would be working 9am until 5pm. There was much to do in terms of administrative tasks. I also had to have the police house signed over to me. What followed was endless introductions to senior officers, experienced officers, other probationers and administration staff. Dave told me very early on, "Under no circumstances ever piss admin staff off. They sign off your expenses and overtime." Expenses and overtime forms were an extremely important part of your paperwork. If you didn't submit them on time, the reimbursements wouldn't appear on your pay slip. If you were stupid enough to upset a member of the admin team, your submissions would disappear to the bottom of their pile of paperwork. Wherever I worked after that, I always made time for people who worked in those roles.

Whilst eagerly anticipating becoming a real copper, I had no real clue about the reality of what I would be doing, getting involved with or the changes it would eventually make to me. We set up home in our allocated police house. It was right in the centre of a large council estate. Everyone locally knew they were police houses. For some of the locals, they were perceived as 'quasi' police stations, with people knocking on the doors at all hours. One woman even deposited a lost dog with me! In my naivety, I took the dog in, jumped in my own car and took it the station, only to be severely reprimanded by the 'office-man', who told me in no uncertain terms that I was to tell future callers to take dogs to the station themselves.

The 'office-man' (because it was almost always a man) was a role reserved for longer-serving officers. They would sometimes be the sick, lame, lazy one, or just too dangerous to be on the streets and often the most cynical voice in the station. On one occasion I witnessed a lad come to the station to produce his documents. He spoke out of turn to the duty 'office-man' who launched himself out of his chair at lightning speed, opened the public entrance door and dragged him inside, telling him he was being arrested "for being so fucking cheeky!"

It was the case that no quarter was to be given to anyone who was disrespectful to a police officer. We always had to win. We always had a bigger army than anyone who wanted to mess with us. That was the culture, not up for debate, end of story. That culture also extended to treating probationers as being the lowest of the low. You made the tea for all the shift members every morning. Question that and you would be ostracised. As a former soldier, I was held in slightly higher esteem, but not by much. You were expected to prove yourself, show courage, understand the law and most importantly, what the unwritten rules were. They were not quite the same as the ones I had been taught at the training school. This was at a time before the Police and Criminal Evidence Act (PACE) 1984 that now governs things like detention, interviewing and search. PACE also brought about the role of custody officer. Prior to that, we managed the cells and booked in our own prisoners. Whilst there was a box on the custody sheet about solicitors, I never once saw a solicitor get access to a detainee. It was just the norm for 'prisoners' (not 'suspects') to be told to sign the three boxes on the detention sheet and told "Just routine stuff". The odd thing was that no one ever questioned it.

Dave drove me around showing me the area I would be policing. Certain calls were reserved for the probationer to attend, as a means of getting experience. The exposure to the streets was a shock at first. Poverty was rife; houses which stank of stale beer, cigarette smoke, cats, dogs, kitchen fat and all manner of other smells was one of the things that struck me. You simply cannot adequately describe the stench. It frequently hung in your nostrils and stuck to your uniform. The squalor that I saw children being raised in was an absolute eye-opener. To a lot of people though, this was the norm. You couldn't fail to notice that almost always they had a top-of-the-range television in the house somewhere. I could never understand how people's priorities in terms of luxury goods came above that of their children. As a young married couple, we were struggling to furnish the house, let alone think about expanding our repertoire of TV channels to beyond the standard three that were available at the time.

I began to understand quite quickly that we were the first responders, called in to sort out all manner of minor disputes. Neighbours bickering, families falling out with each other and children misbehaving in the street were standard fare during the day and I began to wonder what I had signed up for. One thing that was always evident was that when one party didn't get their own way, it would all kick off and you would become the target: "You fucking wankers", "fucking black bastards", and so on. The area was mostly populated by miners and their families. There were several pits in the area and they paid the workforce well. A percentage of the miners had no time for the police, often harkening back to the strikes of the seventies which I knew nothing about.

Dave often had little tests for me up his sleeve, all part of 'learning the job'. One morning, our breakfast was set for 1000hrs. He told me that prior to our meal break, we had an appointment at 0900hrs. He didn't seem to want to share with me where we were going. He drove to a small industrial estate and parked up adjacent to a small nondescript detached brick building. He said something like, "Listen, you're no good to anybody if you turn up at a bad road accident and throw up, so we are going to a PM".

A PM is short for a post-mortem. I had heard the term during training but hadn't given it much thought. We went inside the building and were ushered by an attendant into an area bristling with stainless steel. It was all very clinical, smelling strongly of bleach and disinfectant. The surgeon was already busy at work. He had his back to us. Dave told me to go closer and stand by the wall. There was a man's body laid out on the metal 'slab'. His chest had been sliced wide open, creating a strange upward arching in his body. There was pool of blood on the tray and an assortment of human organs neatly arranged adjacent to the body. The surgeon turned to us both, nodded and exchanged pleasantries. He didn't once stop what he was doing but his sense of humour was evident.

I recall he told me that newspapers were necessary for a PM. If the person being examined was 'posh', then their insides would be stuffed with *The Daily Telegraph* but if they had no money, then it was *The Sun*! This was the sort of jocularity I was familiar with from my time in the services. The sight of the body didn't disturb me. It was, however, difficult to forget the smell.

We left the morgue after about 15 minutes to head back for breakfast, stopping on the way to purchase our bacon sandwiches. As we went to the canteen, Dave put his thumbs up to our sergeant indicating I had done OK. I didn't give it any further thought and we sat down and ate our food, just as if this was normal – which, of course, it was now.

15. Night shifts

After a week of school crossing patrols, taking reports of crime, domestic disputes, road traffic accidents and meeting all manner of individuals, it was time for a weekend off. It preceded seven night shifts scheduled for the following week. I was about to find out how the town took on an entirely different appearance when the sun went down.

Nights started at 10pm. You were expected to be at the station no later than 15 minutes before parade. It was not unusual to get turned out to assist the shift that was on duty if an incident occurred.

I always arrived 30 minutes in advance to make sure my uniform was brushed down and boots shiny. You were not supposed to travel into work in your full uniform – half and half was routine for everyone, consisting of uniformed trousers, blue shirt, boots (polished) with a civilian coat. There was a little ritual for almost everyone in the locker room. You would take your coat off, clip your tie on, slide your staff and handcuffs into the pockets sewn into your trousers, and grab your torch. Every so often on parade you were expected to show your 'appointments', the term for these essential items. Your tunic would then go on, complete with your pocket notebook and pen, then you would head to the briefing room. Here you would be provided with your duties and seven snippets of local intelligence, that would include things such as crimes, wanted persons, suspect vehicles, and so on. The seven items were based on the mind's ability to recall; beyond that it was all very unscientific.

Our stint of nights started on Monday. For the most part, the town was relatively quiet in the earlier part of the week. At the time there were a host of public houses and working men's clubs dotted around the town centre and in neighbouring districts that we were responsible for. Some of the drinking dens were known to be hostile to any intervention by the police, unless of course there was a disturbance that got out of hand, in which case the publican would call for help.

Policing in the eighties was a world away from where it is now. It was long before any real protective equipment was issued. Radios were notoriously unreliable, so you had to think on your feet first and foremost. It was important to talk to people in a language they understood. Our shift numbers were often small. If things got out of hand, assistance was at least 10 minutes away and an awful lot can happen in ten minutes… There was grudging respect of the police though. Where there were challenges to your authority, it was often fuelled by alcohol. Other than cannabis, drugs were not the norm. Unlike our counterparts in the cities of West Yorkshire, we were expected to deal with anything and everything that was thrown at us. The flagship police station in Leeds City Centre, Millgarth, had more officers and assigned dedicated teams to deal with issues such as shoplifting, vehicle crime, and drugs. For us in the 'sticks', the exposure to a wide variety of incidents was good from a personal development point of view.

There was a level of camaraderie on the shift too which meant others would help you out. There was one unwritten rule though. If you asked one of your colleagues for advice, you didn't then go and ask someone else the same question. You would swiftly become unpopular if you did that. As a probationer, you were under scrutiny all the time. If you stepped out of line or were seen to question the system, then word would soon get around and you were labelled a troublemaker. So as a probationer, I found it better to just accept that I was a junior and had a lot to learn. It reminded me of my time in the army and those early beginnings in recruit troop. I was back at the starting line again.

My enduring memories of night shifts were the weekends. The town filled with miners with money in their pockets who were keen to make the most of their leisure time. There was a saying amongst my colleagues that a good night out in the town involved going out, getting pissed, having a scrap, eating a takeaway, throwing up and then going home to beat the wife up. This was no joke. Friday and Saturday nights often resembled a war zone with the frequency of fights and melees taking place. Regardless of the weather, the men wore T-shirts and jeans and the women short skirts and thin blouses.

In many of the pubs, bouncers metered out swift justice if any customers misbehaved. This was well before door staff (as they are now called) were licensed. An awful lot of the men who manned the doors were recruited for their sheer size and reputation. All too often, you turned up to bloodied individuals laid out in the street, where no one had seen anything, there was no CCTV, and rarely did anyone want to make a complaint of assault. It was like the Wild West. We were always outnumbered; you used your verbal skills but under no circumstances could you show any fear. I was a fresh-faced kid in his twenties. If the drunks, troublemakers or members of the criminal fraternity sensed the slightest whiff of fear, they would exploit it mercilessly. Without a shadow of a doubt, the medal ribbon on my tunic from Northern Ireland often broke the ice or engendered grudging respect. Nobody knew I only had a few weeks in the uniform. At times I felt vulnerable and fearful but I managed to conceal it well.

My job was now about enforcing the law, holding people to account and being very, very visible. Once the town began to clear, the domestic disputes started in earnest, interspersed, of course, with fights at the various nightclubs. It was by no means the most violent place I policed during my career, but it certainly had a reputation.

It was during this time that I began to get exposure to the very worst of what people can do to each other in the home. Often fuelled by drink, sometimes the perpetrators being both parties, most often though a drunken male intimidating his wife or partner. On occasions inflicting awful injuries: black eyes, stabbings, hair pulled out, clothes ripped, houses smashed up, doors kicked in and young, innocent children in tears, witnessing the ensuing turmoil. The sad thing is that domestic violence was not recognised as being particularly serious at the time. All too often, calls were written off as 'advice given, no offences disclosed'. It would be all too easy to say that was the fault of the police. It was much more complex than that. There was an attitude that prevailed in society that what went on behind closed doors was nobody's business. Nowadays much more is known about the perpetrators and victims, with early intervention saving lives. I became intimately involved with domestic violence from several perspectives much later in my career.

16. Out of company

'Out of company' was the term used for when you no longer had to be supervised by your tutor. I had benefited enormously from my time 'in company' but after about a month, it was time to step out on my own. I still consider myself fortunate to have been schooled by someone with so many years of experience. However, despite all of Dave's help, it was natural that I would make a few mistakes on my journey.

They say that you never forget your first arrest. I wish I could forget mine. I had been allocated a CID 1 (crime report). It was a report of benefit fraud with a suspect identified from a local estate. It was usual practice as a probationer not to be allowed to drive police vehicles until you attained at least 12 months' service. Therefore, most of the time I was on foot patrol, in the town centre and not far away from the station. This allowed you to earn your spurs, at the same time not being too far away from assistance if you required it. Whilst he lived outside of town, my suspect would likely present himself at the benefits office in the centre to 'sign on'. I made two significant errors. Firstly, I failed to research him properly. Secondly, I was too proud to ask one of my colleagues to accompany me. Despite him ripping off the system, for some reason the Department of Social Security would not allow a police officer to effect an arrest within any building owned by them.

After our briefing, I presented myself in full uniform outside of the main door with the suspect's photo in my hand. He pretty much walked into my arms at the door. Whilst I spent my time ensuring I recited the caution and reason for arrest properly, he pushed me out of the way and ran off at full pelt. Chasing someone when in full uniform with a helmet perched on your head is no mean feat; it slowed me down. I realised I needed assistance and shouted up on the radio. The whole of my shift turned out to help and my man was found about 20 minutes later, hiding under a market stall. Had I taken the time to investigate him in a bit more detail, I would have discovered that he was a 'runner', a term of endearment for those who would always try and evade arrest. I vowed to do better in the future.

On the domestic front, we had settled into the police house and had been busy decorating to make it feel like home. Our baby was due in November. I now had responsibilities for a wife and child so I had to make sure I remained in work. It was no certainty that your job was secure until you had completed your two years as a probationer. If you were deemed as failing in any way during the frequent appraisals, you were gone; there was little mercy. As part of the probationary period, you had to attend regular continuation training at the Academy in Wakefield. Our large intake had begun to shrink; several of us noticed there were one or two absentees. It seemed that one of our training cohort had been arrested for forging a vehicle excise licence, a few more dismissed as being unsuitable, and some had left of their own volition. This served as a constant reminder that your position was fragile.

Each continuation course was normally of one week in duration and residential. Therefore, it was expected you stayed on site and could not go home. Each morning there would be a full inspection and drill parade. The process for this was quite comical. Everyone in the Force around this time knew of 'Tommy' Butler, the drill sergeant. He was a fearsome individual, bald headed, with razor sharp creases in his trousers and tunic, accompanied by gleaming bulled boots. He epitomised the drill sergeants I remembered from my time in the Armed Forces.

With Tommy there was a lot of theatre and humour, but no one messed with him. He owned the small parade square close to the gymnasium; it was his territory. You dare not walk across it if he was conducting a parade. At the top of the square was the police cadet accommodation. One of the lower floor windows was always open in readiness for our morning gathering, a nominated police cadet being responsible for ensuring the antique record player appeared at the appropriate time. Military marching music would resound as we arrived on the square.

The turntable was making the sorts of noises you would only know about if you grew up with needles and styluses. Once we had all arrived on the square, Tommy would inspect each one of us. When he stood in front of you, it was expected that you would shout out your designation, number and surname at the top of your voice. My number consisted of three digits and ended in a nought. On my first attempt, it went something like this: "POLICE CONSTABLE ONE EIGHT ZERO, TANSLEY, Sergeant!!"

Tommy immediately barked back at me in that typical staccato drill sergeant's voice. "A ZERO IS A JAPANESE FIGHTER PLANE, young man!" It was acceptable to smile but you risked his wrath if you dared to laugh. He continued: "The correct designation is 'O', the letter in the alphabet, is that clear?" I, of course, agreed with him.

Tommy was a character and held in high esteem by all those in the police service who met him. Unfortunately, the Force did not treat him well. When a new breed of leadership emerged some years later, it was decided that drill and drill sergeants were old hat and no longer required. Tommy has long since passed and the Academy, which later became known as Bishopgarth, is demolished, now relics of a bygone era. I understand the housing estate that is in its place has a street named after him – very fitting for a man of his standing and influence.

In the summer of 1981, only a few months into my new career, the UK suffered outbreaks of rioting that spread across most of the major cities in the country. Leeds was not unaffected. I had little knowledge of Chapeltown before I joined the police. I knew it to be multicultural and where you went to if you chose to buy cannabis or visit the illegal drinking dens, known as Shabeens. Beyond that, I didn't have an appreciation of the place.

It wasn't long before copycat public disorder broke out in Chapeltown. Every station across the Force had to provide aid in the form of PSUs (Police Support Units). This consisted of a sergeant and ten officers in a marked transit van. The backs of the vans had trestle seats that would seat five or so officers on each side. To say the police were not equipped or ready for this sort of disorder was an understatement. I had received no formal PSU training and neither had many of my colleagues. On our first deployment, we were given Perspex covers that were intended to be attached to the front of our standard police helmet. They were less than useless. Bricks and petrol bombs were the order of the day, so our traditional uniform and patrol equipment could not be considered in any way protective.

Later that week we were provided with green 'Topper' helmets hastily borrowed from the military, the type I remembered from my time in Northern Ireland.

For most of that week, we were parked up as reserves, and although there was rioting, looting and a lot of tension, I do not recall being used for anything of consequence. For our part we resorted to playing cards in the back of the van and eating from our 'happy (sandwich) bags', consuming copious amounts of Maxpax. Maxpax were sleeves of pre-prepared coffee and hot chocolate that seemed to appear from nowhere when large numbers of officers gathered.

Around this time, I became aware of several police vans that bore no livery or other markings: they were red, dark blue and on occasion white. The guys in the vans were dressed differently to the rest of us. They wore dark blue crew-necked pullovers and flat caps, as opposed to the traditional helmets we sported. They had a bearing; they were confident and other officers seemed to be much happier when they were present. They stuck together in their own groups and seemed to command an awful lot of respect. When I asked who they were, I was told they were the 'heavy mob'. If they were here, it meant that there was either trouble or there was going to be trouble. They were the ones in the thick of the riots. It was the first time I had seen members of the 'Task Force', and I knew then that I wanted to join them.

After about a week or so, things seemed to settle down in Chapeltown, but it would not be the end of the troubles in the area. I went back to routine policing and continued to learn my craft.

17. Growing into the job

Back at work, I was slowly but surely getting used to all the paperwork, terminology and the various characters at the nick.

One morning I was out on foot patrol when a radio message summoned me back to the station to see Merv, our office-man. Merv was an old sweat, very wise and a source of counsel for me on numerous occasions. His job was manning the front office and he did it very well. When I arrived, he said to me, "Amelia wants to meet you." He pointed to a female traffic warden sitting behind him.

Amelia was about 50 years old, well past her best, but many years before would have turned heads. She stood up and held her arm outstretched as if to shake hands. I did the same and walked towards her. As I drew closer, her right hand quickly went between my legs, she grabbed my balls and said out loud, "Oh, he's a big lad!" Everyone in the office burst out laughing and after the initial shock, I did the same. I had been set up; it was standard fare for the times and a bit of a ritual for new blood apparently. There was no political correctness then. Things like this happened all time and were accepted as par for the course.

Aside from understanding the culture of the service, there was a requirement for ongoing learning and assessment. I found the frequent visits to the Academy for more classroom work difficult. It reminded me of service days, being 'gated' and confined to barracks. Unlike some of my colleagues, I didn't have the money to drink in the bar and socialise. Neither did I get into Wakefield city centre like some of my fellow trainees, a small number of whom regularly regaled us with stories of what they were getting up to. It was many years later when I discovered what all the fuss was about.

Despite there not being much else to do, I still found it hard to apply myself to the revision that needed to be done. There were exams throughout and if you failed to attain the required marks, then it would be reported back to your bosses back at division. I found learning about HGVs, traffic offences, tachographs and most things road traffic rather uninspiring. By contrast, anything relating to crime kept me engaged.

However, I had not fully developed an effective method of study and was easily distracted. After one notable exam failure, I was summoned to see the divisional Chief Inspector. He made it clear that if my results did not improve then my suitability as a police officer would be reviewed. This was probably the kick up the arse I needed. Things were financially tough at home; I was the only bread winner. It was up to me to take responsibility and sort things out. I knew I wasn't stupid but the exams were a blunt instrument and there to test recall, rather than application. Whilst I wouldn't say I was excelling, I was slowly finding my way around policing. The only way I could get the results needed in the exams was by repetition. I had to read the offences and points to prove, write them out and repeat, read the offences and points to prove, write them out, repeat – and so it went on.

What was also helpful was putting things into practice by dealing with the offences. My lack of interest in road traffic issues left me at a slight disadvantage. The biggest part of me wanted to put all my efforts into catching who I believed to be the real criminals; the thieves, the burglars, the conmen. In all my police service, I never once issued a parking ticket. Some might say that is nothing to be proud of; however, I could never reconcile it with the priorities of keeping people safe. Some of my colleagues loved that sort of thing. It helped them keep the numbers up on their scorecard, something that was required to avoid scrutiny.

I remember being pulled in by a sergeant who felt I wasn't working hard enough. The measure of your achievements were entries in the station 'offence book'. When you reported or arrested anyone, it had to be entered into this handwritten register that was available for all to inspect. The sergeant told me that a probationer of similar service, was, in his opinion, a much higher performer. In his opinion, there was no excuse for not returning similar numbers. However, when I inspected the results, much of the officers' efforts were what was known as CLE/26 offences. All you had to do for them was to walk around on foot patrol, look for an out-of-date tax disc on a motor car and submit a form. Most of the time you didn't even have to speak to the owner of the vehicle. I viewed that as 'hit and run' policing and not real work. I conveyed what had happened to Dave, my former tutor. It was another night shift and he said, "Don't worry, we'll sort that. Come with me."

We did nothing else but park up on one of the busiest roads in town. He positioned our patrol vehicle in a way that ensured it was not easily seen. Shortly after, a vehicle came into view. It was going slightly faster than it should have been, but not speeding. We pulled the driver over and breathalysed him. He was positive and I arrested him. At the time a drunk driver had to have a sample of their blood taken to prove the level of alcohol. It entailed going to a police surgeon's suite at a neighbouring station. Dave had always taught me to try and strike up a rapport with suspects and witnesses alike. It was a slightly longer journey than normal so there was a bit more time to chat and make small talk. The guy told me that he hoped he wasn't over the limit as his daughter was disabled and he needed his driving licence to be able to transport her around. As it turned out, he was very slightly over the prescribed limit, and he did lose his licence. I never forgot that incident, or the man concerned. He was a good sort, very supportive of the police. He didn't jump up and down or complain, he knew he was in the wrong. Of course, he shouldn't have been drinking and driving because he could have caused injury or death to road users or himself. However, there were, of course, others out there abusing the system massively and doing much worse than having a couple of pints after work. This man just so happened to be in the wrong place at the wrong time. I've never forgotten it for some reason. Maybe it hardened my resolve to go after the really bad guys and girls.

Not long after being told that I was underperforming, I was summoned to see the shift inspector. I remember thinking that this was it and that I was going to get the boot. However, completely the opposite happened. It seemed that my direct supervisor thought I was working hard. He thought I was sufficiently mature and trustworthy enough to be posted to one of the satellite stations. I must admit to being puzzled as this seemed completely at odds with what the other sergeant had told me, but I chose not to question it.

I was now destined to work at a place that operated from a much smaller station, formerly a police house. The normal shift numbers were between three and four officers including the sergeant, if one was available. We were responsible for a large housing estate that had been built in the sixties to house miners moving from other coalfields in Yorkshire, the North East, Scotland and Wales, to the more prosperous 'super pit' nearby. I felt quite chuffed to have been 'selected'. Knowing what I know now, I think it doubtful I was 'selected'. I was the youngest member of the shift in terms of service and maybe the one least likely or able to complain or question the decision. I had, however, proved to be reliable and keen to learn so, who knows?

I found out that I would be fast-tracked for a police driving course as that was a necessity. For a short time, I was to be allowed to drive the patrol cars without a driving permit. It felt like I had been promoted. Foot patrol was a good way of learning the ropes, but the real stuff was flying about in cars. You tended to get a better type of call and were even able to put the blue light on sometimes! We didn't have any sirens at the time – that innovation came much later.

In November of 1981, we welcomed our daughter and first child into the world. I was there for the full 23 hours and not ashamed to say that I shed a tear when she arrived. For a father, nothing can equal the joy of being present when your child is born, and I have been fortunate enough to be there for all three of my children's births. Working shift patterns and night shifts made it tough to be fully engaged with childcare at times but I tried to do as much as I could.

My wife had stopped working to look after our baby. Police pay had improved, but I was a probationer. It would take many years of incremental pay rises to become anywhere near comfortable. An auntie and uncle of my wife's lived in the town centre and they were tremendously helpful and supportive. My own mum was miles away in Cornwall, my wife's estranged parents lived some distance away on the outskirts of Leeds, and Dad was in the Midlands. We had no parental support close by, but Auntie and Uncle stepped up to help us time and time again. I also used to call in to their house for a cup of tea whilst on foot patrol as they lived on my beat. Without their support, it is hard to know how we would have navigated the rigours of bringing up a new baby. They were also on hand when a near fatal accident happened whilst I was away on one of my many courses.

My wife had become friendly with one of the neighbours. Her husband was on the same shift as me, another probationer but slightly senior to me by a month or two. She had taken our daughter around to their house. At the time, she was crawling about the floor and exploring everything. Whilst my wife and the neighbour were talking, there was a loud bang and our daughter flew into the air after putting an exposed electric lead in her mouth. It was, in fact, two leads clumsily fixed together with insulation tape behind the sofa. The ambulance was called and she was rushed to hospital with a huge burn to her upper lip. Thankfully she survived with nothing more than a scar in her mouth. The support our quasi parents gave to my wife was amazing. To avoid distracting me from my studies, they persuaded her not to notify me until I returned. When I arrived home and found out what had happened, I held my daughter very tightly, realising just how lucky she and we had been.

18. Starting again

My new nick was a little different. There was no real consistency with the availability of sergeants, so most of the time you were unsupervised. In terms of assistance, if things went wrong, we were isolated and remote. Our closest help was a neighbouring division or another force altogether.

There were several local authority estates, all of which had their individual reputations. There were also some notable characters who lived on them. Two that stick out in my mind were Duggie and Mick, who had the status of local 'hard men'. Neither were related, nor were they ever seen in each other's company, but they had similar characteristics. They were big, strong, liked to drink, and frequently wanted to fight the police. According to local folklore, they had on occasion broken handcuffs, which took some doing. There seemed to be a disproportionate number of criminals who lived locally. There were also, thankfully, some honest-to-goodness Northern folk who had no choice but to try and live amongst it all.

My new posting was a bit of a trek by comparison with the short drive I had become accustomed to. Our shift sergeant was Irish and a stickler for doing things properly. For some unfathomable reason, he had a pathological hatred for HGVs and their drivers. None of my colleagues could explain why. If he chose to accompany you on a patrol, you knew he would have you pulling over a lorry for the sheer hell of it. My fellow PCs on the shift were all quite different personalities. One an old sweat, one who was desperate to join the traffic department, and another who was laid-back to the point of being horizontal. I was the youngest in service and learnt different things from each of them.

The station was a little community of its own; it was a small but happy place. We had our own cleaner who was a laugh a minute. There was a full-time office-man, another long-serving officer who, like many of his ilk, didn't suffer fools gladly. That included members of the public, but young probationary officers didn't escape his venom. The CID office consisted of two Detectives who were a law unto themselves. To say they bore a stark resemblance to the TV programme *Life on Mars* is an understatement. As a young cop, you entered their office at your peril. They were hard-drinking, chain-smoking, time-served, cynical bastards.

I knew that one day I wanted to be a Detective but for now I had to concentrate on getting through my probation. Like my previous posting, the day shifts consisted mostly of attending burglaries, vehicle crime, thefts, neighbour disputes, serving summonses and arresting people on warrant. In terms of petty crime, there was a small hard core of local criminals. It wasn't too difficult to work out who was responsible when something happened.

Proving it, of course, was the challenge. We mostly operated a 'non-casual visitor' approach to formal interviews. Suspects tended to be 'invited' in most of the time for a 'chat' on the pretext of an interview. This was long before the days of tape recordings or contemporaneous notes. Pocket notebooks were used to later record what had been said. There was also what was referred to as the 'voluntary statement' which later fell into disrepute. The major failing with this process was that pocketbooks were supposed to be compiled as soon as practicable after the interview. There were two cells downstairs which were occasionally called into use, should an arrest be required. There was no custody officer and no real supervision of the procedure. In the main if suspects needed to be arrested, they would be conveyed to larger stations. The Police and Criminal Evidence Act, or PACE, turned all of this onto its head. Prior to its introduction, I remember one of the Detectives commenting, "Tape recorded interviews, that will never work!" It did, and it continues to be a safeguard for both officers and suspects.

Night shifts proved to be interesting when the sergeant wasn't working with us, which was frequent. We recorded our own deployments onto a duties sheet. The senior PC was expected to do this in the absence of supervision. The old sweat I worked with almost always ensured that he drove for the first half of the shift. After meal break, it was down to me. It soon became apparent why he preferred this. Meal break was often at 1am and you were allocated 45 minutes. Unless we were called out, the statutory card game often took us well past that. Once refreshed, we set out on the next half of our shift, which either meant responding to calls or driving around the area on general patrol.

However, my colleague often threw a little detour in. One of his friends ran a working men's club, of which there were many in the area. I was often instructed to drive to the rear of the club in question. My colleague would get out, knock on the fire exit door and we would be allowed in. A small group of staff would be sat there having drinks and we would join them for a beer or two. It was all very strange, but I was still young in service so I had little choice but to go along with it.

Drinking on duty was an offence and if we had been caught, as a probationer, I would most likely have been sacked. I took the easy option and drank very slowly, in the knowledge that I was driving until the early hours of the morning. My partner often had several pints of beer. Like the Armed Forces, drinking was the norm. After a run of shifts, most of us would head off to one of the locals for a couple of drinks, but it wasn't something that would routinely happen whilst working.

Dealing with road traffic collisions became a frequent occurrence, some being more memorable than others. At the time, all road accidents had to be attended by the police. One night we were called to a report of a pedestrian who had been knocked down on a main road not far from the station. We were on the scene quickly. A man was laid out on the tarmac. A car had hit him in close proximity to a pedestrian crossing. There were several people on the scene and emotions were running high. I headed straight to the man on the ground. There was blood everywhere and he was slipping in and out of consciousness. The blood was seeping from a head wound. I recall trying to find out where exactly it was coming from. As I lifted his head gently, I expected that the palm of my hand would support the base of his skull. Instead, it went inside his head. He had hit the ground with such force that it had shattered his skull at the rear. The ambulance arrived very quickly and took over, but he sadly died at the scene. He was a local man, in his forties, living no more than 500 yards from the scene. We were acutely aware that news would likely get to his family very quickly, given that some of his friends were present. For that reason, we chose to go to the house and deliver the death warning.

Every officer I have ever worked with dreads doing this sort of visit, me included. It is one of **the** worst things you ever have to do. At around midnight, we broke the news to his wife. It is one of my earliest memories of this type of task and one I have never forgotten. The words "No, no, no," are so often used by the recipients of such a message. Each person reacts differently – some are very quiet, some scream, some cry – but the word "No", perhaps signifying denial, is almost always used.

Because it was dark and we had gone to the house straight from the accident, I had not realised how much blood was on my hands. I am certain the man's wife did not notice any of this. It would only have added to her heartbreak. Finally getting back to the station, I couldn't stop washing my hands. I had no idea then of just how much more blood and guts I would be exposed to in my police career.

By contrast, another road accident was confusing and humorous in equal measure. One afternoon in a relatively busy thoroughfare adjacent to a row of bustling shops, a car had gone into the rear of another. I attended and there was general agreement that the driver who had driven into the other car was at fault, although he was acting strangely. For good measure I requested a breath test, but he was negative. He provided all his details without a problem and after about 20 minutes with paperwork complete, it was time for everyone to go their separate ways.

My vehicle was in front of the offending driver. I was in the process of radioing in the result to the control room when my police car was struck from behind. I looked in the mirror and saw that it was the driver whom I had just breathalysed! Rather than stopping though, he drove off, without even a glance at me. I pursued his vehicle with blue lights for about half a mile and had to get in front of him to affect the stop, such was his oblivion to what had just occurred. I had now been involved in an accident, so had to call out the duty sergeant to take over. It was rapidly turning into a farce.

As it turned out, the reason the driver was acting a little strangely was because he had been taking medication. He hadn't disclosed that, and it wasn't evident to me or the sergeant. The shock of the first accident seemed to have been a factor in his second accident of the day. However, my day was far from over. I drove back to the station with the sergeant behind me in his car. Outside our building was a pedestrian crossing. It was a busy road and at this time of the day, the morning shift were on their way home from the nearby colliery. A pedestrian appeared from nowhere on the crossing and I had to brake sharply. A driver approaching from the opposite direction saw me coming to a halt and felt obliged to do the same. He also stopped sharply, causing a car to go into his rear. The sergeant took the view that I had been a contributory factor, which meant he had another accident to deal with. He was not a happy man…

On the family front, my daughter was growing up fast. We had purchased our first home, a small end-terraced house just outside of the town centre. I had always been encouraged by my dad to invest early in property. The added benefit of a rent allowance from the police made it a no-brainer. It was a struggle nonetheless. The house needed some renovation and there was always something that needed attending to in the form of repairs. I picked up overtime here and there, but we never had enough money.

In terms of the wider family, I was in frequent touch with my mum who found it difficult to be so far away from her first grandchild. She would come to Yorkshire as often as she could. Wherever possible, we would combine our annual holiday with a visit to see her in Cornwall. I saw Dad relatively often as he was not so far away. We were always made welcome at their place in a village in the Midlands.

My sister was in the army, stationed close by in North Yorkshire. She had married a guy from another regiment. With my Armed Forces background, the pair of us hit it off straight away. He was a straight talking 'chunky', a forces term for someone who is strong and thick set. He was also an army boxer. There were times when we all visited Cornwall together and had a whale of a time, drinking, having fun on the beaches and 'beating up' my younger brother. It was all in jest and my brother secretly loved all the attention. Everyone got on, we were young and enjoying life.

One morning whilst at home and off duty, I received a call from one of the office-men at the station. He told me he had some bad news. I had no idea what he was about to say. He then went on to break it to me that my brother-in-law had died. I recall those words, "No, no, no," and fell to the floor. To this day, I will never understand why that message was delivered over the phone. Someone from the station could easily have come to the house and told me in a more compassionate manner, especially as I lived only a matter of minutes away.

My sister's husband was only 26 years of age. He had gone to the Army Hospital in Woolwich for a seemingly minor procedure and died in his sleep. It was completely out of the blue, unexpected and knocked the whole family for six, not least of all my sister. We headed to see her straight away and tried to help as best we could.

One thing that struck me, whilst clearly in shock, my sister did not once shed a tear. The funeral was dealt with by her in a very clinical manner. To my knowledge, she has only visited his grave on a handful of occasions. I initially put this down to our upbringing and time in the services. It wasn't until many years later she disclosed to me that her husband assaulted her regularly; she had even been hospitalised by him after her jaw was broken. No one knew and to see them together, you would never have suspected it. Such is the secretive nature of domestic violence.

19. 1984

1984 is memorable to me for a number of reasons. It was the year my brother-in-law died, when my first son was born, and the miners' strike began.

Shortly after taking my son home from hospital, he became very ill. He was unable to keep milk down and developed projectile vomiting. The condition was diagnosed as pyloric stenosis which causes dehydration and an inability to take on board vital nutrients. He was hospitalised for a while. During my night shifts, I used to go and sit with him. I wasn't supposed to be there, but I wasn't allowed any time off from work. There was no process for parental leave at the time. Even a death in the family only warranted 48 hours or so. My supervisors had children of their own so understood the anxiety and worry my wife and I were facing. Thankfully, my son pulled through, but to this day he sports a large scar on his side where he was operated on to remove the blockage.

Those serving in the police during this fateful year are unlikely to ever forget it. It was the year that Margaret Thatcher and her Conservative government decided to take on the National Union of Mineworkers, the NUM. Policing a mining area was already tough, but it was about to get a whole lot tougher, both at work and at home. Many of my wife's family were miners or supportive of the cause. The miners' strike started in March and escalated rapidly across parts of the country, particularly in Yorkshire. The police were mobilised to deal with pickets. It soon became evident that mutual aid from other police forces would be required to deal with the large numbers of striking miners who would descend on pits to prevent any of their colleagues going to work. These 'flying pickets', as they were referred to, could very quickly overwhelm the often small numbers of police deployed at the gates of the collieries, stationed there to keep the peace. Hence a national coordination centre was put into place to deploy Police Support Units (PSUs) centrally. Some thought the response was heavy-handed, and as a result the relationship between police and the mining community went downhill quite rapidly. We were depicted as 'Maggie's Boot Boys', not helped by the behaviour and attitude of some officers from visiting forces.

In the early days of the strike and mostly because West Yorkshire were a relatively large force, most of the deployments were managed by drawing staff from other divisions. I had regular PSU duties, sometimes on my rest days which would attract overtime payments. It also meant that officers on uniform patrol duties were backfilling because of the abstractions. The working days were lengthy no matter where you were and what you were doing. Thankfully, we now had slightly better protective equipment – the standard tunics and trousers were in no way flameproof. Overalls, riot shields and hard helmets were issued but there was a reluctance to deploy this type of kit because some of the senior officers thought it to be provocative. It was often the case that we had to take casualties before they were even considered. There were times you felt like lambs to the slaughter when encountering the most serious of disorder.

In the initial stages of the strike, policing picket lines was good humoured. It involved a bit of banter with some pushing and shoving thrown in for good measure. However, all too often 'rent-a-mob' would arrive and things would turn quickly. I lost count of the number of times my colleagues and I were subject to brick and stone throwing. Often in the dark of early morning, the cowards amongst them would stand well back and pelt us with missiles. Most of the senior officers had no clue as to how to deal with these types of incidents. It left many of us frustrated and vulnerable. We were held back and not allowed to respond.

However, there were notable exceptions. One or two senior managers were prepared to deal robustly with this type of violence, often only when the likes of the Task Force or large numbers of officers were available. When this happened, we felt like we had won the day because every single time we charged a mob, they ran. That is what cowards do. I for one was angry, being expected to stand there and take the abuse, the violence and general lawlessness. It left a lot of the rank and file to conclude that we were simply cannon fodder.

The strike went on for 12 months. The effects it had on the towns and villages we policed and similar places in the north was profound. Job losses, poverty and a general loss in prosperity were keenly felt. For me and many of my friends in the police, we had families and close friends who were miners. It resulted in huge family divisions, created all manner of dilemmas and made life generally difficult. My wife's uncle was a miner, yet not once did we ever fall out about the strike. He took the view that I had a job to do and respected that. He wasn't into politics and was frustrated by the whole thing.

Other members of my wife's family were not so forgiving. At several family gatherings, I was shunned and ignored. I could live with that, but it did affect my wife. She could be quite outspoken and always supported me. As they were very young at the time, I don't think the kids were adversely affected but it was a concern nonetheless. Things began to get worse as the strike started to fracture with miners wanting to return to work. These 'scabs', as they were referred to, became as much of a target as the police and our resourcing had to take account of their protection. I didn't expect it to cause me any issues directly, but it did.

The house we had purchased had the same street name as one in the centre of town. This caused some issues with the post from time to time. I didn't expect it to cause me to meet a mob on my doorstep though. I had become a regular member of our PSU. This meant starting my shift around 4am to be ready for early morning picket line duties. I tended to go to bed early and leave my blue police equipment bag by the front door. There was no mistaking who the bag belonged to, as it was emblazoned with 'West Yorkshire Police' in large white letters on both sides. Around 8pm I was in bed, asleep, when my wife woke me up in a panic, saying, "The NUM are here and want to speak to you!"

My initial response was less than polite, questioning her sanity, and went something like, "Are you off your head? Why would the NUM want to speak to me?"

I went downstairs in my dressing gown. Sure enough, at the front door stood four or five men, who repeated to me that they were from the NUM. With my right foot, I hooked my police bag out of the way. My immediate thoughts were that this was an attempt at intimidation. It was dark outside and the older guy at the front of the group looked directly at me. The others stood behind him with their hands in their pockets. It was obvious from their demeanour that this was not a welfare check. I looked at them deliberately quizzically and said, "How can I help you gents?"

The older man said, "We're here to stop you going to work, cocker." (Cocker is a Yorkshire term of endearment and not to be confused with copper.)

I replied, "Sorry, I don't understand?"

The older guy sounding exasperated then said, "We know you work at the pit. We're here to stop you going to work tomorrow morning."

I looked at him and said, "I don't work there."

He didn't show any sign of being convinced, replying by saying, "Well where do you work then?"

I felt like telling him to mind his own business but clearly couldn't have told them I was a police officer. However, I was outnumbered, and my wife and children were also in the house. To take the heat out of the situation, I told them that I worked at a local shop; not exactly a lie, as police stations are sometimes known as 'cop shops.' I hoped I sounded convincing as I knew what these people were capable of. Some, but not all, of the cases of beatings had come to the notice of the police. Many miners who chose to go back to work had been assaulted, had their property damaged and were shunned by the community.

As the conversation continued, it became apparent that the man they were seeking lived in the other street bearing the same name as ours. Amazingly, his house also bore the same number. I didn't realise until they left that there were five carloads of them, the remainder being parked at the side of our house secreted out of view. Twenty-plus men had been despatched to deter one guy from going to his place of work! I telephoned the station straight away and spoke to the duty sergeant about what had happened. I found out the next morning that the mob arrived at the other address to a waiting police reception committee whereupon they hastily drove off into the night. I fully expected my windows to go through for several nights after the incident. My wife found it difficult to settle afterwards and spoke of it for many months to come.

There were many occurrences during those torrid times, but one is worthy of special mention. We were on standby one morning close to a cluster of small mining villages and pits. The gradual trickle of miners returning to work, mostly to support their families, had increased. On this particular day, we were in one of the most hard-line areas; they did not tolerate scabs. At this critical moment in the dispute, anyone contemplating breaking the strike by going back to work would suffer the consequences. Those consequences could be brutal; it had included firebombs, damage to property, serious assault, and intimidation of the miner and members of his family. It was thuggery and akin to what happened during the troubles in Northern Ireland.

It was a dark morning and early. A call came across the radio that we were required to attend serious disorder at a nearby colliery. You were acutely aware of when things were going badly wrong. The sheer volume of radio traffic and panic in the voices on the radio network has a language all of its own. Our sergeant hurriedly told us to put our hard helmets on and get our shields at the ready. We raced to the scene with blue lights flashing.

From inside our van, we could see the reflections of our blue light against the shop windows. We also knew because it was dark that this could be seen from some distance away. It provided early notification to the ambush teams on what had become known as 'brick alley'.

As we entered the locality, our van came under a sustained attack with a hail of bricks. Windscreens at this time had a large metal grill to protect the driver and front seat passengers. Nonetheless a lot of damage could be done in a short space of time. We had become so used to these bombardments of missiles that we used to cheer in the van every time the vehicle took a hit. It was a means of dealing with fear. We were hyped up on adrenaline because we knew we were heading to a major disturbance.

Accelerating up the road to the colliery, I could see numerous police vans through the darkened side windows of the vans. It was the sheer volume of noise and sense of chaos that is still a vivid memory. A line of riot shields were being pounded with a hail of bricks. The noise from both sides only adds to an unforgettable crescendo that you become all too familiar with, the more disturbances that you attend. Petrol bombs had been thrown and the flames had caused some of the buildings to catch fire. Walls had been knocked down and the bricks from them were being used to attack the police lines.

Our driver screeched our vehicle to a halt, and the sergeant shouted, "Out, out, out!" The rear doors opened. I was one of the first to exit and we ran towards a group of our colleagues who were holding a line. For some reason, I looked up and saw a large missile in the air. It was heading directly towards us and appeared to be in slow motion. Before any of us had a chance to react, it seemed to speed up momentarily and hit the guy in front of me directly on the top of his head. He crashed to the floor. I somersaulted over the top of him before realising he was a good friend of mine. The missile was one half of a paving slab. His protective helmet had been split wide open. Without it, he would have almost certainly been killed outright. He had been knocked unconscious and was unresponsive. Under a hail of other missiles, we dragged him to safety and then returned to deal with the disturbances.

That morning was an unforgettable baptism of fire. It was ugly and things were getting increasingly violent. I made time to visit my friend later that day. To make it even worse, he had just separated from his wife. At the hospital, they had to cut away the remnants of his helmet to get to his head wound. His face and eyes were so swollen that his features were unrecognisable. It didn't feature in the newspapers. It wasn't covered by any of the media channels. It was as if it hadn't happened, which made me and many of my colleagues angry.

20. Local disorder

There was now a very clear divide between the police and the miners. This was having a knock-on effect in the areas we were desperately trying to police with our ever-diminishing resources. There was an overwhelming sense in the community that the police were being used to suppress the miners and their unions. It came up time and time again when we attended routine calls.

My role at the time rotated from policing the strike to general patrol duties. I wasn't seeing much of my family. Without a word of warning, someone in authority made the decision that I would be appointed to the role of community constable for the largest estate within our area of responsibility. I was mortified, for as far as I was concerned this was 'hobby-bobby' stuff. I had my sights set on joining the Task Force as soon as possible. They were in the thick of the action during the strike. If I am honest, after seeing colleagues injured, suffering abuse and being bricked frequently, then perhaps I saw it as an opportunity to do something about it. Perhaps I harboured a sense of being able to get my own back.

As it transpired, I reluctantly embraced the new position, only because I had agreement from my Inspector that if I did the job for 12 months, he would then support my application for the Task Force.

The role of a community constable was to be visible, engaging with residents and key figures in the neighbourhood. Stories abounded of police brutality on the picket lines, and this fed the disdain on the estate.

Walking around on foot patrol, I was an easy target for abuse. Those responsible would rarely say it to your face. It would come from behind a window, or as a car passed. One afternoon I even had an air rifle fired at me. The pellet lodged in my helmet. I just made mental notes knowing that my time would come; 'what went around came around'. The car that drove by with the yobs mouthing off? The driver would eventually be found walking the street without his mates. We just didn't have the resources available to us to deal with anything that might spark a disturbance.

I slowly made some in-roads. I made a point of visiting the lady who ran the Tenants' Association. Her husband was a miner and staunch supporter of the strike. At first, he made it perfectly clear that he didn't want me in the house. I persevered, we had many conversations, agreed to disagree about the rights and wrongs of the dispute and eventually we became good friends. I did other things like going along to the local youth club and arranging a competition at the local gym for the kids. I even did a reading at the local church one Sunday. It was much more rewarding than I thought it would be and I got a grudging respect from a lot of people. They would often say, "You're OK, it's the other lot in white shirts that we don't like." They were referring to officers from the Metropolitan Police who were deployed on mutual aid.

The shifts were a little better. I rarely had to start at 6am and had a little more say over my own working day. If I had a meeting to attend or a member of the community to visit, then I was at liberty to decide what shift pattern I wanted to work. Those in command had taken the view that community officers were not to be utilised on the picket lines; we were there for the hearts and minds. They didn't want us be seen in riot gear one day, then patting children on the head at schools the next. However, the expectations of the management in terms of what community officers were expected to do as opposed to the reality of staffing the thin blue line inevitably led to me doing patrol duties as well.

One particular night shift sticks in my mind. It was one of those hot, sticky summer Friday evenings. The sort that leads to people drinking too much and generally hanging about instead of heading home. Even though the strike was in full swing, and money in short supply, trade at the local working men's club was always brisk. It was around 10.30pm and I made that fateful comment to my sergeant who I was driving around the area, "Quiet tonight, isn't it?"

"You've done it now," he replied. Within seconds, a call came over the radio: "Disturbance in progress". There were only four of us working our area that night. This club was not the best place to go at any time. On a Friday night there was likely to be trouble, and given the clientele, we were going to have to be cautious. Under the direction of our sergeant, our complement of four officers arranged a rendezvous point so we could arrive together. At the scene we parked our vehicles and went into the club to speak with the manager. As it turned out, he had ejected a couple of drunks and the disturbance was over. There were no offences and no complaints, so we left the building.

In the meantime, a crowd had gathered outside near to our two vehicles. There was obvious hostility in the air, the type you get attuned to quite quickly in the job. It's a gut feeling, you can almost smell it. The adrenaline causes your heart to beat that little bit faster and you enter a state of heightened awareness. The verbal abuse from the gathered crowd, who were about 50 in number, started almost immediately: "Here they are, Maggie's Boot Boys!", "Black bastards!", "Scabs!" they sneered. We were outnumbered and vulnerable. Our situation was being exploited by those with a grudge. The mob (that is the only way to describe them) somehow managed to block the road.

One individual caught my attention; he was extremely vocal, at the front of the crowd and being vehement with his outbursts that were directed towards the four of us. He shouted something and I told him to be quiet. His response was, "Fuck off, wanker!"

Before I knew it, I had grabbed him, told him he was being arrested, and dragged him kicking and screaming to our tiny two-door Vauxhall Chevette. Assisted by one of my colleagues, he was handcuffed and bundled unceremoniously into the back of the car. He was shouting and screaming, "Help me, help me, get these bastards!" I heard someone yell into the radio, "Urgent assistance required!" The mob had now surrounded the car and the idiot inside was laid on his back on the rear seat kicking as hard as he could against the side window. Others had gathered and were now rocking our vehicle from side to side. The situation was deteriorating rapidly. The next thing that happened was that our prisoner managed to kick the window out from the inside and was somehow pulled out of the car by members of the mob. There was no way I was going to lose him, so I returned to the crowd to get him back. We were close to becoming overwhelmed. It had become a tug of war to retrieve him and a matter of pride for me. I'd learnt a harsh lesson about losing a prisoner many years earlier. Then the cavalry arrived, the blue lights blazing their way up the road towards us, with a couple of units from a neighbouring division who were now only seconds away. This caused a slight break in proceedings.

Two of us managed to get our prisoner back into the police car. The sergeant then shouted to me, "Get him the fuck out of here!" As we managed to negotiate our way off the estate, a stream of reinforcements were arriving. There were many arrests that night and it took some time to quell the crowd. Thankfully, none of us suffered serious injury.

Around the same time came the annual Gala, held on a large field close to the local sports centre. Given the tension around public gatherings, the availability of alcohol at the event and general feelings towards the police, there was anticipation of more problems. This was a family event; there were tombola stalls, rides for the kids, candy floss and the like. I was one of a small number of officers on foot patrol in the area. It started around noon and was mostly good-humoured. We walked around and chatted with families.

However, there was a slight undercurrent of hostility with some of the younger lads that had gathered and were drinking. Some of them were miners, some were most definitely not. They were the local thugs who were tailgating on the strike to express their dislike for the police. About 20 of them had formed an obstruction around one of the stalls. This was creating a bit of an issue for young children who were there simply to enjoy themselves. The group were asked politely to move along, but it quickly escalated into a 'them and us' situation. The bating and name-calling started and they refused to step aside. We were outnumbered, but even with only three years of service I already knew that on most occasions if you were confident and assured, they would back down and move.

The sergeant with us decided they were to be forcibly ushered out of the way. We walked towards them, and they were again politely asked to disperse. How it all kicked off I am still not sure, but it turned into a full-on fight very quickly. Assistance was called for and the next thing I knew someone punched me in the face from the left side. All I saw was a youth with long hair running back into the crowd. The next thing I recall was being on the floor with the kicks coming in. Thankfully, a colleague close by had my back and pulled me up. Between us we still had eyes on the guy who assaulted me. He was brought to the ground shouting the usual, "What have I done?" plea and was arrested. I sported a black eye for a while, but it could have been a whole lot worse.

Many months later, I gave evidence at Crown Court about the whole incident. Several of the group had been charged with affray and assault. Despite plenty of witness testimony, my man was found 'not guilty' of assault. As was typical at the time, jurors harboured a lot of public sympathy towards the miners' cause. I felt badly let down by the justice system.

An awful lot of cops in the job at the time felt the same. We worked long hours, trying to keep a lid on things and dealing with the fallout from a strike that was causing hardship for families. We had to deal with all the effects. We were well and truly caught in the middle.

When at home, I was tense and tired. I couldn't put as much time and effort into my two young children as I would have liked too. I don't think they necessarily suffered, but a child's formative years are important. I often wonder what they remember about those times.

During the 12 months of the strike, there were countless incidents of public disorder; minor jobs could rapidly develop into full-on confrontation. Most of the time on patrol, we were outnumbered. You ended up talking yourself out of situations; some you won and some you lost. In the back of my mind, I always knew that there would be another day when the thugs, bullies, criminals and cowards would get their just rewards. I didn't have to wait too long.

21. Task Force beckons

True to his word, the Inspector supported my application and around six months after the strike ended in 1985, I joined the Task Force. My interview had gone well, with questions about my arrest record, my service background and whether I was a team player. Competition for places were fierce; they didn't take everyone and didn't need to.

Looking back, the years I spent with 'TF', as we liked to call ourselves, were some of the most exciting in my police career. We were independent, widely respected and renowned for our zero-tolerance approach. If you had a problem with public order and wanted it sorting, then you contacted us. We were a small army, being about 80 strong, and there were four offices spread across the Force area. Each office had sufficient officers for two PSUs, so 20 officers plus two sergeants and one inspector.

At the time, all officers on the teams were male. It wasn't until several years later that females could join and that initially met with some resistance. Unlike our uniform patrol colleagues, we wore flat caps and a shorter shiny coat. Another staple part of our look was the blue 'NATO' style pullovers, which again were distinctive. We were the only officers allowed to wear them in the Force at the time. I am sure this was done for effect. We were immediately identifiable. It worked particularly well when policing football matches, the downside being you were more easily singled out for complaints. When we were on duty, the hooligans knew there was no messing. If they merely lifted their fingers in a V-sign or dared to shout abuse, they were arrested – it was that simple. It was a different style of policing to the one I had become accustomed to; I liked it already.

Despite my wife and I agreeing that two children were enough, we found out that my youngest son was on his way shortly after I joined the TF. I had, prior to this news, agreed to have a vasectomy at a hospital in Leeds. For about a week after the operation, I had to wear a cricket box so that my very bruised manhood didn't succumb to further damage. A lot of the guys found this highly amusing as it was difficult for me not to walk like John Wayne.

The dark humour and camaraderie were very similar to my time in the Armed Forces, including weird acceptance ceremonies. It was a rite of passage that every recruit was required to undergo some initiation tests before being fully accepted into this 'Band of Brothers'. One morning a character, who shall remain nameless but is part of Task Force folklore, told me and another recruit we had somewhere to go. We were ushered into a couple of vehicles and taken to a field near Wakefield. On arrival I noticed a cage, the like of which you would only see at a zoo, only it looked empty. There were thick bars and a part of the structure had metal panels blocking our view. I had no idea what this was all about. The more senior members of the team that had taken us there were sniggering. The vehicles pulled up just in front of the structure. Both of us were told to get out and stand directly in front of the cage. Under no circumstances were we to move. If we did, then we would fail the test. My fellow newbie and I did as we were told. The horns on both vehicles were then pressed repeatedly.

Much to our amusement, from the enclosed side of the cage came two fully grown chimpanzees. They looked straight at us and without further ado, picked up poop from the floor of the cage and began throwing it at us, attracting much hilarity and laughter from our friends. When we were finally allowed back into the vehicles, our coats were covered in thick clods of monkey droppings. We had passed our first test with flying colours! The next one involved sitting on the floor of the showers at the training school in Wakefield whilst naked and pretending to row across the floor. At the same time, the temperature of the showers had been adjusted so that cold water poured down from above. These sorts of high jinks came to be a regular occurrence and only added to our reputation for being a bit 'off the wall'. The truth was, we all loved it. I felt I was part of something special again.

My first exposure to just how effective we could be as a unit was in Leeds city centre. At the time there was a public house that was a haunt for a group of Leeds United football hooligans who had become accustomed to getting their own way. They frequently caused problems, fights and were generally running amok. Officers patrolling alone were being intimidated and there had been several instances of our colleagues being assaulted. The whole team were called to a briefing by a senior officer. His words went something like this: "Gents, I am sick of these hooligans causing problems for my officers in this city. I want them sorting out once and for all, is that clear?" Nothing more needed to be said, we piled into our transit van and headed up into the city centre. I have no idea who came up with the plan, but we drove into a multi-storey car park behind the pub. Two of the team got out and one of the more experienced members said with a wry smile, "Now we wait." Within less than five minutes, up went a shout on the radio "10/13" and the name of the pub.

A 10/13 was the universally known call for assistance. We drove out of the car park, the transit van revving loudly as we covered the short distance to our two guys who were already battling with members of the gang. The street was filling up as the remainder of their gang left the pub, thinking they had two lone cops to terrorise. There must have been 15 to 20 of them. We took them completely by surprise. For a very short time, I watched as these thugs were shown that we were not going to tolerate them being disrespectful, it was time to get involved. Most of them ran away, those who decided that they would try to fight back went to the floor and were arrested. There were some injuries that night but not on our side. This group of hooligans did not cause any further problems in Leeds city centre. They were taught a harsh lesson, and if I am really honest, it felt good. The reality of these sorts of situations was you simply had to win. Criminals and thugs had to fear the consequences of their actions.

The inevitable post-mortems on the capability of the police to deal with serious disorder in the wake of the miners' strike led to a complete overhaul of training, equipment and command structure. As Public Order Specialists, we were to be elevated to Level 1 PSU response. As far as we were concerned, Level 1 meant that we were the elite. It also meant having to complete frequent training. We were provided with flameproof overalls, better helmets, shields, boots and padding. We trained with the mounted police and performed differing types of baton charges. We were both fearsome and fearless. Primarily a short shield unit, gone were the days of being used as target practice by rioters. We also trained hard with long shields when entering buildings in a cocoon formation, using vehicles as cover, and getting familiar with Molotov cocktails. Having petrol bombs thrown at you during simulations was no less scary than for real, but the only way to learn how to deal with them. Your boots and overalls would occasionally catch fire. Once you understood how it all worked and what you had to do, there was less to worry about. Shock and awe were now the tactics for policing serious disorder. We practiced relentlessly, starbursting through lines of long shields to act as arrest teams. We were extremely effective; if you were on the receiving end, only fools stood about and watched.

Looking back at the riots of the early eighties and the miners' strike, commentators may say it was the main driver for UK policing to become increasingly paramilitary. Personally, I don't think that was the case at all. We were certainly not going to stand there and take it anymore. The constant training and improved equipment was about being more professional and preventing serious injuries. I loved the variety of the work we were given and knew I had made the right decision. We travelled across the whole of the Force area performing all sorts of different roles. We worked in plain clothes as regular as uniform. Where divisions had problems with vehicle crime, drugs and burglary, we would be called in to patrol or conduct observations. We did early morning raids with the CID and Drugs Squad, sometimes in other parts of the country.

Most Saturdays were taken up with attending one of the many football stadiums in the Force area. Leeds United, Bradford and Huddersfield Town were the main venues. Leeds were flying high in the eighties but so was their hooligan following. When visiting teams such as Millwall, Manchester United or QPR came to Elland Road, we were briefed to expect trouble and invariably it came. The thugs knew who we were, and we knew them. We tended to form a reception committee at the railway station in Leeds and escort them to the ground. They would pile off the trains, often drunk, shouting, singing and goading their rivals. Most of the Leeds hooligans would be gathered across the road in a couple of pubs frequented by them on match days. They all knew though that if the blokes in shiny coats and flat hats were there, they had to be careful. If we saw the slightest opportunity to arrest them and ruin their day, we would take it. There was a bit of a league table going on and everyone in the team was expected to make at least one public order arrest per match. The strength of our team was that you always knew you had back up. We were experts in this sort of thing and knew that if you went in hard with a display of strength early on, then it set the tone for the day. I should qualify that and say that no one was ever arrested without good cause, but our collective tolerance for bad behaviour was very low. This inevitably led to us giving evidence in the courts repeatedly and notching up numerous complaints.

I was working long hours again, but the overtime was coming in handy. My youngest son was born in December of 1985; our house became too small, so we now had to find somewhere larger. To reduce overheads and to avoid having to try to find a car parking spot in Leeds city centre, I bought a Honda 90cc motor scooter, referred to by my friends as the 'Honda Clunk'. It was handy in the summer months but miserable when wet, rainy and cold. We eventually moved to a small village outside of Leeds. The house was larger, it was easier to get into work and the children all went to the local school. Life on the home front was going well, even though I was seeing less and less of my wife and children. I had, however, fallen in love with my work. I enjoyed being amongst the lads; the thrills and spills of what we did gave me an adrenaline rush. I wasn't into the partying lifestyle that some of the boys got into. There were odd occasions though when we all abused the 5pm until am shift pattern by drifting off to the clubs and pubs in the city centre on the very loose justification of looking for evidence of drug abuse. We worked hard and played hard.

In March 1986 whilst out on patrol, all of us were summoned back to the office. We were told to get into our vans and head to Morley, a small town in South Leeds. It transpired that a young girl had gone missing the previous night and had not returned home. I recall all of us being extremely frustrated as we sat in the back of our vans in the car park of the station for what seemed like an eternity. 'Hurry up and wait' was an expression often used for some of what we did.

Sarah Harper was 10 years old when she was abducted. She had been sent to the local off-licence for a loaf of bread by her mother and never returned. We eventually embarked upon a huge operation in the local area searching houses, open land and outside buildings for signs of her. If sources are correct, over 3,000 properties were searched, more than 10,000 leaflets distributed, and 1,400 witness statements obtained. I worked both on the ground and in the house-to-house enquiry room during the investigation that kept us engaged for weeks on end. Sarah's body was eventually pulled from the River Trent in Nottingham that April. She had been severely sexually assaulted, killed and thrown into the water. It was horrific and the incident had an impact on everyone that worked on the enquiry. It was many years later when the offender, Robert Black, a paedophile, was finally convicted of her murder.

As a father of a five-year-old daughter and probably as a direct result of that investigation, I became particularly protective of her. On one rare afternoon off at home, I couldn't find her anywhere in the house or garden. I panicked and ran around trying to find her. Just before calling it in, I found her asleep in the back of my car in the garage. The sense of relief is impossible to adequately describe.

22. Undercover

Task Force operated on a buddy system. Most of the time, you paired up with an identified individual. It worked well. If required, the whole team, or teams, would also operate together as a unit. Initially, I worked with a guy whose nickname was 'Ted', after Ted Rogers, the compère of the TV show *3-2-1*. Ted had once made the mistake of swivelling his hand from side to side, using his fingers to indicate the combination of a lock. He was stuck with the name forever. Ted was a good sort, a former soldier like me, but quite set in his ways. The team underwent a restructure a few months after I arrived and I ended up being partnered with 'Billy'. I'd known him at a distance because he worked at a neighbouring division before we were both posted in. He was a bit off the wall, very funny, intelligent and at times deep. He also liked a drink and enjoyed the company of the opposite sex. We became good friends, worked well together and somehow got involved in the investigation of some linked criminal damages in Leeds city centre. The suspects appeared to have their origins in animal rights with connections to elements of the student population in Headingley, an area only a short walk from the city centre.

In Cambridgeshire around this time, there had been car bomb attacks against researchers at an animal experimentation laboratory. This raised the profile of what some perceived to be the exploitation of animals, not least in Leeds and some other nearby towns and cities. Department stores who chose to stock animal fur products were experiencing acid attacks on their windows. The pair of us were given free rein by our Inspector (whom I will refer to as Tom) to conduct our own investigations to see what we could find out. We operated in plain clothes during the day and at night we conducted covert observations. Billy had designs on the Drug Squad when he completed his stint with Task Force. He saw a strong correlation between the persons responsible for the damage and those who were involved in the drugs scene. This was an opportunity for us both to shine.

For this operation we reported directly to our Inspector, Tom, who enthusiastically supported what we were doing. A terrific boss to work for, he was, like us, a bit anti-establishment and liked to rock the boat a bit. At the time, the wearing of beards was frowned upon in the police. So, he deliberately sported one. He would do things his way and despite being told not to, would frequently bring his black Labrador into the office. On one occasion, he even arranged a mating session in the large garage we occupied with another dog belonging to a member of our team. Tom ranks as one of the finest inspectors I ever had the pleasure to work for. He wasn't scared of intervening if you were found wanting or stepped out of line, as one officer found out when he kicked our office door off its hinges because he had forgotten the combination for the lock. Everyone laughed about that, but the miscreant came very close to being returned to divisional policing.

Billy and I hatched a plan to show up at an animal rights demonstration in a neighbouring force area. The demo was to be held outside a laboratory that conducted lawful animal experiments. The enquiries we had made suggested that some of the people we were looking into would be there. It presented an ideal opportunity to gather some intelligence. We were stuck for transport as our work vehicles, whilst unmarked, quite obviously belonged to the police. Tom suggested that we could use his personal car, a tatty, old, silver Ford Granada. On the day of the operation, Billy was sick. I went in to see the boss to break the news. He said in a blink of an eye, "That's OK, I'll come with you!" I didn't expect that, but I wasn't surprised because that was exactly the sort of guy he was. I noticed he had his dog, Jess, in the office. I think he saw the puzzled look on my face so he then said, "She can come too, as a bit of extra cover for us." About half an hour later, after putting animal rights posters all over his car, we set off – both of us dressed in the scruffiest clothes we could muster.

When we arrived, the scene that met us was reminiscent of a hippy encampment. The sun was shining and that was probably why there was in excess of 150 people present. One guy was strumming a guitar, the people surrounding him were clapping and singing along. There was a small group of police officers monitoring the event. We were confident they would not recognise us because it was outside of our force boundary.

Tom's enthusiasm was evident from the minute we arrived. He went straight into the crowd, chatting away to different groups and started conversations about animal rights, as if he was a veteran campaigner. I was chuckling to myself because he was absolutely in his element. He was older than most of the people there, so quite a few of them warmed to him immediately as a bit of a father figure. Before I knew it, he had marshalled a small group of people and began leading them around a tour of the building's perimeter fence, surveying the outside of the premises and pointing out potential places of entry. This was going above and beyond – we were not there to encourage any criminality – but thankfully no one reacted to his enthusiasm.

Because there was an element of risk, Tom had arranged for one of our sergeants to be nearby as our point of contact. We were to slip away to check in with him around lunchtime. When Tom announced to our new vegan pals that we were off into town to get some 'fish and chips', I must admit, we got one or two strange looks. On our return, I noticed that one of our persons of interest was present. From our investigations, we knew that code name 'X' was often quite reserved and didn't readily engage with anyone he was unsure of. By the manner he was moving around and interacting, he clearly knew lots of people. From the intelligence we already possessed, we knew he was a pivotal player. We struck up a conversation with him and found out that he needed to go to a nearby peace camp to run an errand. Peace camps were all the rage at the time, often situated outside of nuclear bases and military listening stations. I casually said to X that we had a car and could drive him there. So, Tom, Jess the dog, me and X went on the short drive. Whilst X didn't say too much, he didn't have a clue that he was in the company of two officers and their undercover dog. The errand involved transporting water. Once that was off-loaded, we sat around chatting and drinking tea. Tom's suggestion about the extra cover provided by Jess clearly paid off; she became the focal point, even receiving a large box of dog biscuits.

After an hour or so, we headed back with one of X's friends in tow. As we all chatted away making small talk, X's friend said to Tom, "Mind if we have a smoke in your car, mate?"

Tom replied, "No problem, feel free."

Once you have smelt it, the pungent smell of cannabis is unforgettable. I realised quickly that the pair of them had started to smoke a joint in the car. Tom and I were both offered a puff but politely declined, saying we didn't smoke, which was in fact true. Sat in the middle of our two new-found friends was Jess the dog, enveloped in a cloak of cannabis smoke. Inside I was falling about laughing knowing that I would dine out on this story for many years to come. I daren't look at Tom because I knew that I would start laughing.

Once we arrived back at the facility, we could see that the demonstration was now in full swing. The police had strengthened their numbers and had begun stopping vehicles to check them. Our two smokers panicked at this point shouting, "Shit, man, it's the filth, get rid of the spliff!" As they hastily stamped the joint out on the rear carpet of the car, I swiftly opened the windows to expel the odour. I couldn't help but ponder the consequences for all of us had we been arrested for possession of cannabis. Thankfully the cop at the entrance didn't stop and check our car, he just waved us through. The operation was a success, we hadn't been compromised, we'd made a few contacts and interacted with a few significant players. There was a lot of laughter on our journey home, and the burn on the car's carpet was doubtless a reminder for Tom for many years to come.

Our investigations eventually came to the attention of the Major Crime Unit (MCU). Like us, they were based in Leeds. We had unwittingly encroached on something they were already engaged with. From memory, the acid attacks had caught the attention of the media. This inevitably had ramifications for senior officers in charge of divisions. Department store owners were up in arms and calling for police action. This was well before city centre CCTV cameras were routine. Catching the offenders would therefore need a lucky break or doing something quite different. The MCU was, as the name suggests, tasked with investigating serious crimes and co-ordinating a response. Unbeknown to us, an incident room had been set up to enquire into the damage. The prevalence of the incidents had begun to increase and was affecting other parts of the Force's area.

One afternoon, Billy and I were summoned to a meeting in the boardroom, located on the upper floor of the station normally reserved for senior officers. This was a place where the likes of us were not generally invited to. When we arrived in our jeans and scruffy shirts, there were about 10 CID officers present. One guy, who was very smartly dressed, then swaggered in. Billy and I formed the opinion that he was in charge because of the way he carried himself. As it turned out, Tony was not the boss but a very well-respected detective sergeant. He turned out to be a great ally for us; another free thinker and someone I really enjoyed working with. It was clear from the outset that he was not enamoured about having to conduct what was effectively a criminal damage enquiry. However, we soon found out he was always open to new ideas and listened to what Billy and I had to say. Sadly, Tony died several years ago from cancer. He was a true professional and a gentleman, although he did get the pair of us into a couple of tricky situations.

Without much more than a phone call, we were seconded onto the incident room team. So began another exceptionally interesting, and diverse, chapter in my policing career. We managed to persuade the team to let us conduct covert surveillance on some of the targets we had identified during our enquiries. We had done quite a lot of work already. It was readily acknowledged that we had gathered plenty of intelligence but little in the way of evidence. Because we were now seconded to a major enquiry, it was much easier to get access to specialist kit. This included a brand-new observation vehicle. From the outside it looked like a tatty old van. Inside it was soundproofed and equipped in such a way that you could observe from several angles and take photographs with little chance of being compromised. Much of our initial work was done in Leeds. However, after a few weeks it became evident that all we were doing was informed guesswork. The acid attacks had dropped off a little. What had replaced them were a number of incidents across the North of England where animals had been 'liberated' from various facilities. These were mostly farms in fairness, as they were easy targets. Grainy videos of hooded individuals claiming responsibility popped up on the news. Still, though, little evidence of who was responsible. What we were pretty sure of was that the various hunt disruptor and animal rights groups were closely intertwined. As a result of our theory, Billy and I came up with another plan. If it were to be suggested nowadays, it would probably get so bogged down in red tape that it would never happen. Times were different then; there was no formal legislation to cover things like infiltration and undercover work.

We had got to know Tony quite well by now. He trusted us, although I think there were times when he thought we were both a bit bonkers. We first pitched our idea to him to test it out. We pointed out that we could be watching potential suspects for months and get nothing. The only effective way to move the enquiry forward was to physically join a branch of one of the hunt disruptor groups. Once we had fully explained our rationale, he agreed to approach management for authority which was forthcoming. Between us, we came up with a couple of cover stories. I was to be an army deserter,

Billy a disillusioned student. Those who knew us at the time would probably say both the identities were not so far from the truth! After making a couple of telephone calls, I attended a meeting of one of the groups. It was suggested that only one of us should attend the first meeting and introduce the other later. I won the short straw, went along one evening and struck up conversations with the various people who were present. Almost immediately, I was accepted and shortly after Billy joined me.

We were keen to impress our new-found friends. They were a motley crew of males and females, all of whom disliked the police and the wider establishment. The common theme was that they were vegans. We therefore had to be very careful about our eating habits in front of them. Billy was already well acquainted with all of that, but as for me, I didn't have much of a clue. Things moved quite quickly. We had an appointed handler who we would meet regularly. A flat was found for us near our targets. For reasons we didn't grasp straight away, Tony decided it would be better if we used his old car, a clapped-out Ford Escort; perfect cover, we thought. There were financial benefits for Tony because he would get an allowance to compensate him for fuel, wear and tear, and so on. It was immaterial to us. The fact that we had a nondescript vehicle at our disposal helped us enormously. We were able to give lifts to members of the group, get them on their own, gain their confidence and learn more about the network.

One such member, whom I will refer to as 'Z', was key to the group. He and his girlfriend were the organisers of events for one of the hunt disruptor groups. Most of the events took place at weekends when the hunts were active. As time progressed, we travelled far and wide across the whole of the UK. One of the aims of these groups was to hamper and ultimately stop fox hunts, which at that time were entirely legal. Most of the participants on hunts were local gentry. They didn't take too kindly when the 'riff-raff' turned up to ruin their day. They often employed groups of local farmers and labourers who would provide muscle to intervene when the police weren't around. Inevitably, we got caught up in that. The tyres on Tony's car were slashed, and in another incident a hunt member rode at speed towards me on his horse lashing out with his whip. I lost count of the number of times we were threatened with violence. Being in our covert role gave us an opportunity to see things in a slightly different light.

Our first trip out with Z almost ended in a compromise. I always drove the car; I cannot remember why but it may have been due to Tony's insurance. We were driving Z around the area allowing him to be as disruptive as he wanted to be. This would often involve him jumping out of the car and getting close to the horse riders. He would then blow a hunting horn to distract the hounds. Another tactic was to run a cloth smeared with a different scent across the ground to throw the dogs off track. On this particular occasion, Billy was in the back of the car and Z was front seat passenger. Z shouted, "Stop!" and jumped out of the car to blow his horn near to some of the hunt. For some reason, I reached over to the glove compartment to look inside. Imagine my horror when I saw a note in there stating 'MAJOR CRIME UNIT, BACK IN FIVE MINUTES'. Something he obviously used to prevent a parking ticket being issued when he was using the vehicle for work purposes. I hastily screwed the note up and placed it in my pocket. I looked at Billy through the rear-view mirror and mouthed, "Fucking hell!" as Z jumped into the car again.

23. Upping the ante

As the weeks and months went on, the powers that be were getting increasingly anxious about our covert operation. Their view appeared to be that two inexperienced, maverick officers were just pissing about on a jolly. As far as we were concerned, their opinion was without any justification and we suspected it to be financially motivated. Operations, such as this, cost money and budgets were always under review, so senior management were always looking at the purse strings and demanding quick results. Tony stood firm; he knew how hard we had worked in gaining the confidence of some key players and they had no clue who we really were. Provided we continued to provide useful intelligence, then he would back us to the hilt. The fact that he received compensation for when his vehicle was in use, could of course have been a contributory factor. An incident with the car though very nearly brought an end to everything.

On one of our Saturday disruption events, I was stopped and questioned by a police officer whilst driving the car. It didn't do our credibility any harm, of course. Z was behind us in another vehicle and he saw me being taken to the police car and given a notice to produce my driving documents. Later when I notified Tony about what had happened, it transpired that his insurance had expired! That effectively meant I was committing an offence. If those who were not happy about the operation had found out, then it would have been enough to shut us down. Thankfully, it all went away quietly. Things were smoothed over without disclosing anything about us or what we were doing.

As young, enthusiastic officers, we were thoroughly enjoying what we were doing. It was exciting, different and an adrenaline rush to be amongst a group of people who had no idea of who we really were. The flip side was that on our days off, we were always on alert just in case we bumped into one of the group whilst out with our respective families. Most of them lived on the other side of the Force's area, about 20 miles away. However, we knew that they came into Leeds frequently for meetings and suchlike. It was important not to be complacent just in case they were secretly trying to find out more about the pair of us. Thankfully, social media was not available, but we still had to be cautious. There was an undercurrent of anarchism throughout the group and some very unsavoury characters in their ranks, as we discovered when attending a gathering in another large northern city.

On the day in question, we all piled into Z's Land Rover and headed off. We had only been told that there was to be a national gathering of animal rights groups at a university in the city. We applied for and received authority to attend. This was an opportunity not to be missed. From the little we had been told, there was to be a formal get-together and then a few drinks at a bar in the city centre. When we arrived, there were in excess of 40 people crowded into a small meeting room. This time, both Billy and I felt the tension in the air. Those attending had come from all over the country. They sported all manner of hairstyles; shaven, pink, green, purple, it was all there. T-shirts displaying 'fuck the police', leaflets about how to act at demonstrations and general anti-authoritarian chatter was everywhere. As the meeting was called to order, a short film was beamed onto a large screen. It openly encouraged violence for the cause. This included civil disobedience with behaviour such as setting fire to and beheading 'pigs' – in other words, people like me and Billy.

My heart was pumping; these were hard-core anarchists. In October 1985, PC Keith Blakelock had been savagely attacked with knives and machetes in London, during riots on Broadwater Farm. They gloated over this incident and used it as a case study. Our small contingent was all sat together on the floor at the front. I could not help but think that we were being set up. The exit was well behind us and if we had to leave rapidly, we had several people to clamber over. It would be almost impossible to escape unscathed.

Once the film stopped, a guy came to the front. He was doing all the organising and had plenty to say about how much he hated the police. My insides churned when he said, "We want each one of you to stand up, tell us who you are, and why you are here." This now felt very suspicious, and I am not ashamed to say I was scared. One by one, each member of our group stood up and said their piece. When it came to my turn, I jumped up in a false show of enthusiasm, cranked up my Southern accent and told them I was new to all this but wanted to do my bit. The guy nodded, said "Thanks, mate," and put his thumb up whereupon I sat back down. Billy did much the same. Inwardly, I breathed a sigh of relief. That feeling of 'getting away with it' has the effect of putting you on a high. We couldn't let our guard down though; we had to remain alert. It was perfectly apparent from what was said during the meeting, that they were alive to the possibility of infiltration. We went for several drinks, had some interesting conversations, gathered some useful information, and later headed back home.

One of our next trips out was to a hunt, perilously close to the police divisions in which Billy and I used to work. We were relatively new to undercover work, but we knew full well that if we were seen by any of our former colleagues, it would cause problems. They may think we had gone rogue on our days off, recognise us, say something, or tell others and blow the operation wide open. By now, my hair was long and dyed blonde. I was just as scruffy and non-conformist, when in character, as the people we were consorting with. My hope was that in a passing glance I could get away with it.

On this particular Saturday, we were amongst a group of about 10 people in the back of an old transit van. The hunt was in full swing and we were trying to get into a position to cause some disruption. However, the police were ahead of us and a roadblock had been put in place. The driver shouted something about 'the filth' stopping us. Billy and I were sat opposite each other and exchanged looks. I crouched and put my head down.

Before we knew it, the rear doors of the van flew open and a uniformed sergeant whom we both knew was in full view. He said something like, "Right, you lot!" then stopped momentarily and for what seemed like an eternity. He had clearly recognised us, but was quick-witted enough not to look at or address us directly. He regained his composure and then said something along the lines of, "I want you out of this area now, or you are all getting arrested!" He proceeded to slam the doors shut. Someone questioned why they hadn't lined us up and asked for our names, like they normally do. For good measure, I said something like, "It's because they are fucking tossers!" Everyone started to laugh, and we drove off.

In quite a short period of time, we had ingratiated ourselves with several of the key figures. Whilst we knew the hunt disruptors shared the same ethos as many of the animal rights groups, no one was saying very much in front of us. We desperately needed to know more about the acid attacks, breaking into establishments and suchlike. The law demands that in the role we were performing, we were not allowed to encourage or incite criminal offences, so we had to be passive in our approach. During conversations with our targets, we suggested that we were involved in other things and needed to keep our distance from the police. It was all to create a bit of mystery and it seemed to work. We even went to the extent of staging an arrest on the forecourt of a filling station. We were both dragged away resisting our capture, effected by Tony and some other officers from the MCU. We later produced fake bail forms to the group, which seemed to elevate our status to that of 'bad ass'. This led to us being asked if we wanted to be involved in a raid on a farm to 'liberate' some animals.

We were now getting closer to the inner circle. This invitation was fed back to Tony who passed it up the chain. The man in charge of the CID for the whole of the Force was getting nervous and was pushing hard for the enquiry to end. However, an event then occurred in another area which had an impact. Some of the intelligence we had gleaned had led to a significant arrest and in turn accelerated the enquiry towards its objectives. More arrests were to follow. It was no surprise to us when we heard that senior officers took the view that our work was complete. We were told we had to extract ourselves from the group and quickly.

We hurriedly arranged to visit Z and his girlfriend. We told him that we had to go on the run because something had happened. We didn't disclose any details and it was deliberately vague. The plan was to leave the proverbial door open just in case we needed to reopen the enquiry at some point in the future. We said our goodbyes, Z shook our hands and thanked us profusely for everything we had helped him with. As far as he was concerned, we had to disappear, he didn't question it. Even though I half-expected to meet him again in an official capacity, I never did. To my knowledge, he was never arrested for anything. I often wonder if he and his friends ever worked out who we really were.

The whole enquiry team later received certificates of commendation for the work we put into the investigation. It was an honour getting that sort of acknowledgement and we both felt proud. The shine was taken off by the then Head of the Force Intelligence Unit (FIU) though. He pulled Billy and me aside and into his office. We were not overly aware of the internal politics of the enquiry. The MCU and the FIU had been at loggerheads about the undercover side of things because the FIU wanted to run it. I'll never forget their Detective Chief Inspector saying to us, "You didn't do so bad given that you have never been trained. Now it's time to put your uniforms back on." The truth was, he had absolutely no real idea of what we had been doing and neither did he bother to ask. It was petty and made me even more cynical about senior officers.

We both came out of the office and simultaneously mouthed the words, "What a wanker!" and burst out laughing. We were heading back to the Task Force and there had been some more changes.

24. All change

Arriving back at Task Force, our friends in the teams were naturally curious about what we had been up to. As you would expect, we regaled them with one or two stories.

There had been some reshuffles at the office. Tom had been posted elsewhere. Our sergeant had been replaced and the new man was already being described by colleagues as a bit of a 'knob'. The guy concerned was performing the role of Acting Inspector and seemed keen to impress. Tales of some of the things that had taken place since his arrival had already filtered back to Billy and I, so we were prepared for trouble. There were also two PCs on our team who had recently passed their sergeant exams. They were very friendly with him and took it in turns to deputise for him. Neither of them were particularly popular with the rest of the team. Their apparent closeness with our new Acting Inspector put them into the bracket of quislings. It became obvious that they were both feeding information to him. This didn't bode well for teamwork; it created divisions such that everyone felt that they had to watch their back.

This was an unfortunate element of the promotion process. The prevailing climate at the time seemed to be that if you had instigated a disciplinary action against a fellow officer, then you were seen to be loyal to the establishment. Promotion had not really crossed my mind. I was too busy having fun.

The biggest part of me though wanted to ensure that I was entirely competent at what I was doing, before I even considered supervising others.

Immediately upon our return, Billy and I were split up as partners and I began to work with a new guy, whom I shall call 'Glenn'. We got on well straight away; he was quick-witted, and like me, a hard-working family man. He was a big man, as hard as nails, and took no messing in public order situations. We quickly got involved in loads of self-motivated arrests together. Glenn had worked in East Leeds before so he knew the area well. It was a stone's throw from our office and catching the bad guys was like shooting fish in a barrel. I could never quite understand why some of the team couldn't do the same thing, in particular the Acting Sergeants who didn't quite understand proactive policing. They seemed to prefer swanning about, seemingly with their eyes closed. We were able to pick off disqualified drivers, criminals wanted on warrant and drug dealers simply by just driving up onto some of the estates.

On one occasion, we were passed some information via another force about a man who was growing cannabis in his garden. On reflection we probably didn't ask enough questions. At the time we believed it was because we had become frequent visitors to the station's intelligence office to see if we could assist with local crime problems. We had the luxury of having a relatively free rein. Our colleagues on routine uniform patrol were going from call to call and had little time to do the sorts of work we were able to apply ourselves to. We were told that a local man had come to notice in another area and that they wanted to know more about him. He was believed to be involved in drugs and some unsubstantiated information existed that he was a big-time dealer. We were informed that if we wanted to do some development work on the drugs side of things, then we were welcome to it. Being as keen as mustard, we jumped straight in.

First, we did a bit of research and that afternoon Glenn, me and a couple of others went to the man's house. In the garden amongst the tomato plants were masses of cannabis plants. Our suspect wasn't at home, but his girlfriend was. Typical of the area, she wasn't a fan of the police and denied all knowledge of the plants, telling us she cleaned the house for her boyfriend. She did tell us that our man was expected home tomorrow. Being proud of our seizures, we uprooted all the cannabis plants and departed. Glenn and I arranged to come back early the next morning, a Saturday as I remember.

The pair of us were not expecting any problems. As far as we were concerned, it was a routine drugs arrest and the offender had no prior convictions or history of violence. It was around 8am and we were in plain clothes. I knocked on the front door a few times and then to my left I saw the curtain open. In view was a man who was taller than me, well over six foot. He did not look at all happy. He beckoned us to go to the rear of the property. We duly went to the back and he met us stood square in the door frame. I am certain to this day that he knew who we were and why we were there, but he decided to make a big song and dance about it. I identified myself and Glenn and informed him that he was under arrest for both possession and distribution of controlled drugs. He made no reply and just stared at the pair of us, as if weighing us up.

You develop a sixth sense in the police of when things are just not right, and this just did not feel right. After a short interlude he said, "Wait there, I am going to get dressed."

I then said to him, "Sorry, we are not waiting anywhere, we are coming inside." I stepped into the house with Glenn behind me.

Our suspect then shouted, "Get out of my house!" We had no intention of doing that because he was under arrest and the last thing we wanted to do was to give him the opportunity to escape. He turned his back on us and quickened his pace from kitchen, into the hallway, turning right into the front lounge of the property. Before we knew it, he turned back towards us, brandishing a large machete and shouted at the top of his voice, "I said, get out of my house!"

There was little room for manoeuvre. When you are faced with a weapon like that and have no protection, the best option is to retreat. I don't think we ran but we certainly headed out of the house quickly before he kicked the door shut. Glenn and I looked at each other. I will always remember him saying to me, "Well, what the fuck do we do now?"

This was an embarrassing situation to say the least. Hindsight is a wonderful science, but we should have given consideration to back up before going to the property. In our defence, we were doing this type of arrest day in day out. You cannot predict every eventuality. We had several options, but going back in without help was not one of them. Without any warning, the door re-opened. Our suspect presented himself dressed in a pinstripe suit and said, "Let's go". Without further ado, we conveyed him to the local police station to be booked into custody. Other than demanding a solicitor and not being overly chatty, he was co-operative. It was obvious we needed the machete as evidence to prove that we were threatened, so we quickly headed back to the property. We searched the house from top to bottom but there was no sign of the weapon.

In court some weeks later, the missing machete proved to be a huge issue. A barrister had been instructed to represent our man in the Magistrates' Court, which is quite unusual. All sorts of allegations were levelled at both of us during cross examination, including the fact that we had fabricated a story about the machete. It also transpired that the Force providing the information about the cannabis were interested in the prospect of a firearm being at the address. A firearm that was believed to have been used in a murder, something that had not been shared with us. Our man was eventually convicted of two offences of assaulting a police officer and got a very minor financial penalty for the drugs charge. For both of us, it made the whole episode completely pointless. We had not given too much thought to what might have happened. It clearly had the potential for serious injury or death though. If you dwell on incidents like this for too long, nothing would ever get done.

Back at the office, there was increased discord about our new supervisors. Our previous bosses knew not to micromanage, but it was happening more and more. In our collective opinion, the best supervisors won our respect by trusting us to get on with the job.

There were other changes afoot. We were redeployed into separate 'bomb search' and 'firearms' teams. Some years previously I had qualified to be a firearms officer. I never quite got on with the police issue revolver, having been more accustomed to an automatic pistol during my time in the Armed Forces. I subsequently failed a refresher course. I didn't bother reapplying as there was a nationwide cull on temporary firearms officers. There had been an incident in London in 1983 where a man called Stephen Waldorf had been wrongly identified as an armed suspect and was shot by the police. The subsequent enquiry changed the direction towards the use of full-time firearms officers. There had also been a significant increase in the use of lethal weapons, so more capability was needed.

Glenn and I became bomb search officers. We were responsible for the clearance of buildings and areas prior to the arrival of VIPs and royalty. This supplemented our other duties and kept us busy. We were also regularly deployed on major crime enquiries. We were the ones on our hands and knees conducting fingertip searches, lifting drains, searching through rubbish at municipal tips, and looking for weapons and evidence. We really did see every type of waste on those tasks. Whether it was the sheer pace of the work or the fact that we had very little respect for our current supervision, from time to time we would get into minor mischief. This was all par for the course and it was a way of letting off steam.

On one notable occasion, we had all been deployed to a pop concert at Hyde Park. It was a hot summer's day, and we were kept busy responding to public order incidents, dealing with crowds and generally being run ragged. Our 'happy bags' (refreshments) provided for the day were left in the van and many of us did not get the time to eat our food. When the event finally concluded, we returned to our van, climbed in, and as was normal, all headed straight to our meals. This often included a yoghurt. Someone decided to flick a spoonful of their yoghurt straight into somebody's face and all hell broke loose. Yoghurt was being thrown about inside the van and a general melee ensued.

At some point, the rear doors were opened by our Acting Inspector. An instruction had come down from on high that all the teams were to congregate for a debrief by the Chief Inspector and to thank us for our hard work that day. Our boss looked incredulous at the state of all of us dripping in all flavours of yoghurt, shouting obscenities at each other and generally carrying on. He uttered something under his breath and slammed the van doors shut. Nothing more was said about it, but he clearly was not happy and from then onwards our cards were marked.

An incident in the early hours of the morning, whilst on mobile plain clothes patrol in an area of Leeds, sealed my fate. I was involved in a road traffic collision with one of my colleagues. It resulted in my police driving permit being removed whilst the matter was investigated. It emerged later that our Acting Inspector was going out of his way to look for evidence to support non-existent driving offences. This made me nervous about my future within the team. Without a driving permit, I was left to rely on colleagues to drive me around, which was fine for a while but the novelty soon wore off. By this time, I had completed around three years on the teams, and it was unusual to stay much longer than that. My master plan was to get into the CID, pursue promotion and go on from there. First, though, I would have to go back to uniformed patrol work. I started to make my own enquiries about my preferred posting rather than being landed with a fait accompli. I'd had three years of adrenaline-pumped excitement and experiences, disorder, major crime enquiries, policing public events and plenty of interesting investigations. It all provided a solid foundation for my career trajectory. On the downside, the hours were long, and I had spent little time at home with the family. When I was there, I was tired and at times irritable. Now it was time to get serious about the future, I decided it was time to study for my sergeant's examinations.

25. The long road to promotion

Prior to leaving Task Force, several of us decided to work together to ready ourselves for what we all knew was going to be an arduous process. Personally, I loathed studying, and my previous track record had not been great. I didn't want to fail the exam though. To give me the best possible chance, I knew I would have to study hard. The fact that we acted together as a little support group to help each other out was a great move. It served to provide an element of competition, and we also motivated each other as a group.

What also drove us, was a collective and perhaps conceited view that many of the people getting promoted around us were incompetent. Certainly, there were some questionable individuals getting advancement. It naturally led to conspiracy theories, including Masonic influence, favouring minorities and so on. Whilst I have no concrete evidence about any of the speculation, there were many examples of completely hopeless supervisors and managers in the ranks. Some had been promoted with little operational experience and had proved themselves as unfit for the role. I have always held the view that promotion in any organisation should be about merit, hard work and technical competence.

I now felt ready to begin the process and certainly felt much more confident about my abilities. The next part of the journey was the written examinations. For me, this was the process I knew would be the most difficult. In fact, it was only the beginning. Once I started to progress, it became all consuming. I developed a competitive side, always wanting to better myself. However, in my quest to do that, there were some casualties along the way.

I began cramming as much study as I could at home. I would lock myself in the kitchen each evening so I could concentrate. It meant that I didn't spend as much time with the kids as I wanted to. However, I wanted to provide them with the best possible life, so in my view sacrifices had to be made. I prepared piles of flash cards with key words to help me remember the legislation. A key aspect of the examinations was the ability to recall and quote legislation. It was a memory test, when all is said and done. I trained my brain as much as I possibly could to help me remember. At work we would test each other on the core subjects: crime, road traffic and general police duties. They all had their own quirks and individual question papers.

I took the exam in 1988 at Leeds University. You were expected to attend in uniform, desks were set apart from each other and we were closely supervised. It was strict exam conditions and took most of the day.

Some months later, I was overjoyed to find out I had passed. I knew that whilst all the legislation was fresh in my mind, it would be best to take the next written examination for the role of inspector. It was a bit more involved but a similar format. My rationale was that if I left it too long, I knew I would lose the impetus.

I finally left the Task Force of my own volition, doing a mutual swap with another officer at a division in Leeds. After the standard leaving do, I emptied my locker and departed. I would never experience the same level of comradeship and belonging in the service ever again. I was very at home with the macho culture in the teams, but knew it was close to having its day. The police service changes and adapts continually, trying to keep pace with the society it serves.

Referred to as such by a chief inspector who welcomed me to the division, the town I had been posted to was the 'ring in the doughnut'. It was a small town on the outskirts of Leeds surrounded by some challenging and large local authority estates which we were not directly responsible for. There were several new housing estates and an influx of professional people into our area because of the proximity to the city centre. It was beginning to grow at a pace. Unfortunately, this made it a prime target for all manner of villainy. House burglary and car crime were rife, most often perpetrated by criminals from elsewhere. Crime was topical; I saw an opportunity and made it abundantly clear on my arrival that I wanted to get into the CID. The system at the time was that you first had to undertake a six-month attachment, known as the 'aide' to the CID. It was an apprenticeship of sorts. Competition was fierce and I soon came to understand that there was already a queue of budding detectives.

Being a new face, I took it upon myself to introduce myself to the divisional Detective Inspector (DI) one afternoon. Fairly typical of the times, he was an irritable sort who strutted around the station as if he owned it but was better for knowing. One of the DSs I later worked with told me, "I'll never forget the day you walked into our office and told the DI you wanted to be an aide." He qualified his remark by telling me, "I thought you were a cocky little twat." It was one way of being remembered...

It was now December 1988. I only had seven and a half years of service but was one of the most senior members on my new uniformed shift. There had been a large intake of probationary officers and experience was lacking across the board. My time in the Task Force had given me exposure to many different facets of policing. This, coupled with me passing the sergeant's examination, put me in a strong position. Being at the back of the CID aide queue, I also knew that I would have to work hard to get noticed.

I was first posted to the main station in town and my first set of shifts were nights. Almost as if to remind me that I was at the bottom of the pile, I was given foot patrol duties in the town centre. Compared to my previous role, I found it mind-numbingly boring. Whilst there was a small amount of public disorder to deal with, I no longer had the reassurance that the person next to me would have my back. My adjustment was going to take a while.

In a very short space of time, I was told by the shift inspector that I would be joining one of the satellite stations. I must admit being more than a little disappointed. It seemed a little 'déjà vu'. My first thoughts were that this would likely limit my opportunities to get into the CID. I would be 'out of sight, out of mind'.

On the flipside, in terms of home life my journey to and from work was reduced dramatically so it wasn't all bad. My hours became a little more structured again and I was able to spend a bit more time with the children who were all growing up fast. My salary dropped significantly because there was much less overtime on offer. There were opportunities if you made arrests towards the end of the shift, but it was becoming increasingly standard practice to hand over prisoners to the oncoming team. I was never overly comfortable with that approach as I preferred to see the job through. My motivation was never a financial one but the opposing argument from the bosses was that someone would have to pay you overtime. The 'lock 'em up and leave 'em' culture had become pervasive. It provided reasons for officers not to follow through, and it also had the effect of deskilling officers who lost out on conducting investigations from start to finish.

As I settled in, I became more adept at 'thief-taking', sometimes getting home mid-morning having arrested burglars in the early hours when they were at their most active. I soon realised that my early misgivings about the satellite station were completely misplaced. There were a lot of criminals that would travel into the area because of the shops, expensive cars and lovely houses. Burglary and levels of car crime were high. During the quieter night shifts, I would prowl the streets looking for someone doing something they shouldn't be.

Amongst the 'self-motivated' work came the run of the mill domestic disputes, shoplifters and road traffic accidents, all of which were expected to be dealt with during our shift. The place had several arterial routes connecting several large towns and cities together. We were lucky to have two very good road traffic officers attached to our team. They were both proactive and supportive. The division was a busy place for drink drivers at night. I was well past my misguided guilt trip from the early eighties, having now seen much more of the accompanying misery drunk drivers cause with collisions, injuries and at times, deaths.

One particular night shift there always sticks in my mind. We were called to assist our road traffic colleagues who were on their way to a serious incident. Instead of turning at a T-junction, the offending driver had completely misread the road layout, and had headed straight across the road into a large tree. It must have been at considerable speed because the driver was dead when we arrived and his body was not in a good state. His male passenger was inside the vehicle, unconscious with his head down but appeared to show signs of life.

Between us, we managed to get him out of the car and laid him on the ground. In an effort to resuscitate him, I performed mouth-to-mouth. Whilst I had been taught to do this in both the army and police, it was something I had never had to do for real. Even as I recount the event, I am propelled back to that scene. I blew into his mouth and pumped his chest as I had been trained to do. His breath smelt so strongly of intoxicants that I nearly threw up. I was so desperate to bring him back to life, trying for so long that I had to be physically pulled off by my colleagues. As it turned out, he had broken his neck in the collision so my attempts to revive him had been pointless.

I was never a lover of dealing with road traffic related work but equally didn't shy away from blatant law-breaking. That same week, another drunk drove his car straight over a roundabout, plunging down an embankment and very nearly onto the motorway below. I found him hiding nearby but he emphatically denied being the driver. Unfortunately for him, a witness had provided an excellent description after watching him exit his car. He was breathalysed, arrested and taken into custody. I didn't recognise the guy and don't ever recall meeting him prior to the event. He was dealt with fairly, properly and there were no issues. As it turned out, my daughter was in the same class as his daughter. I will never forget her being the only member of the class who was not invited to the girl's birthday party, a week or so after the incident. This was the sort of petty crap that you had to endure from time to time. It comes with the territory, but my little girl was so upset, she was only seven-years-old and thought she had done something wrong. I felt guilty, not for him, but for her. There were several occasions during my service that my family were affected by the job; however, that one I cannot forget.

It didn't take as long to settle into my new role as I expected. I became friendly with a few of the guys in the CID. I was a frequent visitor to the cell block and got to know most of the custody staff. One of the pivotal roles in relation to the Police and Criminal Evidence Act (PACE) is the custody sergeant. That person is the equivalent of God. They authorise the detention of suspects. As the Arresting Officer, you had to stand in front of him or her and relate the circumstances. Some custody officers were great, but some were almost anti-police. After taking a mother into custody for child neglect, one sergeant and I had a heated discussion about the legality of my arrest. Once the legislation had been confirmed, it turned out I was in fact correct. There was no point scoring as far as I was concerned. I just happened to remember it from my recent studies. From then onwards, he couldn't be more helpful when I arrived with prisoners.

Uniformed patrol work often gets a bad rap; some people loathe it, others love it. My experience was that you were given great opportunities to deal with all sorts of things, if you put yourself forward and made the effort. You could also get some very strange jobs to deal with.

One afternoon, I was called to a report of a man acting suspiciously in the rear garden of a house. The property was not far from the police station and I happened to arrive first on the scene. As I pulled up in the police vehicle outside the caller's address, a man resembling the TV character Catweazle was walking away quickly and, as is said in the trade, furtively. He was pointed out by a young woman who said, "I think he has stolen my underwear off the washing line!" I drove alongside him, stopped him and during a search of his pockets, sure enough he had secreted knickers and a bra. I arrested him for theft which seemed fairly straightforward.

As I spoke to him, it became apparent that he was not from our area, neither was he recorded on any of our systems. It was strange because most often the men who do this sort of thing are local. They are often associated with Peeping Toms and suchlike. As it turned out, he came from a neighbouring county, seemingly travelling many miles to steal underwear, which was again very unusual. My colleagues, including our shift sergeant, had now arrived. After a few more questions, the man admitted having a car nearby. We searched it and found two bin liners crammed full of women's underwear. This man was stealing women's lingerie on an industrial scale. Whilst we tried, it proved extremely difficult to discover the owners of the smalls. Our suspect freely admitted that they had been acquired over a period of several weeks and across different areas of the country. He was subsequently charged with a number of offences.

Once released from custody, he turned and thanked me for dealing with him in such a professional and non-judgemental way. It was some years later when working on a specialist unit, that I came to realise that the sort of behaviour he displayed is often a precursor to more serious sexual offences.

26. Supervisor

In the late eighties, vehicle crime figures were going through the roof across the UK. The term 'Twoccing' (from the offence of TWOC, taking a vehicle without consent) was born at about this time and vehicle pursuits were frequent. On arrival on your night shift, you often found yourself being pilloried by your inspector or sergeant about the crimes that had been committed the previous night. The CID did not see vehicle crime as their responsibility as their time was taken up with burglary and other serious offences. There was clearly a void which was being ruthlessly exploited by the criminals involved. In some of the other areas of the Force, small teams of officers had been set up to counter this, often with great success.

One evening, I took the bull by the horns. I went to see the local Chief Inspector to suggest that a team of officers should be formed to deal with the problem. I added that I would be more than happy to be involved. His response was lukewarm, but he listened with interest and dismissed me a short time later. I did not discuss my suggestion with anyone else. Given the Chief Inspector's apparent lack of enthusiasm, I just went back to work.

Some weeks later, I was asked if I would be interested in being the Acting Police Sergeant (APS) for the newly formed Project Team, who were to be formed to tackle vehicle crime in our division. Each of the four uniformed teams was to provide one officer and I would be their supervisor. I was over the moon because this was exactly what I wanted. We were to be semi-autonomous, work in plain clothes and I would get hands-on experience as an Acting Sergeant, which was something I had to have under my belt to be put forward for promotion.

We made the Force newspaper and the local media. Big things were expected of us. I was told that if we got results, I would run the team for six months. As it turned out, I did it for well over a year. Other officers cycled on and off the team every few months. The first three I worked with all had less service than me, but we all got on well. It was like being on the Task Force all over again. We would play stupid tricks on each other, get involved in banter, laugh and joke but we worked hard. I had read in a magazine called *Police Review* that crime mapping was proving to be an effective means of understanding patterns of offending. I put a map of the division up on our office wall which helped us identify what are now referred to as hot spots. We did observations in those areas and had a lot of success. We dealt with suspects who had been left in the cells from the previous night and got admissions about other crimes. It wasn't long before the local villains knew who we were, and we knew them.

There were a couple of local gangs that we were arresting frequently. They had been operating with impunity for long enough, mostly young men with little to do who were breaking into cars for fun. The media often called this 'joy riding'. There was no joy in this type of crime for the police or the owners of the cars. It invariably involved stealing a high-performance car and driving it hell for leather, baiting the police in high-speed pursuits. The cars favoured by them would include the Ford Fiesta XR2, Ford Escort RS, Sierra Cosworth and Vauxhall

Astra. It was dangerous for the public, for police officers and of course the idiots driving the stolen car. All too often, road collisions ended badly. As is normal for this sort of thing, the media rounded on the police for 'chasing' the criminals in the first place. For us as plain clothes officers, we were not involved in the pursuits but we did pick up the pieces. We interviewed countless offenders, dealt with the witnesses, searched houses and made sure that evidence was properly secured. Criminals rarely engage in one sort of crime. They may steal a car to travel around in, but they will often commit other offences whilst using it. Making off without paying at a petrol station, burglary and ram-raiding were the types of crimes committed in their wake. Whilst we were primarily formed to investigate vehicle crime, we ended up dealing with all sorts of things. It was great experience. We had become so effective that questions were being asked by certain inspectors about what the CID were doing. I didn't buy into that, even though it did create some friction and rivalry. As far as I was concerned, we were all working to a common goal: taking criminals off the streets and making people feel safer.

Around this time, my wife and I took the decision to get a slightly larger property with a bigger garden, so the kids had somewhere decent to play. She originated from the small town I was now working in. Her parents and wider family all lived close by and it was her preferred option. I had some reservations given that our office was there. It was a relatively small place and as a cop I was readily identifiable. I could live with that, but I didn't want the children to be adversely affected. On the plus side, the house was within striking distance of the town centre and close to schools. I was always acutely aware that because I policed the area, it may cause the children problems. Children of police officers can be singled out by bullies and the thought of that happening always troubled me.

There was the occasional humorous episode though. One day whilst off duty, my two boys asked if I would take them to the shops in town for some sweets. As I crossed the road to walk across the car park, I noticed that on one of the kerbstones something had been scrawled in black marker pen. It read: "PC TANSLEY IS A WANKER". My eldest boy was only around six years old at the time and recognised his surname, but thankfully the swear word didn't register with him. He asked me what it was. I replied, "It's someone thanking me for helping them". I struggled to contain my laughter. I knew that a little gang of local idiots had penned it, because they were being arrested frequently by the team and me.

I had the privilege to work with some outstanding officers during my time on the project team. I learnt a lot from them, and I believe I was able to share my experiences. They were all different. One guy, who I'll call 'Steve', was a formidable thief-taker and we worked really well together. We had very different personalities so, good cop/bad cop came easily during our many suspect interviews. Steve's paperwork, however, was an abomination. As a result, he was always getting into hot water with the divisional Process Sergeant whose job it was to check prosecution files. They were a law unto themselves, tended to be long in service, had their own idiosyncrasies and would pore over your submissions looking for grammatical and evidential errors. This sergeant took it upon himself to make Steve's life a misery. As a result, given that I was the supervisor, I also got it in the neck. It became our mission to get Steve's reports past him first time. It was hard to do, but we did achieve it and consistently.

It reinforced to me that report writing is an essential skill and just as important as arresting people. Better files contributed to an improvement in our detection and conviction rates.

Whilst this was important for us as a division, it only serves to illustrate a very blunt measure of effectiveness, whereas the reasons why crime was happening rarely came under scrutiny. It was a numbers game and equated to how much crime was being reported and whether or not we caught the people who perpetrated it. It sounds simple, but it's much more complicated because there is no means to measure crimes that are not reported or why the ones that were reported took place. Drug abuse was doubtless a causation factors and heroin had become mainstream, the effects of which in some of the areas we policed was horrendous. The word 'rattling' had become synonymous with the need to get a fix. We were increasingly dealing with offenders who were addicts. They were stealing cars, and things from cars, to fund their habit. There were times when we searched the houses of offenders who had children and saw at first hand the deprivation that they suffered due to their parents' drug habits and behaviour. It is a sad fact that with this type of exposure at such a young age, some of those kids had no structure in their lives. They would be sucked into a world of crime and anti-social behaviour. It was a vicious circle. It made me very protective of my own children. I am sure they will remember their dad interrogating them as to where they were going and who they were spending time with.

All good things come to an end, and I was eventually reassigned to a different uniformed shift. There had been a lot of changes, including another major intake of probationary constables. There were also several newly promoted sergeants in place. My new inspector was a man of many years of service. He was one of the few people I ever met in the police who did not swear or curse. The most he would ever say was "Flipping heck". Also noticeable was the number of new female officers; they were almost equivalent in number to the men that had been recruited. It didn't go unnoticed that some were attractive. It wasn't long before some of the 'players' were making their moves on them and the scandals started. Men and women working together anywhere can result in affairs. There's something about the uniqueness of the police though. Whether it is the time officers spend together, the irregular shift patterns, the experiences the job throws at you, or maybe it is just the opportunities it provides. I remember being present during a briefing for a night shift and being told that I was the only PC on the shift (of eight) who was not divorced, going through a separation or had left home for another partner. That was just how disruptive the police service can be to your domestic life.

I was happy at home, completely devoted to my kids and loved spending time with them. There was nothing better for me but to snuggle up with them on my weekends off and watch movies. I would have one either side and one sitting on the floor between my legs. My wife though would be on the sofa on the other side of the room. I'm not saying for one minute that she wasn't close to the children because she was – like me, she adored them – but the two of us were gradually becoming different people. The move back to the town she originated from meant she was spending more time with her family. This would involve her going to the local working men's club on Saturday evenings with her sisters and friends. I, on the other hand, hated the place. On the few occasions I went there, I would invariably bump into people whom I had dealt with, and it felt like everyone knew what I did for a living. I just couldn't relax there.

The inner me was saying that these people didn't understand my job and that I couldn't talk to them. My wife thought I was becoming a bit of a snob. For my part, I much preferred going for a drink with work colleagues. I had much more in common with them. You could compare notes, talk about the jobs you had been involved with, partake in general police gossip and discuss the courses you had attended. Everyone understood each other and there was always a leaving or promotion party to attend. These events also put me into contact with the CID officers who enjoyed a drink. Like my time in the Armed Forces, it was the case that unless you 'took a drink' and were the social type, you were not joining the club. It didn't matter how good you were. I'd often use this as an excuse to go out and attend the various functions.

Up until this point in our marriage, I had been faithful. There were one or two occasions when it came close, but I never anticipated having an affair or leaving my wife. I had seen the fallout from my parents' divorce and the effect it had on me. There were a couple of times when I could have advanced things with female officers; I was tempted, but I didn't. I knew it would be grief all round and I also knew how the rumour mill and gossip-mongering worked at the nick. I've always been a private person and the thought of my personal life being the subject of that sort of discussion did not appeal to me one bit. Some didn't seem to care less – it never ceased to amaze me where and how people were caught. Doing stuff when they should have been working – some of them supervisors and managers, who were supposed to be setting an example! So, on seeing this in the workplace I distanced myself and got on with the job. I was being given occasional Acting Sergeant duties and receiving good reports and appraisals from my supervisors. I managed to pass my inspector examination too. Approximately 18 months after leaving the Task Force, I was told I would be starting my six-month CID aide-ship. It had seemed like a long time; it wasn't, but I have always been impatient.

27. Welcome to the CID

In common with a lot of the CID offices at the time, ours had no female officers or ethnic minorities. I don't think that was down to any overt discrimination. To get into the CID, you had to have some experience and the lack of diversity in the service meant that the pool of potential candidates was not large enough to draw from. Things are very different now with the police being much more representative of the community.

In the office, there was a distinct pecking order. It was made abundantly clear to me from day one that I was at the bottom of the pile. I had an allocated Senior Detective Constable (DC), whom I will refer to as 'Sam'. He was experienced, competent, jovial and he became another good friend. It was his job to guide me through my aide-ship and get me recommended for the ten-week course so I could qualify as a detective. The first thing I was expected to do was to make the tea for everyone in the office and whenever it was required. This was standard practice and I had been briefed to expect to be treated like a nobody. If you reacted, then you were not going to make it. The DI I had met when I first arrived was still in post. He was still as ill-tempered and rarely did he have anything good to say about his uniformed counterparts. He took great pleasure in berating junior officers either to their face or in writing.

I recall one episode when he decided that a young in-service officer was incompetent because he failed to collect enough information at reports of crime. He sent an instruction to him that he would take witness statements at every crime scene that he attended for a month. Nowadays that would likely result in a complaint of harassment or bullying. The officer concerned is still a great friend. He did what he was told and went on to become a highly successful investigator and senior officer. Obviously not entirely down to the actions of the DI, but it did instil in him a need for high standards. Characters like the DI existed across the Force and were the stuff of legend. Police officers love stories, particularly about their bosses. I guarantee even now, that if I got together with a few of my old friends, those individuals would creep into the conversation very quickly. I managed to cross swords with one very shortly after my arrival at the office. More about that later.

There were two DSs in the office. They were completely different characters. One was flamboyant, outspoken and had traits of a bully. The other was much more quietly spoken and laid-back. Both enjoyed a drink, and I soon came to understand that the culture in the CID was that boozing greased the wheels and was actively encouraged. After a hard day at the office, it was expected that you would all go to the pub together. For some, it was a daily ritual.

I'd been briefed to expect a deluge of crime reports from the DI. It was his way of trying to overload you and test your mettle. They kept coming, for there was no filtering at all. In those days, every house burglary had to be passed to a Detective for investigation. Within two days, I had around 30 crime reports in my tray. Burglaries were prevalent and I was expected to pay a physical visit to each address. My second shift at the CID office was what was known as a half-night. You started at 5pm and finished around 1am, depending on what the evening presented. For some reason, Sam wasn't about and I was to be working on my own. I arrived early. I thought I would use the opportunity to get out and do some follow-up calls on my allocation of crimes. At around 5.30pm everyone that was in the office gathered. I thought they were going home.

"OK, come on then, let's go," said one of the detective sergeants. "You coming?"

I looked up naively and said, "Where?"

They all started laughing, and someone said, "You're in the CID now. We are going to the pub; it's what we do every Tuesday."

I declined the offer, stating that I had things to do. I was keen to impress. I wanted to work and I also didn't have spare cash to spend at the pub. Things were still hard financially at home. The kids were growing up quickly, they seemed to always need shoes and clothes, and I was still the only earner in the household. I also wasn't keen about drinking on duty. You never knew what you might have to do, or where you would have to go.

The next day, Sam pulled me to one side. He informed me, in no uncertain terms, that declining to go to the pub with the guys from the office was a bad move. Like it or not, I had to be part of the club. There is an old saying that goes something like this: 'never trust a man who doesn't drink because he's probably a self-righteous sort, a man who thinks he knows right from wrong all the time.' That summed it up really. I wasn't against a drink, but I wanted to work so I just had to learn to slow down. I related to Sam my financial concerns and he explained how that worked too. There was an unwritten rule that whilst you would have to work for it, everyone would get at least 20 hours of overtime each and every month. Most of the time that would be exceeded because there were always prisoners in the cells to deal with. There were never enough CID vehicles to go around, so private mileage was also a way of bumping up your salary. At the time there was a scheme called the 'county loan' which meant if you were an 'essential user' you could borrow money from the West Yorkshire Police Authority to purchase a motor car for personal and work use. All officers in the CID did this and later in my service I benefited from the system too. As I was the aide, for now I would always be allocated one of the CID vehicles and almost always be the driver.

What followed was six months of long hours, hard work and exposure to all manner of investigations. If I was to pinpoint a time in my career when I changed, then this was it. I became much more hard-nosed, more suspicious, and if it was possible after 10 years in the job, a little more cynical. I was drinking more, socialising more and not at home very much. The shift patterns were predominantly Monday to Friday. We, of course, covered weekends, but the work was much more reactive.

As a result, the shifts tended to fit better with the kids' schooling and I was able to see much more of them at weekends. The boys were both playing football and my daughter was horse riding and had a passing interest in cross-country running. At work I was dealing with serious assaults, sexual offences, house burglaries and all manner of offenders. Every so often, you would encounter some heavy-duty criminals. Some would try and intimidate or threaten you personally, with the "I know where you live," or "I know where your kids go to school". Most of the time, that was bravado, although you couldn't help at times being concerned for your family.

It didn't take me long to get into the groove of the drinking culture. I became a regular at what was often referred to as 'choir practice', mostly held on Tuesdays. You also got to meet detectives from other divisions and some of the more senior officers. I quickly found out that the CID had a much more relaxed approach about rank as compared to the formal hierarchy in uniform. A lot of the senior officers in the CID enjoyed a good drink too. I discovered that on half-nights, it was customary to drop in for a couple of pints at various pubs across the division. There was an age-old tradition that was used to justify it. Detectives were expected to have informants. Going to the pub was used as an excuse for mingling with potential informants. If the truth be known, informants are best recruited when you have something on them, or they want something from you. This was most often when they were in the cells during an investigation. I don't ever recall going to a pub frequented by villains. Most of the detectives I knew tended to go to the more decent places, to relax, have a chat and on occasion, chat women up. We were also partial to frequenting nightclubs from time to time. I don't want the reader to form the opinion that being in the CID was just one big party. It most definitely was not; it involved hard work and very long hours. When, for example, you have multiple offenders in the cells, a detention clock running, statements to take, houses to search and solicitors to chase for interviews, it is stressful and tiring. The drinking and getting together were a means of letting off steam. I had experienced it all before, but I don't think I understood why we were 'all' doing it or appreciated the effects.

One evening I was partnered with a veteran detective before going for a "swifty", as he called it. I heard him telephone his wife, and the call went something like this.

"You OK, love?" He smiled at me and then said, "Look, I've got to take the aide out for a quick drink, I'll be home about half past, OK? See you later." When he put the telephone down, he turned to me, winked, tapped his nose, and said, "You'll notice I didn't say which half past !" The pair of us just fell about laughing.

The first CID Christmas party I attended was a memorable one. It was organised weeks in advance and cover from a neighbouring division was arranged. The event commenced at lunchtime with a local pub commissioned for the day and closed to the general public. If you were not part of the CID, then you had to be invited. Preference was always given to policewomen, local (friendly) solicitors and anyone else who had a loose association with the office. To say it was raucous was an understatement. When I arrived just after 1pm, an inflatable sex doll was being thrown about the pub, which was already packed. When police officers let their hair down, they really go for it. Hence, it is better for the general public to be nowhere near the venue. Rarely was there a time when there wasn't some sort of scandal that fell out of a Christmas do. Women being touched up, constables being abusive to senior officers, clothes being removed, so on and so forth. Pretty much everyone got steaming drunk, as the alcohol flowed freely. It was a great night and as time went on, my memory became 'cloudy'.

Apparently, I called my wife to collect me around 11pm. According to her account, I moaned at her all the way home saying that she was a rubbish driver. The only thing I do remember is waking up freezing cold in the front seat of the car at about 3am where she had left me. I had fallen asleep during the short ride home. My wife was always tolerant of my work; she rarely complained about the long hours, she knew it was for the greater good in terms of the family and my career. However, I was enjoying work and the social side so much that the job had now become more important than her. It was exciting, I loved the thrill of the chase when investigating, the socialising and had built up a good reputation for both. I was enjoying myself again and had become totally immersed in my work.

Things in the CID office were not entirely harmonious. One of the DSs had singled me out for attention. I was used to having the piss taken out of me. My way of dealing with it was to give as much back. It was the norm in both the army and the police. It was run-of-the-mill banter; "You cocked that up!", "You fancied that woman!", You said something out of place", "Your car's a mess", so on and so forth. The police are renowned for it. However, when someone repeatedly homes in on your personal features or the clothes you wear, then that is something altogether different.

The guy concerned came up with a rather uncomplimentary nickname for me and always drew attention to what he perceived to be my cheap suits. The truth was, I couldn't afford more expensive clothing. My salary went towards providing for the family and propping up my drinking habits. I knew that if I had taken him on verbally, it would have ended badly. He was influential with the DI and would have submitted an adverse report about me, regardless of how hard I had worked. I had to grin and bear it. Thankfully most of the time he was on an opposing shift pattern. I wasn't alone though, for one morning he walked into the office, and without warning, took a pair of scissors to one of the other detective's ties because he didn't like the pattern. The remains of the tie were pinned to the noticeboard. I used to dread going into the office when he was there, but wasn't going to let him win. It frustrated the hell out of me that this DS played golf whilst on duty, was having multiple affairs and always took home more overtime than anyone else. Because he was a large and intimidating character, no one in authority ever questioned it.

Intimidation was the weapon for some, but thankfully not all, of the CID managers and supervisors I worked for. I found that the vast majority were not overly authoritarian and didn't act like zealots. Overwhelmingly I was treated well and like an adult. The bosses gave me responsibility and let me get on with the job. I hate to be nagged and micromanaged because I know I can be trusted to get stuff done. However, on one Sunday I was on the receiving end of treatment from a senior officer who was well known for his confrontational management style.

It was a Sunday morning. Sam and I arrived for work with the intention of tackling our mountain of paperwork. You were always expected to wear a suit and tie in the CID. Any move away from that was seen to be a lowering of standards. West Yorkshire Police were big on standards, something which I entirely agree with. Because it was a Sunday, I had taken a decision to dress down slightly and wear a blazer, shirt, tie and slacks. This was something which had been perfectly acceptable on previous weekends.

Overnight and unbeknown to us, an incident had occurred at a house where a man had turned a shotgun on his female partner. He had killed her with one cartridge fired at point blank range. The remains of her head were plastered across the living room. He then turned the shotgun on himself, placing the gun under his head and discharging it. His weapon of choice was of the double-barrelled variety. He had positioned the empty chamber directly under his chin, with the loaded barrel partially exposed. Once he pressed the trigger, the shell exited, killing him and blowing half of his face away. It was a macabre look and one I have not forgotten. The offence we were investigating was the most serious of all, a murder. Despite the offender being dead, it still required that the on duty Senior Investigating Officer (SIO) would be required to attend. In keeping with the times, this would generally be a detective superintendent. I was in the CID office when the on-call SIO arrived. He took one look at me and boomed out, "Who the fuck are you?" I had only met him once before during my Task Force days. Billy and I had found a knife down a drain during a search of a murder scene, when he had seemed OK.

I responded to him, "I'm the aide, Sir."

He immediately said, "Well why the fucking hell are you dressed like that?!"

What I said next just tripped off the tongue and was a poor attempt at humour. "Well normally I go to church on a Sunday boss. I didn't expect a murder, sorry."

I saw the look on his face and instantly knew I should have kept my mouth shut. He launched into a litany of expletives about being insolent and that it was a requirement for aides in his division to always wear dark suits, no matter what the day was. Over his shoulder, I saw Sam walk into the office. His face said it all: 'What the fuck has been said to him?' When his rant was over, he ordered me to make myself useful and get him a cup of tea, asking Sam to brief him.

When I returned with his tea, rather than thank me, he said, "Right, you cheeky fucker, get yourself down to the scene. There is a poisonous spider and a snake in that house, and you are going there to find them." I wisely chose to do as I was told and say nothing. I looked at Sam, shrugged my shoulders and headed to the house. By the time I arrived, Forensics had finished what they needed to do and the house was cleared for entry. I then spent a very uncomfortable few hours on my hands and knees at an extremely gory crime scene looking for the missing exotic creatures. There were dark puddles of blood soaking into the carpet, there were bits of bone and brains dripping off the walls, and the house was not the cleanest I had ever seen. That scene is easy enough to describe, but it is the smell that never leaves you. Unless you have experienced it, there is no accurate way to convey it in writing. I had no success finding the pets and was not even sure what I was supposed to do with them if I had found them.

I headed back to the office dreading reporting the failure of my enquiries to the SIO. To be honest, he wasn't in the slightest bit concerned when I told him, reinforcing my view that he did it purely and simply to exercise a bit of power. The whole of the CID office had now been called out and by the time I got back, it was well after lunchtime. His coup de grace came when he called the canteen to order refreshments. He asked everyone present in the office to shout out what type of sandwich they wanted. He made a point of ignoring me and just before putting the phone down, he said, "Oh, and a jam sandwich for the aide". Everyone thought it was hilarious. I just thought, 'What a childish twat!' Sam and I often laughed about that day; he even conceded that the guy was a bully. It didn't trouble me at the time; it doesn't trouble me now. When I hear of officers taking the service to an industrial tribunal for what I perceive to be trivial stuff, it takes me back to that day. A sergeant once summed it up when he said to me very early in my service, "If you can't take a bit of banter from your colleagues, then you cannot police the streets."

I completed my CID aide-ship without any significant problems. The grumpy DI even praised me in my final report as, 'The best aide we have had during my time here.'

I knew that crime investigation was where I wanted to be and where my skills lay. However, the job had other plans for me. There was a huge backlog of detective officers waiting to be appointed. First though, I had to complete and pass the ten-week CID course at Bishopgarth in Wakefield.

28. More training

I was again returned to uniform duties for a time, before attending my Detective Training School (DTS). For some reason, domestic violence and child protection issues were in the news and had become a political hot potato. Critics believed the police didn't understand the complexity of the problem and were largely ignoring it. Specialist units, known as DVCPUs (Domestic Violence & Child Protection Units), had been set up to provide a better service to victims. Changing the attitudes of long-serving officers was a challenge. Some didn't see it as 'real' crime, even referring to the local units that had been established by the rather unflattering name of 'Knob Squads'. In those early days, the units were predominantly staffed by female officers. There was a mostly unspoken view that they were incompetent, doing women's work and similar nonsense.

Someone from the command team at headquarters put the cat amongst the pigeons though. An instruction was sent out that all officers completing a CID aide-ship had to complete at least a month with their local DVCPU as part of their training. The attachment also had to be completed before attending DTS. I had little experience of investigating child protection matters. It was not an area I was familiar with. I recall having reservations about the work and what effect it would have on me, given that I had three young children of my own. I was no stranger to the domestic violence side of the work, having attended many incidents in my career. But I really didn't know what to expect when I reported to their office for my first day.

The DS running the team turned out to be another great supervisor. He was experienced, knowledgeable and nurtured the people that worked for him. He cared about his team, and he cared about the victims of crime. He also knew how to get the best out of his staff by talking to them, listening and delivering on promises. I learnt a lot from him about managing people.

In the broader sense, I began to get an understanding of the value gained from partnership working during these types of investigations. The unit had to interface daily with social services and a range of other agencies. This was cooperation on a level I had not experienced before, although it must be said that some of those we worked alongside had a very jaded view of the police. They were suspicious of us and acted as if we all wore jackboots and beat people up for a hobby. I initially struggled with some of them because of their politics, the way they dressed and their approach was often at odds with my own. However, some were exceptional, performing demanding jobs under very difficult circumstances. Working with families is problematic and challenging. I also had the opportunity to work with some remarkable female officers. The stereotype of the 'Knob Squad' was completely misplaced. On my return to normal duties, I became one of their biggest advocates.

The joining instructions for my ten-week DTS course arrived. It was made clear that this was one of the most challenging courses I would complete. Unlike some of the students (as we were all referred to), West Yorkshire officers had to pass the final exam. If you didn't, you would not get appointed as a detective. Some other forces didn't insist on the same standard, so for certain officers it was a bit of a holiday. I knew already that as part of the course you were expected to know definitions of criminal offences off by heart, so therefore more studying would be required. The purpose behind this was so that you fully understood the points to prove, for the countless offences you would come across during investigations. I can still recite many of them now. You were only supposed to go home at weekends – this was designed to engender a team approach in each of the various classes.

That teamwork also extended to regular drinking sessions, another key element of the course. I was told by my CID colleagues that I should have savings of at least £1,000 for the social side. This was to be spent in the local bars and nightclubs. In 1991, that was a lot of money which I didn't have to hand. Without my wife's knowledge, I cashed in an insurance policy and opened a separate bank account. As it turned out, most of the attendees on the course had a secret stash set aside. My wife and three young children waved me off as I began the next journey. I didn't enjoy being away from my kids. There was always a lot of horseplay at home with them, wrestling on the floor and playing football at the park. They brought out my inner child and I loved them for it. I missed them terribly when we were apart, even if it was for just a few days.

There were around six classes of students for the course. We all congregated in the lecture theatre for the welcome address by the Head of Training. It was always expected that everyone was read the Riot Act, such as 'you must not bring anyone back to the accommodation, you must moderate your drinking, you are not to have landing parties, and you are not allowed into the dining room after hours.' You had only to be on the floors of the accommodation block in the evenings to know that virtually every rule was completely ignored. We were assigned our course tutors, a DI and a DS. They were polar opposites – one was a party animal, the other much more reserved and at times sombre. They both had different teaching styles, one being very didactic accompanied by a lot of humour, the other being more serious but more supportive.

There were 17 of us in our class, several West Yorkshire officers with the remainder from across the country, including Cleveland, Derbyshire, Durham, Greater Manchester, Norfolk, North Yorkshire, Suffolk, South Yorkshire, the Isle of Man, Nottinghamshire and North Wales. Police officers the world over have lots in common, so it wasn't long before everyone was getting on. If I were to put police officers attending a course into categories, it would go something like this: the womanisers, the drinkers, the workaholics and the coasters. There were, of course, individuals who had a foot in all camps. I think I was a drinking workaholic and for the most part I gravitated to those who shared the same interests.

We were all assigned our room and classroom for the 10 weeks. The living accommodation had not been updated since I joined many years earlier; it was spartan, comprising of a tiny bedroom with a small wardrobe, a table for studying and a sink. There were no en-suite facilities. Toilets, showers and a bath were on the main corridor. Each class occupied one floor of the tower block. Female officers at the time were in a separate area and males were not allowed onto that floor – well, not officially. We had assigned cleaners who we got to know well. They were your typical Yorkshire types, plain speaking, hard-working and not afraid to tell you where to get off if you were too demanding.

I had been to Bishopgarth several times so knew the drill. Others from outside forces were not so accustomed to it. The canteen food at the time was not great. For lunch you were required to sit at a designated class table with food delivered to you in metal dishes. The canteen area was run by a lady who bore similarities to a famous comedian, one Stanley Baxter. However, if she heard you say that, then it would directly affect the amount of time that you waited for your food.

In the classroom, we were told to expect to work hard and play hard. Each night, we would have to complete periods of self-study. Every morning, we were subjected to 'welly sessions'. Two or three of us would be singled out to stand up and recite offence definitions verbatim from the previous day. If you didn't know the answers, you were belittled by the trainers and your colleagues. It motivated me to learn, and it worked.

We were further advised that when lessons finished for the day, we should take part in some sport. Study was to be undertaken until at least 9pm. We were then free to do whatever leisure activities took our fancy. We were repeatedly advised not to go home because you were expected to be a team player. This translated as hard drinking. It became part of a routine that we would meet in the on-site bar very shortly after 9pm, have a couple of pints and head into the town centre for more. Wakefield was teeming with bars, clubs and takeaways in the nineties and was affectionately referred to as 'Benidorm without the sunshine'.

With the various drinking establishments came the camp followers. Women who you would see night after night, looking for a good time or husband material. These ladies were comedically referred to as 'Fixtures and Fittings'. Some were adept at identifying budding detectives, even possessing insider knowledge of what each week of the course involved in terms of the content. For those away from home and so inclined, Wakefield town centre was a target rich environment. There were plenty of opportunities for one-night stands and affairs. One guy in our class met a woman one evening and from then on did not spend a single night in the accommodation. To be perfectly honest, I just wanted to get out for a few drinks, relax and have a laugh. With a small circle of like-minded friends, that is what we all did. I wasn't interested in chasing women. I was happy at home, and I made sure I telephoned the family every night whilst I was away. That is not to say that there weren't any drunken nights, some horrendous hangovers and an awful lot of money wasted on booze and takeaway food.

Friday mornings were never the best for learning as everyone had been out the night before and energy levels were low. We also knew it was standard practice to finish shortly after lunch so not much would get done. This was primarily to allow those who had longer journeys to get home in plenty of time. There was still lots of work to do in your own time at the weekend, as on Monday mornings there was always another exam.

Most of the time, I arrived home on Friday and flopped out on the sofa, completely wrecked from a heavy Thursday night in Wakefield. When the kids came home from school, I gave them all a cuddle and caught up with what they had been doing. One memorable afternoon, my youngest son asked me if he could go out into the street on his bike. Of my three children, he was the most headstrong and had been the most rebellious of all. He was only six and knew that he was supposed to stay in the cul-de-sac where we lived. All three of my children went outside to play together. I drifted into a sleep.

The next thing that I remember was that my daughter woke me up shouting, "There's been an accident, Dad! He has been knocked down!" I ran out to see my youngest son laid out on the tarmac in an adjoining street, about 25 yards from our house. A car was close to him and his bike was crumpled in a heap. I sprinted over; when I arrived, I could see there was blood oozing from his ear, and he was completely unconscious. I had been to enough road traffic accidents to know that this was not a good sign. I learnt that an ambulance had been summoned, and very shortly afterwards an on-duty colleague, whom I knew, arrived at the scene. The ambulance, though, seemed to take an eternity.

When they got there, my son was quickly placed onto a stretcher, then we blue-lighted it all the way to hospital. He groaned and made a few noises on the way, but other than that he was out for the count. It is at times like this when you see things from the perspective of a victim or their loved ones. It reminded me to be supportive, caring, and empathetic.

Thankfully, my son made a full recovery but not without spending the weekend at the hospital with me at the side of his bed. I returned on Monday to the course. I failed the weekly exam, receiving an almighty bollocking from one of the instructors. I didn't disclose what had happened to either of them. I didn't want to be seen to be making excuses.

I made some great friends during that ten-week course. It was one of the most intense learning experiences I had ever undertaken. I passed and attained high marks; I was chuffed but glad it was over. The habitual drinking had caused me to develop a 9pm thirst for alcohol. We lived close to a public house and several times I found myself sniffing the air in our garden. It was a difficult habit to break and easy to appreciate how, for some, it becomes routine.

I returned to work all fired up and with the expectation that I would shortly be joining the ranks of the CID. Sadly, that was not going to be the case. The huge backlog of trained officers had grown ever larger and there were no vacancies. To get a place, you either had to know one of the CID bosses very well, or be prepared to put yourself forward for a post that nobody else wanted. I was crestfallen; some of my friends from other forces had walked straight into CID appointments, but I was back in a queue again.

Back in uniform, I was again given periods of Acting Sergeant Duties and tutored less experienced officers. The lack of any movement was frustrating; it was 'dead men's shoes'. The Force was a large beast, and with estimates of two years before a vacancy could arise, it was demotivating.

For a short time, I was employed across the division as a plain-clothed crime scene visitor. One of a team of four, my role was to attend reports of house burglaries. It was designed as the primary response to these sorts of high-volume crimes in order to conduct a more thorough assessment, giving victims a better service and fast-tracking reports with identified lines of enquiry for the CID. It worked well in terms of improving service to the public and prioritising crimes that stood a chance of detection. It kept me in the eye of the CID supervisors, but we all knew the situation was not going to change. It was a chance meeting with the DS from the DVCPU that provided an opportunity for me. One of the male DCs on his team was going away on his CID course. It meant they were going to be short-staffed. He asked if I would be interested in filling in. To say I jumped at the chance was an understatement. It proved to be a defining moment for me in a variety of ways.

29. New direction

Whilst I had some exposure during my earlier attachment, I hadn't had the time to fully appreciate the complexities of a child protection investigation. The complete lack of understanding within the Force for what the units did was obvious. I lost count of the number of times colleagues made comments such as, "You're wasting your time in the knob squad," or "What are you doing women's work for?" The ones making the most noise had never conducted these types of enquiries. Some saw it as below them; others feared opening themselves up to the emotional roller coaster that accompany these types of cases. A common response was, "Oh, I couldn't do that," said in a manner that reminded me of when you step into something unpleasant.

The unit tackled everything from domestic violence, to allegations of sexual, physical and emotional abuse in children. I was astonished by the sheer volume of referrals that came into the office every day, few of which could be ignored. The workloads of each officer were staggering. I was no stranger to hard work and loved being kept busy. My concern though, was that I would let a vulnerable person down because I did not have the experience. To counter this, I set out to learn as much as I possibly could about the subject.

There is a common misconception about child abuse, to an extent fed by the messaging we have all heard in relation to 'stranger danger' and bogeymen. The sad fact was most of the offences that came to our notice were committed in the home by persons known to the child. Some victims were too young to be able to communicate, so the lack of any other evidence made investigations notoriously difficult. Sometimes the best outcome you could hope for was the removal of the child, or children, from the situation to protect them from further harm. That was inherently difficult when one of the parents was in complete denial and refusing to acknowledge that their partner had committed an offence against their own child, another common occurrence. I felt like a fish out of water for the first few weeks, but I watched carefully as members of the team dealt with their victims in a compassionate and sensitive way. They were also able to turn into highly competent and incisive interviewers when dealing with offenders. These types of investigation were frustrating but also highly rewarding. There was no better feeling when you were able to protect the most vulnerable members of society by making them safe.

The team were mostly female officers, including the civilian assistant who worked exclusively for us. One or two of the women were attractive and it was common to be reminded by my male colleagues that I was very fortunate to be working with such good-looking co-workers. Some went a little bit further with their comments. Police stations are rumour mills and if you were seen in the company of a female officer for any longer than a few minutes, then you were a target for gossip. This was the first time I had partnered up with females for extended periods and it took some getting used to. Because they were more experienced than me in this field, the female officers often took the lead, something I was also not accustomed to. Without doubt the macho qualities firmly entrenched in me from my previous experiences in both the Armed Forces and the police were, at times, challenged.

This was more a sign of the times, as females were still in a minority, particularly in detective roles.

The Sergeant encouraged trips to the local pub after work, where we all came together, relaxed and had a giggle. It was a way of decompressing after dealing with what could be harrowing referrals. By now, I was well accustomed to dealing with violence, the fall-out from violence and violent offenders. There is no way I could have prepared myself for what I was being exposed to when dealing with child abuse. Some of the things that adults do to children are horrific. I hadn't previously realised that even very young babies are sexually abused, savagely assaulted and damaged emotionally. It wasn't the sort of conversation you could have with your wife, a friend or anyone who had not worked in that environment. I still remember the words of the late Ray Wyre, a therapist who worked with sex offenders. He came to train us in how to deal with them effectively. He said, "You have to believe the unbelievable," – that was so true. I've never forgotten those words, they proved prophetic.

Whilst we drank at the same pub, many of the local CID largely ignored us, most of them thinking we were a bit odd. The Sergeant and I would often be the only men amongst the girls from the office and it naturally led to more rumours. Despite what some of my colleagues thought, I was not having an affair, nor had it even crossed my mind. However, at home, the fact that I was now spending more time at work, or in the pub 'and' in the company of female officers, did create tension between my wife and I. We had started to argue more. Once again, I was at work a lot and she was spending more time with her family. I hadn't really noticed how much we were becoming different people. My exposure to the type of work I was doing also made me extra alert in terms of my own children, in particular my daughter who was approaching her teenage years. When you are in an office all day long hearing about children, mostly girls, being indecently assaulted or raped, thoughts naturally turn to those close to you. Keeping them out of harm's way was a priority for me. My daughter would probably say I was a bit of a nightmare when it came to her and the opposite sex. At one point after finding out she was at an address on a local council estate, I burst in, got hold of her and marched her out of the door. I don't think she has ever forgiven me for that.

My attachment was over in a flash. After three months, I was returned to uniform patrol once again. I must have made an impression at the office because I was then encouraged to make an application for a Child Protection Investigation course. Apparently, I had the right qualities for the type of work. I had shown I could relate to victims and was a proven investigator.

I now had a real dilemma on my hands. I had just over ten years of service, I desperately wanted to be in the CID, but had already been told that it would be at least a two-year wait. My annual appraisals were good, I was performing well, had been recommended to apply for promotion and was being pushed for that too. I had many conversations with colleagues and senior officers about what to do. In the end, I decided to apply for the course, at the same time putting myself forward for promotion in case there were more vacancy issues. If I was successful in my promotion application, all well and good.

Like the CID, there was a long list of successful applicants for the rank of sergeant. Divisional commanders could select who they wanted. I duly made my written application for the course whereupon the deputy divisional commander promptly blocked it. I was livid, not least because there was no explanation. My application had been returned with the words 'refused' written on it. I did nothing more than knock on his door and ask to see him. In fairness, he shared his reasoning that someone else from the division was going on the course and he couldn't spare two officers. It was with a degree of disappointment that I returned to my uniformed duties. I was informed that support would be forthcoming next time and that is what we settled on. I often wonder what would have happened if I had gone on that earlier course.

Simultaneously I launched myself into the promotion process. Applying for any form of progression in the police can be an arduous process. Arguably attaining the rank of sergeant is the hardest because there are so many hoops to go through. In my time, you first had to pass written examinations, get supervisory experience by performing Acting duties, provide evidence of competencies against a framework, and then be supported by your inspector before even setting foot in an assessment centre.

I had already suffered one failed attempt and it was an awful experience. There were about ten of us in a room sat in a half circle. The mediator provided a subject to discuss amongst yourselves. Invariably, those who shouted the loudest were successful. I could barely get a word in edgeways, but when I did it was incoherent and rambling. I didn't like speaking in large groups of people and it showed. As a system for identifying prospective supervisors, it was appalling. It manifested itself in some awful sergeants with minimal management skills who resorted to ordering people about.

When I applied for promotion for the second time, things had altered, something the police service had a habit of doing. The system had become much more scientific; advice had been taken from psychologists and a whole new department had been created in its wake. The process was to be based upon a series of scenarios. A role player would come into a mock inspector's office where a fictitious incident would unfold. As the candidate, you were then expected to respond and deal with it. There were cameras in the room and an independent marker who sat quietly in the corner scribbling away on a notepad. You had around six different situations to deal with during your assessment. The tasks consisted of anything from people-specific problems, serious crime scenes to major incidents. Much as I like to think I had prepared for the process, I hadn't; I bombed again. My failure was in trying to beat the system rather than understanding the scenario.

Despite the process being shrouded in secrecy, rumours always abounded before and during the assessment centres. The well-informed would claim to know what the scenarios were about, the buzz words you should say and how you would be marked. Most of the time, they were wrong. Conspiracy theories were also rife about rebalancing the representation of females and those from minority groups in supervisory posts. When I saw and heard about some of the successful candidates, I must admit to having believed that narrative. There were people on the list who had a reputation for being incompetent and lazy, yet they still managed to succeed. I was annoyed with myself for failing and angry with a system that, in my view, did nothing to support hard-working coppers.

Several months later, I received word that my attendance on the next child protection course had been approved. It was three weeks in duration and held at Bishopgarth. It would be attended by mostly West Yorkshire officers, none of whom I knew or had experience of working with.

The course proved to be quite different from my CID course in several ways. Oddly I was in the same classroom; however, this time, instead of the traditional layout of rows of single desks and chairs, there was a horseshoe formation with no desk to hide behind. I looked around on that first day and felt very much in the minority. There were three men and approximately nine women, and both instructors were also female. I got an early impression that the training was going to be challenging and it was. After the normal rounds of introductions – who you were, where you were from and so on – came one of the strangest ice-breaking exercises I had ever participated in. We were all told to pair up with someone and come up with a list of as many words for the sexual organs as we could within five minutes. Thankfully, I was paired up with a girl who had a terrific sense of humour, and we laughed all the way through our list. All the words then went up onto the whiteboard at the front of the class. Each of us took it in turns to shout out a new one. Some, I had never heard of, with the majority originating from two girls in the class who it turned out were both vicars' daughters! The whole purpose of the exercise was to get comfortable with each other and not to show embarrassment or shock in the future when dealing with the victims of sexual offences.

Like all the courses I had attended previously, there was a social side. It wasn't quite the same as the CID course. Some of the class didn't stay at the centre overnight and others didn't drink. A smaller group of us would go out together and the drinking was more measured. I also made the time to go home at least one night a week to see my children. Compared to the CID course, it was nowhere near as intense from an academic point of view.

In terms of content, it was tiring and demanding. It was about empathy, emotions, a deep understanding of deviant behaviour, child psychology and a lot about you as an individual.

Both instructors later became very good friends of mine. They worked exceptionally well together as trainers, sharing their very personal experiences of dealing with rape victims, abused children and coping with a very male-dominated world of police managers. They were both pioneers in the field and had been much maligned and mistreated by some senior officers over the years. It was sobering listening to their experiences; it caused me to reflect on what it must feel like to be in a minority.

Like all the other courses I had attended, it didn't take long for the group to gel. I found myself getting on very well with most people in the class. One girl, who I'll call 'Janet', I found to be quite difficult to engage with. She was a little outspoken, well-educated, clearly ambitious and always had an opinion. Her endearing feature was that she possessed a very sharp sense of humour, a quality I have always admired. My dad is like that; he can be sarcastic, but is very quick-witted and always finds a way to make people laugh. There were many times when he was in full flow when I laughed so much my ribs ached. Mum would always say that sarcasm is the lowest form of wit, possibly because of her experiences with him, but I must disagree; Dad was a class act with his brand of humour. Janet confused me because she could be very funny but also quite cold. I got the impression she wasn't keen on me. During the course we all spent a lot of time in pairs or groups doing exercises of one sort or another, yet I don't ever recall there being much of a connection between us at all. Even over coffee and during lunch breaks, I am not sure we had many conversations.

In common with tradition, on the penultimate day of the course the class night out took place. It had been two years since my CID course but Thursday nights in Wakefield had not changed, they were still as mad. The pubs and clubs were full of partygoers and off-duty police officers. It was a heady mix; one I had become familiar with and made the most of. Several of us were in Yates's Wine Lodge, a pub and popular music venue. It was close to the end of the evening and a few of us from the class were stood together when the song 'You're The One That I Want', from the film *Grease* came over the speakers. It is one of those tunes that gets everyone singing and dancing, so we all ended up jigging about. At the point where the chorus features in the song, Janet looked at me, outstretched her finger and mouthed exactly that.

About an hour later, we were together in her room where we spent what was left of the night together. To the best of my knowledge, nobody else knew and we went our separate ways when the course ended. It all should have ended there but the whole thing threw me into some considerable emotional turmoil. I began to question myself and my marriage. I felt extremely guilty but had an overwhelming urge to contact Janet again. We had clandestine meetings and a brief affair. For a short time, I even believed I was in love with her. Janet was married and unhappy at home. I had three children who I loved dearly. The pair of us lived miles apart and our backgrounds were quite different. It was a non-starter. It was also a stupid thing to have done. It unsettled me from then onwards. I found myself doubting the longevity of the relationship with my wife. I still don't know what Janet saw in me, or what prompted the interaction that night. We made the sensible decision to stop seeing each other and never met or spoke again.

30. Promoted

Having got over the distraction and upheaval after the affair, I refocused myself and concentrated on work. After successfully passing the course, I was placed on the Child Protection Unit (CPU) succession plan. Because of the deadlock with CID vacancies, there was likely to be little, if any, movement hence the prospect of an appointment in that department being unlikely. I was reliant on somebody retiring, dying or getting into serious trouble. There was no prospect of advancement. I was getting increasingly frustrated and became irritable at home. It seemed that no matter what I did or how hard I studied, I couldn't get to where I wanted to be. I was back in uniform, again performing Acting Sergeant duties.

I took the decision to apply for promotion again and received support which I was thankful for. There were many of my colleagues thinking the same way. There were no available detective posts, so the only option was to pursue promotion. Whilst many of my colleagues seemed relaxed about the wait, I wasn't. I had now reached all my annual salary increments. The kids were getting older and the overdraft was getting larger by the month. Being back in uniform meant limited opportunities for overtime. At home, the financial position was not good. My wife was not earning a wage, preferring to be at home for the children, so we just rolled with the punches. In the meantime, I paid for some additional tuition to assist me in dealing with the assessment centre. The additional support clearly helped; in Autumn of 1992 I was successful in my bid to be promoted. I told my wife and children then telephoned both my parents. They were all proud; my kids loved the idea that their dad was going to be a sergeant. I still have the drawings that they did congratulating me.

In July of 1993, I was notified that I was to be transferred on promotion to another division. This was not unusual, the thinking behind it being that newly promoted sergeants should not be put in the position of supervising their friends or people they had worked closely with. I was heading to yet another hard-line mining area. It was also a significant distance from where I lived. What the service gives you in one hand, they often take with the other. My pay increase was now to be swallowed up in the fuel bills getting to and from work as the round trip was over 40 miles. It was pointless complaining. I was a newbie sergeant, I wanted to be promoted, so I just had to suck it up.

Before I could leave Leeds though, there was the small matter of a leaving do to arrange. I still had a great relationship with the guys in the CID. I spent a lot of time in and out of their office, so it was natural that they would encourage me to have a get-together in a public house. I arranged a private room in a bar local to me, with the standard finger buffet included. I turned up with my wife for the send-off. Leaving parties, like Christmas dos, have a reputation for getting out of hand but I didn't anticipate much of a problem. I had a broad representation of guests from across the division, including several bosses. The speeches were delivered, then came time to settle down to the business of drinking and eating, or so I thought. As I was about to leave the room to visit the gents, a blonde girl appeared in the doorway. "Are you, Colin?" she asked.

I didn't recognise her as being on the invite list and naively replied, "Yes, who are you?" Before she had the chance to answer, the room erupted in laughter and loud clapping. I then realised that the CID had arranged a stripper. When I looked again, this very attractive blonde girl had taken off her long coat. Underneath she was clad in an extremely short black leather dress, wearing stockings and carrying a leather whip. This was the stuff of nightmares. I hated being the centre of attention for anything and to make things worse, my wife was in the room. Before I knew it, the stripper was sat on my lap, topless and rubbing her bare breasts into my face. I noticed that someone was taking pictures; thankfully, this was before the advent of smartphones and social media. When I finally got home, rather worse for wear, my wife was not best pleased about the antics. My excuses about it being part of the job were beginning to wear a bit thin.

The station I was posted to was a relatively new building, which made a nice change. The shift I was taking over was comprised of officers who were young in service. Many were local to the area, and a few were miners who had joined the police after the strike of 1984. This was quite a brave and noble thing to do. Residents of the area were staunch supporters of Arthur Scargill and his policies. There was an extremely strong anti-police sentiment amongst sectors of the community. Eight years after the strike had ended, the term 'Maggie's Boot Boys' was still a common verbal taunt when we arrived at any disorder. I was acutely aware that as a newly promoted Supervisor, I would now be under the microscope from all angles. The PCs want to test you, the CID want to know about you, fellow sergeants and your shift inspector are watching you to see if you can set yourself apart from the rank and file. Everyone wants to know whether you are competent, a maverick, a zealot or a complete idiot. I worked for all those categories of boss in my time and had engaged in these types of amateur assessments in the past. I was entirely confident in my investigative ability but running a shift of officers, being responsible for them and everything that went on in the area, was at first a daunting prospect. All the books in the world cannot prepare you for it. I was fortunate to have a very good inspector though. He was a former trainer, very personable, supportive and competent. I heard many a boss over the years say to me, "Any problems get in touch, anytime." For some, those words were hollow. I could tell that this guy meant it. I knew if I had any issues then I could talk to him.

One of my very first incidents as a Supervisor was to attend an address following a request from a PC. He wanted authority from me to force entry into an address. Neighbours hadn't seen the man who lived there for a while. He suffered with depression so there were concerns for his welfare. My first thoughts were that if it had been me, I would have just kicked the door in and worried about it later. It was what is known in the trade as a 'no-brainer'. As I was to find out, certain constables always wanted to pass responsibility for their decisions to a Supervisor. The front door was forced open. When it eventually gave way, we saw the stairs directly in front us. On the landing above, a man was hanging from a rope secured in the loft. As is typical with hangings, the man's head was tilted to one side, his eyes were bulging from their sockets and his face was contorted. It was a sad sight; whilst by no means was it the first suicide I had ever seen, this one stuck in my mind. The guy was so young, his life in front of him, dying alone, and for what?

It wasn't always doom and gloom though. Later that week, I responded to another call, this time from two different constables who needed assistance at a domestic dispute. Both officers were characters; competent, hard-working, quick-witted, and always up for a laugh and a joke. On my arrival, the male protagonist was sat on a sofa in the living room, engaged in an argument with his female partner, deliberately ignoring our presence. He was refusing to leave the property. There had been no injuries to either party, but to avoid a breach of the peace he was told he had to leave. Somehow, I ended up stood in front of him, conveying firmly that he was departing the property or would be arrested. His response was, "Fuck off".

At this point in my service, I rarely gave second chances. When he replied to me in that manner, I said, "OK, fine, you're locked up". I leant down and picked him up from the sofa by his coat. As anticipated, the struggle and fighting started. It wasn't long before we were both rolling about on the floor. The two officers with me were now trying to get a hold on him as well. The next thing I knew, my right leg was being pulled backwards and I was being dragged across the floor. I had no idea why this was happening but refused to let go of my prisoner. It turned out that one of my men thought it was the prisoner's leg. Once the fighting and struggling was over, we managed to manhandle the prisoner into the waiting police van.

The PC responsible for pulling my leg said, "Really sorry, Sarge, what a way to make an impression?!" We just fell about laughing. Our detainee, thinking we were giggling at his misfortunes, then decided to have a kicking fit, causing a whole load of damage to the rear door.

Many police sergeants will tell you that holding that rank is the best place to be in the service. I would tend to agree with that. I must admit that making the transition from being a constable was difficult at first. I still liked being in the thick of it, making arrests, etc., and never wanted to stop doing that. However, I had to learn to step back at times. It was just as important to set the standards, be a role model and provide direction for younger officers. I was quite glad in those early months not to have been put into the position of supervising my friends in Leeds. I think I may have struggled to strike the necessary balance between respect, trust, and discipline.

I found the role to be multifaceted. I was now responsible for others under my supervision, I had to monitor incoming calls and ensure that my people did not come to any harm. During our shifts, I was the one responsible for them and the delivery of operational policing, once again quite remote from any assistance. It could at times be a lonely world. It was important not to finish duty and go home until you knew that all your staff were accounted for. Whilst it was usual for officers to operate alone and be single crewed on patrol, I considered that to be risky, especially at night. So, whenever I identified I had a single-crewed officer, I would go out with them.

For one night shift, doing that nearly saw the end of me. On reflection, I am glad I was there. I had only one female officer on the shift, and she was quite inexperienced. The male officers didn't hold her in high regard. To me, she just needed a bit of nurturing and guidance. Whilst crewing with her on the night in question, we received a call that a vehicle was travelling in the wrong direction along an extremely busy arterial route that passed through our division. When the call came in, we were at a petrol filling station having a cup of tea – something we did when time allowed, as it served as a preventative measure, deterring criminals who often saw filling stations as easy targets for robbery. On receipt of the call, we dashed out of the door, got into the car and the officer concerned turned directly into the oncoming traffic lane of the carriageway. It was the early hours, and the road was quiet, but I shouted at the top of my voice, "Stop! What are you doing?" The thought of us blue lighting it towards who knows what, in the opposite direction to oncoming traffic, and in the dark, filled me with dread, "Reverse, now!" I said and we pulled back into the service area. There are times like this when adrenaline takes over. That can be when people make questionable decisions and mistakes. It was a perfect illustration for me about the role of a supervisor. The thoughts of us dying in a needless collision or causing innocent members of the public to be injured, or at worse die, were terrifying to think about. We were not trained for that sort of specialist intervention. Our involvement extended to acting as spotters until the incident was successfully resolved by the road traffic department.

As a new sergeant, I had to receive periodic reviews on my performance. It was during those meetings that it became apparent to me that to advance further in the ranks, I would need better educational qualifications. The Force at the time was advertising for recruits who possessed degrees. These people were being fast-tracked for advancement. It filtered down that the 'management team' of the Force would prefer future candidates for promotion to have evidence of academic achievements. My smattering of secondary school qualifications counted for nothing. I only had operational experience to call upon. However, the Force was offering some educational support programmes. I applied for funding and embarked upon a Higher National Certificate and Higher National Diploma at Bradford College.

Once again, I found myself in the classroom and hated it. I wasn't connected in a strategic sense to policing. I just went on the streets and did my bit. I had trouble correlating how things like accountancy and politics equated to what I perceived to be the 'real world'. I had to put in additional study at home in exchange for being allowed to attend college sessions during work time. Time with my children suffered yet again as I ploughed more effort into improving my prospects. I mitigated that by telling myself that it would give all three of them a better chance in life. I knew it was far too early to consider putting myself forward for the next rank, but I wanted to lay foundations for the future.

A couple of months later, I attended the newly promoted sergeants course. All the attendees were male, all from West Yorkshire and fresh in the role. The course was run by a stern, old-school inspector. It involved a lot of sitting in horseshoe formation again, discussing issues such as race, equality and how to deal with difficult members of staff. Some of it was quite tedious at times and I found myself drifting off, only to be confronted with, "What do you think about that, Colin?" the blank look on my face only confirming to the Inspector that I wasn't paying attention.

One of the biggest takeaways from the course for me, was that as a newly promoted sergeant, I was just like everyone else – we were all in the same boat. When you cut to the chase, we all had similar concerns about our ability and how we were perceived by others. I think that gave us all the confidence that we were not alone. It was a normal process, I heard it described as, going from 'being consciously incompetent to unconsciously competent'. The course was once again residential. There was of a lot of socialising, drinking, frolics and trips into Wakefield but again nowhere near the scale of the CID course. There was a slight relaxation of the rules in terms of staying at the accommodation and I again made time to go home midweek to see the family. Despite me feeling I was doing my bit, there was more than one conversation with my wife around this time about me being increasingly wedded to the job. I mostly ignored the comments and her concerns because I was happy at work, advancing and enjoying my new responsibilities. There was probably quite a bit of truth to what she said. The police service will do that to you if you allow it. It is easy to lose sight of your own domestic matters and become completely engrossed in your work. I lost count of the number of divorces and separations that were taking place around me.

With the course completed, I returned to normal duties but was already finding the journey to and from the place wearing. Quick turnarounds, finishing at 10pm and back in for 6am were part of the shift pattern. If you finished late one evening, then it ate into your sleep time. As the Supervisor, I took the view that I had to be in earlier than the rest of the team to ensure that everything was ready for the morning briefing, hence five or six hours' sleep becoming routine. There were times when I arrived home completely drained and had little time for the family. I knew I would have to complete at least 12 months at my new posting before I would even be considered for a move closer to home.

After around eight months, I started to put the feelers out and plead my case. I had felt little financial benefit from my promotion but had gained so much experience.

31. Back home

After about a year, I was successful in securing a transfer closer to home. Those first 12 months were in many ways a baptism of fire, in a violent, unforgiving place; I loved it. It allowed me to grow into the role of a Supervisor. I had exposure to all manner of issues and incidents. There was a man on the roof of a building pelting all and sundry with tiles, a siege in a working men's club, staff welfare and performance issues, plus the odd spell in the custody suite which always presented its own unique challenges.

My new position was to be a completely different experience. No longer was I to be autonomous. I was one of four sergeants running a much larger team. It quickly became apparent that the inspector in charge of us was laissez-faire, to say the least. He left the sergeants to run the show and rarely got involved with anything. We were all a similar age and length of service; all having been promoted around the same sort of time. Each of us had our own individual ambitions and professional goals. The problem you have with our Supervisors managing a team is maintaining consistency. Frequently, all the sergeants had a different opinion on how to do things. Certain officers would shop around amongst us to get the advice they wanted to hear. I found it quite frustrating. I knew I performed better if I was left in charge of a team and not having to get buy-in from other Supervisors about my decisions.

We policed an area of Leeds that was suburban and semi-industrial. It had its sink estates, poverty and high volumes of crime as part of its overall make-up. The population levels were higher, and that meant more officers were required, there were more calls for assistance and ultimately, more problems. Most of our crime had a correlation with drugs – heroin was emerging as a common feature with persistent offenders.

My kids loved the fact that I was closer to home. They were proud as punch and loved seeing me in my uniform. When I was able to, I would pop home in a marked car or van, and they would come and look inside in awe, asking the sorts of questions only kids do. Once or twice, they even had a play with the 'blues and twos'. My daughter had started secondary school by this time. Now that I was back in the local area, I harboured a concern that all three of them were at some point likely to encounter the "Your dad's a copper" nonsense when they finally arrived there. Thankfully, the school had a smattering of children whose parents were also police officers. To the best of my knowledge, my concerns were unfounded. I rarely discussed the darker side of what happened at work with them, always choosing to talk about the positives and who we had helped. It was never lost on me that the job had an element of danger, but it was always important to me that I came home to them. When I suffered injuries at work, I never related what had really happened. It was my way of protecting them and I think most cops do that with their kids.

There is a propensity for violence during night shifts; it's difficult to pin down why but my experience was that this was when you had to be extra careful. Very shortly after transferring, I was out on patrol with another sergeant when a call came in about a man in a house, armed with a knife and threatening a woman. It was around this time that we had all been equipped with body armour, rigid handcuffs, pepper spray and PR24 batons. This was largely due to a surge in assaults on officers and the recognition that the traditional piece of wood – the truncheon – was not effective as a defensive tool. Thankfully, it had seen its day.

We were first on the scene. My colleague loved to drive the van, so being in the passenger seat, I was first out of the vehicle and ran to the door which was opened by a female. I established that it was her partner in the kitchen and he did indeed have a knife. I could hear my colleague on his radio, requesting back up, a firearms team and the helicopter. Frankly I thought it was over the top as we hadn't had the opportunity to properly assess the situation. I opened the kitchen door gingerly and sure enough the guy was holding a domestic carving knife. The blade was around six inches long. He looked troubled and fearful; it seemed to be the case that a domestic argument had got out of hand. He pointed the knife towards me. I have no idea why, but I got the sense he was not going to use it. I decided to speak to him calmly by asking him to put the knife down so that we could sort the matter out peacefully.

To this day, I have no idea how long we were in the kitchen, although it felt much longer than it probably was. I knew it had the potential to end badly, but I also knew I had a stab proof vest and spray if I needed to use it. Not wanting to escalate the situation, I just talked to him, asking what had happened, why it had happened and just talked him down. He eventually dropped the knife, and was handcuffed, arrested and we walked out of the house together. By this time, there were around 15 officers in attendance. I don't recall feeling elated – more relieved and quite pleased that things hadn't escalated into a siege or worse.

After booking him in at the police station, I bumped into our Inspector coming the other way along the corridor. The conversation went something like this.

"Get that little job sorted, Sergeant?"

Feeling quite proud of myself, I responded with, "Yes I did, boss. Managed to disarm him of his knife."

His reply was, "Oh good," and at that, he walked off! I was utterly aghast at his reaction. I didn't expect a Chief Constable's Commendation, although I have seen them awarded for much less. However, some words of encouragement, 'well done' or 'great job', would not have gone amiss.

My lack of confidence in him was compounded still further some months later during another night shift. I happened to be the only patrol sergeant working the area when there was a report of a fire at a local chemical works. This had to be treated as a major incident because of the potential for injury and loss of life. When he didn't answer his radio and was nowhere to be found, it smacked of neglect on his part. He didn't attend as would be the norm. He was nowhere to be found and when he finally surfaced after the event, not once did he ask me what had happened at the scene. He showed no interest at all; something I had never experienced before from someone in his position. He didn't impress me at all; he displayed little interest in the job, or the people that worked for him. I never did understand it but said to myself if ever I reach that position, I would do things differently.

Being back in Leeds meant that I was in frequent contact with my former colleagues from the CID and the Child Protection team. It wasn't long before I was being encouraged to apply for the DS positions that were being advertised. This had the potential for yet another long wait. In an effort to break the deadlock, the Force introduced a system called Tenure of Post. This meant that you were only able to serve in a specialist position for a set period before being returned to uniformed duties. There were pros and cons to this and a whole load of controversy. Training costs money and the biggest argument was that this continual recycling was inefficient. The flip side was that greater breadth of operational experience could be dispersed across the organisation. The CID and traffic departments were most affected by this move and were up in arms. It seemed to have the reverse effect of what it intended to do, with people digging their heels in and refusing to move.

Regardless, I applied, had a good interview and was told that I had been successful. However, all the sergeants on my shift had also applied and had been accepted as well. During annual appraisals, my next career move was discussed. I had the local DI telling me he wanted me in the CID, but he had no vacancies. I had other managers encouraging me to apply for promotion to Inspector. It all sounded very familiar. I performed occasional periods of Acting Inspector duties and was supported for my application for the upcoming assessment centre. Once again, I found myself on the proverbial merry-go-round of work, study, work, more study and not seeing too much of the family. I failed the assessment centre, so for a short time I went into 'poor me' mode. I was nowhere near ready for promotion to the next rank if the truth be known. That first attempt only served to get me some exposure to the system.

Getting knocked back for advancement in any employment is a part of the journey. The hardest part is watching other people getting promoted when you know they aren't ready for it either. Successful candidates were eventually appointed at the division. On the odd occasion, normally because of staff shortages or holidays, you could end up working alongside them. Despite a rigorous assessment process, it was apparent that some had limited experience or exposure to serious incidents. As a result, and rather than be seen wanting in front of PCs, they would turn to the nearest sergeant for help. I had absolutely no issue with this, it was a perfectly sensible thing to do.

I recall being asked by one such inspector to accompany him to a suspicious death, as he wasn't overly confident about what he needed to do. On our arrival at the house, I went up the stairs and into the bathroom – what I saw was awful. The body of a man in his fifties, quite large, was stood upright in the bath, where he had been taking a shower. His whole body was bright red, swollen and covered in large blisters, a gruesome sight resembling something out of a horror movie, and another incident permanently etched into my memory. There was no sign of an attack, no sign of forced entry and no indication of a crime. It appeared to be the case that the man had died after suffering a heart attack. The shower, being unregulated, then overheated the water, which in turn caused the severe burns to his skin.

32. Protecting children

In another quirk of fate, I again ended up working with the CPU, this time as a sergeant providing cover. It was a short stint of around six weeks but brought me to the attention of their management team. The incumbent, who was in fact one of the trainers from my CID course, needed to perform some Acting duties. He needed to update his operational experience to apply for the next round of Inspector promotion assessments. Because I had completed the Child Protection course prior to being promoted, the wheels were put in motion for us to do a short-term mutual swap. This set in train a change in my career path.

I have always said that working on the Task Force was one of the most exciting times in my career. Child Protection was undoubtedly the most rewarding. It ensured that the most vulnerable members of society were safer. I started my attachment a bit like a fish out of water, for one thing I had never supervised so many female officers. Men were in the minority in the office – it was me and one other. The attachment went well, it flew by, and a glowing report was received at headquarters. Subsequently, the DS who ran the unit was successful in his bid for promotion and I was offered his position. I had now completed around two years as a uniformed sergeant, gained bags of experience and had now got into a branch of the CID. Whilst no one said so to my face, I sensed that one or two of my fellow supervisors thought I had short-circuited the system. Nothing could have been further from the truth. I had not approached anyone. I happened to be qualified for the role and in the right place at the right time. The CPU set-up appealed to me. I was autonomous but also shouldered a tremendous weight of responsibility. The workload was huge, as we received far more referrals than we could effectively respond to. Not only did we provide cover for child sexual, physical and emotional abuse, but the Force had also decided that female officers had to provide night cover for adult victims of serious sexual assault and rape.

Because of the nature of the work, it was mandatory to attend an annual counselling session with an independent therapist. Like many of my colleagues I joked about it, felt I didn't need it, but went along to 'play the game'. My enduring memory of the first ever counselling session I attended was chatting to the therapist about his farm and the fact that he grew peat in his spare time. If anything had been wrong, I very much doubt whether I would have said anything anyway because I had zero trust in the police service to have kept it confidential, despite all the assurances.

In truth, despite everything that was going on, I really didn't feel I wanted that type of support. I had developed a certain resilience over the years, probably emotional detachment; something that many serving and former police officers will be familiar with. It is a survival mechanism; you had to be able to close parts of yourself down, or you simply could not function in the job you were paid to do.

I soon came to realise why the annual assessment was necessary though. The role was utterly relentless, and you were exposed to the very worst of humanity. As a sergeant, I couldn't stand back and watch the DCs deal with all the investigations, so I took on my own case workload. Of course, I had the luxury of being selective, but I also wanted to learn more about these types of crimes, the offenders and their victims. The only way to do that was to get involved. It was a steep learning curve and not quite the same as having minimal ownership when on previous attachments. It was a balancing act – if I took my eye off the ball in terms of overall supervision and something went wrong, then there was the potential for children's lives being put at risk, a full-blown case review and the adverse media exposure that can go with it. Thankfully, we were not alone; the burden was shouldered to an extent by the agencies we interfaced with.

Partnership working had accelerated significantly since my very first attachment some years previously. Multi-agency case conferences were now in vogue and there was a culture of openness where parents were invited along. This was alien to me, even more so when they were the suspects. My previous investigations had almost exclusively been a police matter, other than the Crown Prosecution Service (CPS) rarely did anyone else have much of a say. During these case conferences, you would discuss previous convictions, details of the case and make recommendations. On occasion, those meetings led to children being removed from the family home, pending investigations. Other agencies were much more intimately involved in the case, routinely attending and participating in interviews with children that were recorded on video tape. For the most part, I had extremely good working relationships with social services. One head of department even referred to me as someone who brought calm and reason to difficult situations.

Seeing, reading, and hearing about what some adults do to children was emotionally draining. As the supervisor,

I had to review every case file. There were times I had to read things several times over in order to fully comprehend what was alleged to have happened. Often a lack of forensic evidence and a victim too young to talk determined that you were unable to advance the investigation. It left you feeling helpless. In my opinion, it also made you a better investigator because you worked harder to solve problems by identifying other lines of enquiry. You had to be an agile interviewer; one day you may be talking to a very young child, the next a seasoned and cunning offender. For suspects there was no benefit in admitting to what they had done. No one would respect them for it. If, for example, they were convicted and went to prison, they would be put into isolation and become the target of other prisoners. It was a battle of wits in the interview room, the standard 'no reply' a regular occurrence.

I have never been able to fully erase one case from my memory. One morning, I arrived in the office faced with an extremely serious referral that was developing rapidly. The allegation was that a young baby had received life-threatening injuries at home. Mother and father were not providing any plausible explanation. One of my officers had already taken responsibility for the case. It had the potential to be a murder enquiry such were the severity of the injuries. If the child were to have died, then we would have had to hand over the investigation to the divisional CID. For now, we had to attend at the hospital to establish what was known of the child. We arrived at the Intensive Care Unit to see a tiny baby girl wired up to all manner of tubes, cords and wires. The frequent beep of the instruments and flashing lights served to underline the gravity of the situation. The available medical opinion was that she had been violently shaken or thrown with force, probably against a wall. Improbable though it may sound, the parents said they had no idea what had happened.

Both were arrested and interviewed on suspicion of GBH (Grievous Bodily Harm). Neither parent had a high intellect. They were, however, acutely aware of the fragility of their situation. As was their right, both instructed a solicitor for advice during questioning. During the investigation and early interviews, we formed the opinion that the father was responsible for the injuries the baby had suffered. He had not exercised his right to silence but was maintaining his denials.

What comes with experience of suspect interviews is the ability to read the signs when someone is lying and when they are on the brink of telling you something significant. We reached a point in the interview when I asked him if he was responsible for the injuries to his baby daughter. I deliberately held the silence and just looked at him. It is a common tactic used by experienced interviewers because silence is uncomfortable and difficult to maintain – at some point, someone will crack and say something. Our suspect looked directly at me and there was a non-verbal acknowledgement that he was about to say something. As he opened his mouth to speak, the solicitor recognised it too. He intervened and advised his client not to answer further questions. The solicitor knew full well the father was guilty, but he was doing his job, just as I was doing mine. That said, I was never able to come to terms with his intervention. We later found out that the baby was permanently damaged; she suffered cerebral palsy, would most likely never be able to walk properly and had her lifespan severely limited. I cannot remember the father's first name, but I still recall the child's full name. He got away with what he did. The mother, whom I feel sure knew the full story, to my knowledge never disclosed the truth.

Cases such as this leave an indelible mark on your inner consciousness. I have often spent time wondering if I could have done more to hold someone to account, such was the nature of these types of offences. Finding sufficient evidence to prove them could be challenging and frustrating.

Having continued exposure to investigations such as these made me even more protective of my own children. I would not leave them in the company of other adults unless I trusted them implicitly. I spoke to them in what I felt was age-appropriate language about the potential for abuse and being able to speak to their mum and dad when they didn't feel comfortable about things. My daughter, who was about 14, again came under increased scrutiny from me. I make no apology when I admit to having made certain enquiries of her boyfriends to ensure they had not come to the attention of the police. I was incredibly close to my kids and was always very open about things. For instance, if they had a question about sex, as so often kids do, they got an answer. Sometimes their little giggles and sniggers felt as if they had set me up, particularly the boys.

On a personal level, we were now much more financially secure. I was feeling the benefit of my promotion along with annual salary increments and overtime. For the first time, I was able to purchase a good car by utilising the county loan system. I used it for work purposes attracting mileage payments. I tended to get most weekends off, so we also purchased a caravan. That gave us greater mobility in terms of getting away during my time off. As a result, the children all developed a love of camping and the outdoors, something which they all continue to enjoy as adults.

We were also able to travel down more frequently to see their Nana (as they loved to call her) and have holidays in Cornwall. Mum missed her grandchildren and would frequently knit cardigans, send presents and letters for them. When we travelled to Cornwall, she would fuss over them and they loved it. My relationship with my dad was also good during this time. We would travel to visit him and my stepmother as well. Her parents had both passed away around this time and the pair of them had come into a sum of money, allowing them to extend the house, buy adjacent land and build a tennis court. It was a fantastic space and very safe. The children loved to visit; we were always made welcome, and I have many happy memories of family meals, fun and games there. My two boys were keen footballers and had joined local teams. I was able to take them to and from their matches and spend time with them.

I wouldn't go as far as to say that my wife and I were living separate lives, but our closeness had diminished further. I don't think she was ever overly happy that I was working in an office mostly staffed by females. Her concerns were unfounded though. I had no interest in developing any form of relationship with anyone I supervised. Most of the girls in the office were in serious long-term relationships. From my perspective, I was more interested in getting the work done, earning the respect of the team and doing a good job. All the people who worked for me eventually became friends of my wife and kids, and I remain in contact with many to this day. It just wasn't the sort of place for affairs, despite what some people thought. The subject of sex was a daily discussion but in a very different context – if you happened to walk into our office unannounced, you would often be privy to some very strange discussions. It was all in the context of investigations, but visitors sometimes wondered what they had unwittingly stumbled into. Very occasionally, you would still hear the term 'knob squad' or something equally disparaging. My way of dealing with silly comments like that was to invite the individual to come along on an attachment to get a better understanding of what we did.

Over time I began to see a steady stream of short-term secondments, even from the CID officers. It was a great initiative because we were also able to feedback the signs of child abuse to front line officers. They were then able to engage us more readily and we could then pass information to our partner agencies. There were, of course, one or two individuals who didn't quite know what they were letting themselves in for. One female officer, quite young in service, turned up one morning wearing shorts akin to hot pants. Whilst quite a distraction for me and my male colleague in the office that day, the fact that she was going to accompany another officer to interview a sex offender determined that she had to be sent home to change into something a little more appropriate.

33. A very different type of offender

Trying to understand why people commit crime has confounded researchers and academics for years. A wide range of issues play their part including: socio-economic factors, poverty, deprivation, a lack of parental intervention and, to an extent, peer pressure. I have dealt with lots of criminals over the years. There are those who steal property – some do it out of greed, some out of need. You tend to see the same old faces time and again; they get to know you and you get to know them. There are even times when you have some empathy and understanding of their situation. If ever you have been poor or short of money, then you will understand what I mean.

However, many of the sex offenders we dealt with in the CPU were a different breed altogether. Their motivations were alien, strange, complex and had roots in power and control. You had to develop a rapport to get the job done, but never wanted to go near them again unless you were feeling their collars. Individuals committing these types of offences hail from all sorts of backgrounds, but they also have to be devious to conceal their desires. Their victims were, for the most part, defenceless, so I got a great deal of pleasure in putting guilty parties into prison or protecting the people they harmed.

For reasons I was never entirely clear about, our office was the point of contact for a law firm in Leeds who protected the interests of a body of clergy when allegations of abuse were made. One of the male Detectives explained to me shortly after my appointment to the unit that he had to visit the firm to meet a solicitor there. He suggested that it would be wise if I accompanied him because of the nature of the allegation and the suspect. What followed was a roller coaster of an investigation, and despite our very best efforts, we were outwitted at every turn.

We arrived to meet an affable, middle-aged and very well-attired lawyer. The offices were in a part of the city where the more 'up-market' firms operated from. I found over the years that you were able to assess how well-heeled the firms were by the quality of the coffee and crockery they produced. It was the very best, accompanied by the thickest of chocolate biscuits. The lawyer explained to us that a woman had come forward and made allegations of sexual abuse against a prominent member of the church that had occurred many years ago. He went on to say that his role in the proceedings was to provide us with details of the allegations, assist as best he could and feed back to the church hierarchy about the progress of the case. Essentially, he was a go-between. It was lost on me initially, that the church was paying the firm handsomely for legal advice and did not necessarily have the victim's best interests at heart.

Because of the gravity of the situation, immediately after the meeting I went to see the Detective Chief Inspector in overall charge of the Force Child Protection Teams. Given the sensitive nature of the investigation, I needed to brief him on what we had been told. Somewhat reluctantly on his behalf, it was decided we would put together a small, confidential enquiry team. I say reluctantly because the police can never do right by the public or media with these types of investigations. It seemed a no-win situation most of the time. If the allegations are not probed thoroughly enough, the police get criticised. If a suspect is arrested for historical abuse based on the word of one person, it is an uphill struggle. Getting good, admissible evidence is exceptionally hard in such circumstances and it often relied on other victims coming forward. A tactic used in the past, now understandably frowned upon after some high-profile cases, would be to name the suspect in the press at some point. This often had the effect of encouraging other victims to come forward. It was a risky strategy because if the allegations were shown to be groundless or malicious, reputations were ruined irreparably. Regardless, the police service is duty-bound to investigate the matter, it simply cannot be ignored.

We arranged to meet the woman making the allegations. She lived in another police area, was a child at the time of the incidents and had disclosed details of the abuse during psychological therapy. It was immediately apparent to us on the first meeting that she was a troubled individual with some severe emotional issues. From a prosecutor's perspective, she would not be viewed as a competent witness. However, as an investigator you must question what was it that made her that way. Was it the abuse that had caused her psychological damage?

A lengthy statement alleging several incidents of sexual abuse was obtained over a few visits. The interviews took place in the presence of her psychologist, a very well-qualified professional. She felt strongly there was truth to what was being disclosed. We knew that despite her instincts it would make no difference to the CPS if we were only able to rely on the witness statement. At that point in time, her account was uncorroborated. What followed was weeks of tracing and interviewing members of a long since disbanded church group, the majority of whom spoke highly of the suspect, yet very few had any recollection of our victim.

Thankfully, no one was in touch with the subject of our enquiries. Google was not available and social media was unheard of. The suspect lived in the south of England, so there was potential that he could discover that we were investigating him. We always swore our interviewees to secrecy – being God-fearing people, it was a tactic that appeared to work. After several weeks, our enquiries eventually led us to his home, a large private dwelling on an affluent private estate. I arrested the man, who was in his seventies. Whilst retired from mainstream work with the church, he was still very well-known and respected. To say he was outraged at our arrival was an understatement. He demanded that we leave the property whilst he got himself ready. We declined his offer, not least because we needed to conduct a search of the house.

A DI from our Force, new to the units and not having any real experience of Child Abuse investigations, had been foisted upon us for the arrest phase. Whilst we conducted the search and prior to transporting the suspect to a custody suite at a nearby police station, the DI announced that he had agreed with our prisoner that he could drive himself there. I was outraged. Not only was this a complete breach of protocol, but it also gave him the upper hand.

Later on during questioning, he totally denied the allegations, at one point slamming his fist into the wall and shouting at the top of his voice, "This is utterly ridiculous!" His whole demeanour and attitude throughout did not strike me to be that of a member of the clergy. Evidentially that counted for nothing – we did not have enough evidence to charge. Bail was afforded and when all our enquiries were completed, we headed back home. Several days later, we became aware of a press leak about the case naming our man. I can say with certainty it did not come from me or any member of the team. There followed some frantic telephone calls between our Force and colleagues in the south of England. There were now threats of legal action against both forces. The solicitor we had met in Leeds was under pressure from his clients and wanted assurances that we had not informed the media.

Then, out of the blue I received a telephone call. An elderly lady, an author, whom I cannot name, asked if I would be prepared to visit and speak to her about a sexual assault that happened to her as a child. She didn't want to say too much over the phone but named our suspect as the man responsible. Further, she had not realised until the newspapers broke the story, that she lived no more than a few miles from him. We were to travel to the south of England yet again.

Our new witness was credible, well-educated, had fantastic recall and was a writer. She had not previously disclosed details of the assault on her for fear of not being believed. This is a common characteristic with victims of abuse. As a young orphan, she had found herself in a convent in Ireland. She related to us how she met our suspect. He was in his twenties at the time and had indecently assaulted her when she was alone in a secluded garden at the property, something which she had never forgotten. A comprehensive witness statement of many pages was obtained. Ireland was not under our jurisdiction and the CPS lawyer was not convinced that the statement would be admissible in an English court. I was instructed to send the witness statement to the police in Ireland.

Despite repeated requests, no confirmation was ever received of any investigation there and I strongly suspect it was filed as NFA (No Further Action). It was ultimately decided by the CPS that there was insufficient evidence to support any prosecution. Just prior to that decision being received, our author witness called us in tears. That morning she had been visited by two men who claimed they were representatives of the church. They had threatened her, stating she was to say nothing more to the police. The church solicitor refused to speak further to us about the allegations and we were forced to close the enquiry. Someone somewhere had exerted some influence.

Approximately seven years later, whilst working overseas, I was contacted by a newly appointed supervisor to the CPU. Fresh allegations had emerged about our suspect. The records and files, which we had painstakingly put together and stored within several cardboard boxes with the operational name thereon, had been moved. I knew exactly where those boxes had been located, because every time I went into the store I had seen them on the top shelf. A permanent reminder to me of the frustrations I had about not having been able to finalise that investigation.

On another occasion, one of my female Detectives came to me about a case she had picked up over the weekend whilst covering the Force. It wasn't in an area of West Yorkshire that we had direct responsibility for, but she had developed a rapport with the victim and for continuity purposes she wanted to keep hold of it. Whilst there was a protocol for this, rarely did you get any resistance from another unit if you said you would complete the investigation on their behalf. They were equally as busy and welcomed the assistance. The officer briefed me about what had happened. I reviewed the victim's witness statement. It was lengthy and made disturbing reading.

What this man had put his wife through was the stuff of nightmares. He had whipped, burnt, cut and bullied her. One cold Christmas morning, he had even made her stand outside in her underwear. He was a drinker who, rather than feed his family, preferred to visit pubs and clubs. He was sexually violent to her as well, inflicting the most awful internal injuries in the process. She had somehow tolerated his behaviour for many years. It was only when he began to show a sexual interest in underage girls that she decided enough was enough and went to the social services. This case was without doubt the most serious Domestic Violence investigation I ever came across in my service. How the victim had endured the levels of brutality and survived so long was a miracle. We knew that we had to do everything possible to protect her and the children from further harm. In the short term, they were all in a women's refuge and safe.

Our suspect was elusive. He must have reached the conclusion that the authorities were aware and fled. He was subsequently circulated as a wanted person. It was the following weekend when we were notified that he was in custody in the north-west of England. Fortunately, we were both on duty so headed over the Pennines to bring him back for questioning. The nature of the allegations was so serious that we already knew that once interviewed, we would be applying to keep him in custody to put him before the courts. This man was a danger to his wife and children. Once we charged him, if given bail, he would do absolutely everything in his power to intimidate his wife into withdrawing the allegations. Worst still, there was every chance, given his previous conduct, that he would seriously injure or kill her.

When we met our man in the cell block, he was typically charming, polite and told us he had no idea what had led to the allegations. As far as he was concerned, he was an upstanding member of the community and innocent. He told us that he was willing to help us with our enquiries. You become accustomed to responses such as this, so the pair of us just nodded and said everything would be sorted out in good time. There was something about him though. Instinctively I knew he was not to be trusted. Experience provides you with a sixth sense about people. I knew that if given an inch, he would take a mile. He was a manipulator. I took the decision to handcuff him to me.

My female colleague began the drive back. What was immediately evident was that he completely ignored her, deferring to me all the time. My instinct was that he thought women were second-class citizens. It became obvious that he had a problem with females in positions of authority. He tried his best to befriend me, showing disingenuous respect, being careful to refer to me as Sergeant, asking lots of questions about how the allegations had come about and trying to make small talk. He was doing his utmost to play us. It was going to be a verbal game of chess. One thing we could not do was to question him about the allegations and I think he knew that. It would be a breach of the Police and Criminal Evidence Act which, amongst other things, gives suspects the right to legal representation during interviews. Any chatter about the allegations, no matter how innocent, could be construed by the courts as an interview, be exploited by the defence ruthlessly and potentially disallowed in any future proceedings.

His next ploy was to state that he needed to go to the toilet urgently. At my instruction and prior to leaving the custody suite, he had already paid a visit. I had to explain that I thought he would try to escape, hence any trip to one of the motorway service area toilets could be embarrassing for both of us, because I would be unable to remove the handcuffs. My response seemed to work. He remained quiet for the rest of our journey.

The next morning in the presence of his legal representative, I started the first interview, going through each allegation. He seemed to think that as a male, I would side with him as he made make comments like, "You know what women are like", inferring his wife was lying. I wanted to shake him off his pedestal; he was too cocky. I asked my female colleague to take the lead for the next round. It was apparent from his demeanour that he did not like having to answer to her. He was riled and began to show his temper when answering questions. He denied absolutely everything, stating his wife was making it all up. The medical reports told a very different story. Some of the things he had done to his wife over the 20 plus years they were together cannot be conveyed here. They were utterly horrific; she bore the physical and emotional scars from his behaviour. The children did not emerge unscathed either; they were extremely fearful of their father. Even with the medical evidence, there was an element of her word against his. We had to make the case as strong as possible. We charged him with what we believed we could prove. He was remanded in custody and we then embarked upon strengthening the case further. It involved travelling to the south of England where he originated from and speaking to people who knew him.

He subsequently appeared in the Crown Court and was imprisoned for ten years. We were congratulated by the prosecuting barrister, and both commended for our work by the Chief Constable. It was great to be recognised but most importantly, we had helped set the victim and her children free so they could build a better life for themselves. It was a great feeling.

34. Not a good year

By late 1997 I had accumulated over two years with the CPU. I was supervising a fantastic group of people, some of whom I had recruited. I had fostered excellent relationships with the management team, my peers and the local CID. At home I was seeing more of the family; things were good and I was feeling settled. However, unbeknown to me, the rest of the year was to be one of the most tumultuous I would ever have to live through.

In the space of a few weeks, two of my female friends were diagnosed with cancer. One was a Detective in my office. One morning, she asked if she could speak to me for a minute. This was a regular occurrence, so I thought nothing of it initially. As a supervisor, I always tried to make time for everyone and understand what was going on in both their work and personal lives. I was shocked when she told me in a very matter of fact way that she had cancer. It was in her mouth and would entail an operation. I didn't know what to say at first; I hadn't been exposed to it before. All I could say was that I would support her as best I could. Thankfully, after a few months, she recovered and bounced back; it was caught early. But it was worrying nonetheless, because she was young and wanted to start a family.

Shortly after, I discovered that a female DI whom I knew had also been diagnosed. She was one of the instructors on my Child Protection course, and we had worked together frequently since my arrival on the units. We had become good friends and always had a laugh and a joke together. For some reason, I ended up driving her to several meetings and events. It became a standing joke and I referred to her as Lady Penelope and she called me Parker.

It transpired quite quickly that her cancer was life-threatening. I watched over a few months how she became a shadow of her former self. She was very well thought of, exuded professionalism and understood people. Despite her illness, she was always telling me to slow down, not to work so hard and make time for myself. Officers in the CPU were, for the most part, the caring type. We were all affected by her illness. Sadly, she passed away some weeks later. It was the first time one of my close police colleagues had died of cancer and the first police funeral I had attended. There were some fabulous eulogies on the day, all bearing testament to one of the finest female officers I ever had the pleasure to work with. The latter part of the year had been emotionally exhausting, but it had not finished with me yet.

Mum was always a hard worker, holding down several jobs, including cleaning, being a school playground supervisor and whatever else she could fit in. She took the decision aged 62 to wind down and take it a bit easier. Due to work commitments that year, it was a challenge getting time off for the summer holidays, so she decided to come and stay with us in August for a well-earned break. Due to his own work, my stepfather was unable to make it. We still had a great time. Mum travelled up by train and she spent quality time with the children which they loved. She had always been a fantastic baker and cook, so we were treated to her speciality Cornish pasties, cakes and buns. She also loved getting out and about in Yorkshire and the surrounding area. We had a lot of fun, visited tea rooms and went for walks in the countryside.

One afternoon, we drove to Ladybower Reservoir in Derbyshire. Having grown up during the Second World War, Mum had a fascination for the history of that era. Ladybower was where the bouncing bomb of Dam Busters fame was tested. We were all walking along; I was slightly in front and keeping an eye on the kids. For some reason, I looked round and saw that Mum was hanging back and rubbing her side. I asked her what was wrong, and it soon became apparent that she was in a lot of pain. It transpired that the soreness she was experiencing had been troubling her for some time. Typically, she had kept it quiet and not thought to seek any medical advice. Mum was going back to Cornwall the next day so I made her promise she would make a doctor's appointment as soon as she got home. I cannot describe how I felt when she telephoned me to say that the pain in her side was lung cancer. I didn't know how, or indeed if, I would tell the children. Mum was always a worrier and I knew she would be thinking the worst. I tried to play it down over the telephone, assuring her she would be OK. Sadly, that was not to be the case.

Some weeks later, we all drove to Cornwall as she had been taken into hospital. I walked onto the ward that day and did not recognise her. In her hospital bed, she was sat upright and gaunt. In the weeks since we had last seen her, she had aged so much. Frankly, she resembled someone from a prisoner of war camp. I tried my best to hide my shock, but I knew this was not good. I remember sitting with her, holding her hand whilst she told me with tears in her eyes that she simply couldn't understand it. Like me, she hated smoking and smokers. When she said to me, "It's so unfair, I've never smoked," it broke me inside. Here was a woman who had worked so hard all her life, had raised four children, wanted to spend time with her grandchildren and was about to embark on a well-earned retirement. For my own sanity and to try and help in the only way I could, I felt I had to find out what the prospects were. I set about searching for her doctor.

Unceremoniously, in the corridor of the hospital, he told my wife and I that she would be unlikely to survive more than a few months. The cancer was far too advanced. I couldn't take it in, I didn't believe him. My irrational and emotional brain kicked in: 'people survive this stuff', 'my mum was Superwoman', 'no way would she be dying, no way'. When she asked me to 'look after' my stepfather if she died, I told her not to be so silly. That was Mum all over, always thinking of others.

We stayed for as long as we could and later travelled back to Yorkshire. Mum came out of hospital and for a short time, things were a little better. But as always seems the way with that awful disease, her immune system weakened and she went downhill rapidly. My stepfather was struggling to cope with the rigours of caring for her.

At work I had been asked to take on additional responsibility. I was given the role of Acting Inspector which meant managing several of the teams and operating from another office. I was out of my comfort zone but knew I could do the work. I was heavily conflicted, as part of me refused to accept that Mum was going to die. My reaction was to throw myself into my work, partly out of loyalty and responsibility, but also to distract myself from what was going on.

In September that year, my stepsister was married in Cornwall. Mum was allowed out of hospital for the day, although she was clearly struggling and looked very frail. Always up for a party, she did her best and stayed for as long as she could. I still have a photograph of the pair of us dancing together on that day.

Shortly after the wedding, the decision was taken to move her into a hospice. It had become obvious that she needed intensive support and a level of care that was not possible at home. I called Mum at least once every day during this time. I wanted to make sure she was OK and kept telling her that she would get through it.

One day, I recall she ended the conversation prematurely because she was having difficulty talking. The cancer was affecting her ability to breathe properly. That same evening, I arrived home and went to the local sports centre to attend circuit training. I returned about 7pm and as I opened the front door, the telephone was ringing. I picked it up and my stepfather said something like, "You need to come home, it's not looking good." Even 20 years on, he referred to Cornwall as my home, as did Mum. I was in my sports gear but was out of the house and on the road in less than ten minutes. My wife asked me if she should come with me. It was out of the question, given the kids and their schooling.

With a complete disregard for any speed limits, I drove to Cornwall from Leeds as quickly as I could. There were no mobile phones, so I had no idea of how things were. I didn't want to stop, I wanted to be with my mum and she wanted me there. If these were to be her dying moments, then I had to be present. As far as I was concerned, it was my duty as the eldest child to be there for her.

I was about 20 miles from the hospice when the car suddenly went very cold. It felt as if someone was in there with me. I recall looking into the rear-view mirror and a shiver went down my spine. It was the strangest of feelings and I shrugged it off. I arrived at the hospice, pulled up outside and dashed up the stairs to be met by my sister. The look on her face said it all. "She's gone, I'm so sorry".

I was utterly devastated and unable to talk for several minutes. I went into a corner of the room and stared at the wall. I didn't want anyone to see my face. As far as I was concerned, I had let my mum down in her time of need. My stepfather came to me – he could see I was completely broken – and said, "She knew you were on your way." That didn't really help. I asked if I could see her on my own. I held her hand, sobbed and just kept telling her I was sorry. I just could not take it in; she was invincible as far as I was concerned. After all these years, I still find it very difficult to talk about without getting emotional.

The next day, my wife and children arrived by train. My children knew their Nana had been ill but hadn't expected her to pass so quickly. From staying with us in August, it was less than three months before she died. My wife was very close to Mum. My daughter was 16 years old, and my sons 13 and 12. It was not the first time they had suffered loss, as my wife's father had died some years earlier. They were much younger then, and this hit them hard. Mum always made both time for and things for them. They still have the handmade individual Christmas stockings that she knit for them.

We went to the Chapel of Rest to see her and say our goodbyes. I then spent time keeping myself occupied, helping my stepfather, registering the death, deciding on the music for the funeral, cuddling the kids and meeting with family. I wept in private; it was not the 'done' thing to do that in front of anyone. In my eyes, I had to be strong for everyone else.

Mum's funeral was well attended; she was popular and known to many more people than I knew. To his credit, despite not speaking to Mum for many years, Dad drove down to support me, my sister and brother. It was a lovely gesture, doubtless difficult for him, but I respected him enormously for that. One of the tracks I chose for the funeral was 'Your Love' by Diana Ross. Mum adored music, and this song epitomised how I felt, with words like, *'Your love has kept me going through good and bad times; It's kept me growing like a steady flame'*. It saddens me deeply that I cannot recall ever telling her that to her face. I had been brought up and conditioned that expressing how you felt was soppy. How wrong I was.

I returned to work after a few days of compassionate leave. It was a welcome distraction. I was back to being extremely busy, dealing with anything and everything that was thrown at me. If anyone at work asked me how I was or expressed sympathy, I acknowledged it and thanked them, always saying I was OK. There was no other answer. I was a man, you had to get on with it.

It wasn't necessarily evident straight away, but Mum was the glue that held the wider family together. In the years that have passed since her death, there have been numerous family fallouts. Some to this day remain unresolved. My brother blames my stepsister, wrongly in my opinion, for Mum's death. My stepfather feels that my sister should have done more to help Mum when she was ill, so on and so forth. She did not leave a will, hence my stepfather has made his own decisions about who is to benefit from the estate when he dies. That will not apparently include my brother. I have the greatest respect and love for my stepfather, and I don't necessarily agree with everything he has done, but Mum asked me to look after him and from a distance I continue to do that as best I can. I speak to him about once a week and whenever possible I visit him in Cornwall. I used to have a very good relationship with my brother and sister but as my stepfather advances in years, they appear to have become ever more resentful about the situation. I have not spoken to my brother for three years and for the last 12 months I have heard little from my sister. These sorts of petty squabbles would not have been tolerated by Mum. It would have been sorted out.

35. Teacher

I spent two more very happy years working in the CPU. I was supported for promotion and despite putting as much work as I could into the preparation, I failed to get through the assessment centres.

My tenure of four years was fast approaching. It was time once again to start thinking about my next posting. During this time, I volunteered for some uniformed Acting Inspector duties, swapping with a sergeant who wanted exposure to Child Protection. I remained on the qualified CID Detective Sergeant list and had been told I was earmarked to replace a soon-to-retire DS.

Out of the blue, I received a telephone call from a colleague who worked at the Force Training School. He wanted to know if I would be interested in joining a specialist team there. This was completely left field, but I had always harboured a desire to improve my confidence with public speaking. I still didn't enjoy standing up in front of people and I knew this would be a personal challenge. I spoke to the DI who was holding my place at the CID office. I had expected him to go ballistic and he did. In a small way, I suppose it was a backhanded compliment, to discover that he wanted me working for him. The truth was that nobody had any idea when any vacancies would be realised. Certainly, the incumbent was telling everyone he wasn't ready for retirement yet. I applied for the training position and was accepted on the condition that I had to pass the National Police Trainers course. This involved another lengthy, residential course at a place called Pannal Ash near Harrogate. It felt like I would be returning to my early roots as a soldier.

The course was renowned to be both difficult and mentally challenging. Some described it as having your brains transplanted, meddled with and replaced. I shrugged that off; surely it couldn't be that bad, I thought. However, I knew of some trainers who came back as very different people to the ones that left. That may sound a little sinister but for those susceptible to a bit of brainwashing and political correctness, this was where it all took place.

We arrived for our first day and sat around in the standard horseshoe formation, which I was now very familiar with. In our classroom, we watched a PowerPoint loop presentation for about ten minutes. There was very little chatter other than the exchange of polite formalities, as people tend to do when they don't know each other. Our trainers then entered, one a civilian and the other a sergeant. Instantly and from our initial stand-up introductions, I knew this was going to be a 'very' different course to the ones I had become accustomed to. Everything we did was pored over in almost forensic detail and debriefed not just by the trainers but by your peers. Questions like, "How did that feel?" and "How do you think that made 'x' feel, when you said that?" were all standard fare. This course was not going to be so much about knowledge, but more about emotional intelligence, getting your message across, having an awareness of people and being confident.

After that first day, I went back to my room totally exhausted. Four of us from the class were allocated bedrooms on the top floor of one of the accommodation blocks. It had an area with some soft furnishings where we gathered to debrief the day and find out more about each other. Each of my three new friends had CID backgrounds, were grounded and practical coppers. I knew we would look after each other during what was going to be a mentally tough few weeks. John, Mark, Bob and I became firm friends; we always supported each other when there was confrontation during lessons. The class was about 15-strong with some I never warmed to. Some were too strait-laced for my liking, had never dealt with an angry man, been in the thick of a fight or a serious investigation. My view was very much you had to have done the job before you could even think about training anyone how to do it.

We covered countless models of learning, including the use of exercises to help identify our own individual styles using something known as Honey and Mumford. It provides four categories, and one tends to be dominant. They are; Activist, Theorist, Pragmatist, or Reflector. It didn't really surprise me that I fell into the Reflector category. I was assessed as one who observes, gathers data and uses experiences to reach a conclusion. We also learnt about ego states and how rapidly you can move from being Parent, Adult or Child. You only had to think about an argument with someone to understand how it all fitted together. It was also useful in the classroom to gauge behaviour.

Alongside all of this was the need to prepare detailed lesson plans where you had to identify the type of delivery and activity for every part of the lesson. It became apparent to me that standing in front of a group of people to teach, involved much more than simply being on your feet.

At times conflict in the class would be deliberately, but subtly, introduced by the two trainers. You could liken it to a hand grenade at times. John, Mark, Bob and I were partial to a drink and we would all pile into town whenever we could to escape the centre. On one occasion, we had been out until the early hours and were the worst for wear when we arrived in class for the morning's activities. It was announced that we were to study race and diversity. Some of our group were singled out to wear turbans on their heads to make them look different. As it happened, the four of us ended up together and working in a separate room where we had to discuss the subject. Frankly, I thought it was childish and stupid. We didn't take it serious, eventually giggling and laughing.

One of the trainers came into our room to see how we were getting on. He was clearly not happy and questioned what we were doing. We finally got back on task and completed it. When everyone gathered in the classroom, the trainer who had been in to see us, said, "OK, everyone, before we debrief this exercise, I just want to pose a question to you all. Let's say that you are back at your respective training schools, you set an exercise for the group, but four people on the course are clearly drunk... what are you going to do?" There was a deathly silence. I knew who this was aimed at. He had a point, but I was more than a little bit annoyed because we were not drunk.

I remember looking at him and saying something like, "I think that is meant to be for us? Personally, I think it is a little unfair. Hands up we were not taking things as seriously as we should have been, but I found the whole thing a little ridiculous, if I'm honest." There followed a debate for over an hour about every subject under the sun. I was enjoying the course, but this sort of tedious nonsense just got me down.

That evening with the perpetual psychoanalysis eating away at me, I grabbed my suitcase and started to pack. Thankfully I came to my senses, got my gym gear on and went for a run. I didn't know it at the time, but becoming a trainer was one of the best moves I ever made in my police career. I passed the course just prior to Christmas of 1999, also gaining a City and Guilds certificate in adult teaching practice. I had some time off with the family and in the new year I joined the training school staff. I was excited to hear that I would be travelling to Miami to attend a specialist course designed to equip me to train the subjects I would be teaching.

I will always maintain I went to Harrogate on two separate occasions and each time came back a different person. Something happened during my time whilst training to be a trainer. I began to reflect even more, but mostly on my personal life and circumstances. I had nearly 19 years of service and 11 years left to progress beyond the rank of sergeant. It would be wrong to say I was dissatisfied with where I was, but I knew those 11 years would fly by. My children were getting older and they were becoming less reliant on me. I think I began to feel insignificant at home. I knew deep down that my wife and I had grown apart; our common interests were the children but beyond that we did very little together as a couple. We argued more and didn't agree about very much at all. I was, however, torn, as this woman had supported me through thick and thin. She was a fantastic mother to my children but in time I knew they would be off and doing their own thing. I parked my feelings, threw myself into work once again, concentrating my efforts on becoming a good trainer and learning new skills.

My trip to Miami didn't materialise. Unbeknown to me whilst away in Harrogate, the training school negotiated with the company in the USA that I would be instructed by in-house staff. There were three other guys in the department I was posted to, one of whom was hostile and unhelpful from day one. As it transpired, he and the guy who invited me to apply for the position were always squabbling over something or other. What I didn't know was that he had raised objections to me being brought in. It soon became clear that he was going to make my life difficult. Having qualified as a trainer at Harrogate was only part of the story. I had to be tutored and assessed for at least six months. I was lucky to have a good mentor; he was great at giving feedback and very supportive. He was required to sit in on my lessons and review my progress. It helped that he didn't understand the subject matter because it allowed him to focus more on my teaching skills.

However, the trainer who had objected to my appointment decided one day, without any notice, that he would assess me. Whilst this was out of the ordinary, he justified it by saying that he was best positioned to comment on the technical elements. He sat stony-faced throughout, copiously making notes; he was like a man possessed. It was a distraction to me and not the way my assessor worked. I could not help but think something was afoot.

With the teaching finished, the classroom emptied and he asked if he could give me some feedback. The term feedback was something I had become accustomed to. The process was a means of offering critique on your performance with suggestions for improvement. However, what followed was nothing less than a character assassination. It was not the sort of feedback I was used to – more criticism with not a single positive comment. It was obvious he was trying to stitch me up. Other than make a few very minor comments, I didn't challenge him at the time. I thanked him for his time but inside was raging. I asked for a copy of his notes which he reluctantly provided to me. There was not a scrap of positivity anywhere. As far as I was concerned, he had set out to come in and try and take me down a peg or two. I couldn't let this lie, so took it up with my assessor and the Head of Training.

Some days later, the pair of us sat down and cleared the air. It was obvious we were never going to be friends. The annoying thing was it had all to do with a feud between him and somebody else. Internally though, I had already decided that if he thought I was not cut out for the role, then I was going to prove him wrong. I worked harder to understand the ins and outs of the subject matter and became a much better trainer. I was more confident in the classroom as a result, gained respect from my peers and began to embrace being in front of a group of people talking, answering questions, and imparting knowledge. It is something that has never left me. I continue to train to this day. I enjoy it and the police service helped me find that niche. Things were going well, but my world was about to be plunged into complete turmoil.

36. Emma

Emma (not her real name) came to a training course I was leading. She was not a member of the police service but an analyst from private industry. The Force was into revenue generation at the time, so it was a way of earning money. We had met a month or two earlier when one of the trainers and I went to sell the course to the company she worked for. Emma was in her thirties, brunette, slim and attractive. My initial assessment of her was that she was demure and lacking in confidence. At her offices, she smiled sweetly at me and brought me a coffee. I didn't think too much of it at the time. As I left, I politely said to her, "Hope to see you on the course soon."

She arrived on the course and from the outset she gave me the impression that she didn't want to be there. On the first day, it was customary for each delegate to tell everyone a little bit about themselves as an introduction. When it came to her turn, she went bright red, spoke very quietly and quickly. I immediately felt for her, as I knew what this was like. Prior to getting into teaching, I would have done the same thing.

Later that day, each delegate had to complete a short research exercise which then involved them standing at the front of the classroom and explaining their findings. I was an observer for this part of the session and could see just how uncomfortable Emma was. My colleague had either not noticed this or didn't really care. When she stood in front of the class, her head was down, she mumbled and was incoherent. Rather than letting it go, my fellow trainer launched into a lengthy feedback session. This only raised Emma's anxiety and before we knew it, she ran out of the class in tears. I looked at my colleague accusingly. I felt that it could have been handled better and went to see if I could find her. One of the other female delegates left with me and we found Emma downstairs in tears. It was something she was not accustomed to and openly admitted to both of us that public speaking was a huge fear of hers. Everything was sorted out, we broke for afternoon coffee and continued.

At the close of the session, Emma came up to me and thanked me. Nothing more was said, but it was clear that I had made some sort of unintended connection with her. The course I was teaching lasted two weeks and I got to know my class quite well during that time. Whilst I don't think I spent too much time with Emma to the detriment of the other delegates, there was the odd conversation over lunch or coffee. I felt quite protective of her for some reason.

On day one of each residential course, we were required to explain what the city centre entailed. It hadn't really changed much, still having many of the same bars and clubs. On the last Thursday of the course, it was normal for class members to go out into Wakefield for a drink. It had become the norm that as their trainers, we also would join them. At some point during the night after consuming too much alcohol, I got into a conversation with Emma. The conversation led to a dance and the dance led to us being up a side alley. Like me, she was married. She went on to tell me how unhappy she was, that her husband was violent and she wanted to leave him. The pair of us walked back to the accommodation at the training school, where I kissed her goodnight and caught a taxi home.

There are times when you wake up in the morning after drinking too much with that realisation or 'Oh shit' moment and this morning was no exception. My wife made comment about the time I had got home, which was around 2am, but I brushed it off and made my way into work. Emma and another girl were in the classroom when I arrived. I said, "Good morning" and made small talk, trying not to mention the previous night's events. Everyone was rather the worse for wear and it seemed apparent to me that what had happened had not gone unnoticed by the rest of the class.

The course finished at lunchtime, everyone said their goodbyes and I thought that would be that. However, I walked over to the reception area to collect some mail and bumped straight into Emma who was heading for her car. There was a short conversation about keeping in touch, and we exchanged emails and mobile phone numbers. That was the blue touch-paper that started a full-blown affair. An affair that had huge implications for me, my children, my wife and the wider family. I had absolutely no idea what I was getting myself into.

I was now the proud owner of my very first mobile phone. I used it to speak to Emma daily, we emailed each other and sent text messages. At the time, each message cost around 15p hence I soon racked up a hefty bill which I tried to keep out of sight of my wife. There was only one computer in the office that had an internet connection, and I was often found on it sending messages to Emma. She was heading to Cornwall on holiday with her husband and told me how much she was dreading it. I recall coming to my senses about a week after the course, telephoning her and saying that I didn't think we should continue to see each other. Her reply was, "Well go back to your fucking family then!" It would be all too easy to blame Emma. I was also unhappy at home, so talked myself into continuing the relationship. I think I felt needed by her and was getting the attention that was lacking at home. That is not to say that I didn't feel incredibly guilty, because I did. I had been here before and it was an uncomfortable place to be in many ways.

One day we arranged to meet for lunch, close to where she worked in Leeds city centre. I parked up at the agreed meeting point and saw her running up towards the car, clearly distressed. I then saw a male chasing her. She leapt in and shouted, "Drive, drive!!" The male caught up to her as she jumped into the passenger seat, then he tried to open the door as I drove off. It was the only time I saw her husband, who she went on to tell me suspected she was having an affair and had threatened to kill her. The seriousness of the situation we were both in was obvious. My wife was also suspicious, so we were both coming under pressure to reach a decision as to what we were going to do.

By sheer coincidence, not by design, we both disclosed to our partners what had been going on during the same weekend. This reverberated through our respective homes, but the whirlwind was only just beginning. Emma told me that her husband was becoming violent towards her and as a result she now needed to leave the marital home. Between us, we decided to move in together and hurriedly got a rental property in South Leeds.

The most painful thing was having to tell my children that I was leaving. I wasn't prepared in any way, shape or form for the backlash. My daughter was in the process of moving in with her boyfriend and didn't seem overly concerned, or even surprised. My two boys reacted badly; my eldest, who was 17 years old, refused to talk to me for many months. My youngest son, who was 15, began truanting from school and went downhill rapidly from then on.

The house we rented was a terraced property; it was OK and only meant to be temporary. Initially things were good; it was new for both of us, but we had only spent small amounts of time with each other. Getting used to living together was something very different. Emma was very set in her ways, things had to be done in order and at set times. She was also obsessively tidy. I had always viewed myself as being a well organised and tidy person, but this was beyond the pale. Everything had a place, and everything had to be in that place. One of the first things she did was to buy me a completely new set of clothes. In her words, I needed tidying up. I didn't think too much of it at the time.

I also noticed a side to her that I had not been privy to before, which was that she could sink into a very dark mood and almost at the flick of a switch. The slightest little thing could do this. At first, I put this down to the stress of the situation we found ourselves in, with divorces being discussed and both sides speaking to respective solicitors. The financial burden did not help either. I had promised that I would continue to pay the mortgage for my former home because the last thing I wanted was for anyone to suffer, least of all my children. Money was tight.

Emma had not met my daughter before so I arranged for us to get together a few weeks later at a pub for something to eat. The meeting went as well as could be expected. My daughter was very friendly, but for some reason Emma took an almost instant dislike to her. On the drive home she launched into a tirade of abuse about her and that she was clearly spying for her mother. This, in my view, was completely unjustified. Nothing was further from the truth. I sensed that Emma was jealous and threatened by the fact that I had children. My kids were never a secret and I had made it plain how much they all meant to me. I was confused, I didn't expect things to change overnight, but this reaction was a strange one and completely disproportionate. Something was not right, but I could not put my finger on it.

If any of my children called me on the phone, Emma would become sullen and moody. She was demanding of my time and had little patience or understanding of what they were going through. Ever the peacemaker, I tried to keep everyone happy; however, it was a stressful time.

It was just before Christmas when I left home. Some months before, Emma booked a holiday for her and her husband to Eilat, Israel over the festive season. Before I knew it, she had removed her husband's name from the booking and replaced it with mine. The fact that I was going away on a seemingly expensive holiday with my 'floozy' did not go down well with my wife or children. I must admit feeling guilty, but nevertheless another part of me wanted an escape. I don't think I realised it at the time, but I was in a state of self-inflicted emotional turmoil.

On reflection many years later, some of Emma's comments were an indicator of trouble ahead. "She has had you for twenty years, you're mine now," was one that still sticks in my mind. I was blinded by love and lust; she was younger, attractive and had a good job. We had without doubt rushed headlong into the relationship without thinking it through. Don't get me wrong, the relationship with my wife had broken down years previously. It was inevitable as far as I was concerned that we were going to split up. I would have preferred that to have happened when the children were a little older, but we are not always responsible for our destinies.

I cannot remember how long it was before we argued, but I recall it being quite a nasty one. It started about my children and Emma made her feelings plain. There was an outpouring of insults about me, how useless I was, that I needed to grow a pair and leave my children to it with their mother. To me this was completely heartless and I felt an impulse to leave so I got into my car and drove off. I had no idea where I was going but heading to the former marital home was not an option. I returned a short time later to a very emotional Emma crying inconsolably and begging me not to leave her. Once again, I made excuses for her and put it down to the stress of the situation.

Things were fine for a while, but the slightest issue could cause an adverse reaction from her. What was also strange was how quickly she would bounce back and act as if nothing had happened. Always apologetic afterwards, she had me completely and utterly baffled. Emma's mother and father were estranged but refused to divorce. They lived in separate houses and could not abide the sight of each other. I got on reasonably well with them both. There was never any overt comment about what I did for a living, that I was older than Emma or that I had children. They didn't really seem to care about that, arguably I am not sure they cared for their daughter very much either. There seemed to be an emotional disconnect between the three of them.

We lived in rental property for several months and then purchased a house in another area of South Leeds. It was handy for us in terms of work and it was a modern property. Life was relatively stable until, of course, my children were mentioned or I arranged to meet them. Emma had for some time chosen not to accompany me to see them. Her view was that they didn't like her because she was the other woman and felt that any efforts to alter their view would be a waste of her time. It was difficult for everyone, but I felt torn as trying to manage the various sides to the relationship was like a minefield.

I introduced Emma to my dad and stepmother and that went OK. My sister, now living in Egypt, was less impressed. Emma kept her distance, so my sister formed the opinion that she was not to be trusted. I brushed that off because she had always been overly protective of me and not exactly an expert on relationships given her track record. After her husband died, she suffered several less than happy couplings with men. This had led her to Egypt to complete a diving course, where she had started a new life with a younger guy who after marrying her, left her for another woman. Eventually, she found love with a local man and that is where she remains to this day. As a result of the bad feeling amongst the parties, Emma became reluctant to have anything to do with my children and certain members of my family. This continued to be a source of friction between us. I struggled to understand why she couldn't make more effort, and in turn she thought I was not being supportive of her.

It is fair to say that these tensions began to cause problems for us quite early in our relationship. I became resentful of Emma because in my view, I had given up a lot so that we could be together. From her perspective, I think her expectations were that when I was not at work, I should be spending all my spare time with her. The mood swings were becoming ever more frequent and I repeatedly tried to have conversations with her about seeking medical advice. Our respective divorces were progressing through the courts; Emma's sailed through, it was unchallenged and a straight 50/50 split, the legal bill being minimal. Unfortunately for me, mine was more complicated.

Whilst only one of the children was still at school, my wife was making a claim of not being able to work enough hours and demanded a percentage of my pension, monthly maintenance, plus wanted me to pay the mortgage. Reading the demands was eye-watering and the legal fees began to mount up. I was no longer able to earn any overtime to try and supplement my income. I had already promised my wife that I would not stop paying the mortgage because I wanted the children to have a home.

Emma, however, would have been happy for her and the children to live in a council house. As far as she was concerned, my wife was common, and the children were no better. I knew that not to be true. Whenever finances or issues related to the divorce cropped up, there was always tension and it seemed to drag on forever.

37. On the move again

By contrast with my domestic situation, work was on the up. It seemed that my commitment to get to know as much as I could about the subject matter that I was teaching had not gone unnoticed. I was asked to take responsibility on behalf of the Force for the development of a national training course. I was informed that I would be one of two Force specialist trainers collaborating with three other forces.

West Yorkshire had a very good reputation for its training and trainers. It was a very well-respected Force and regularly participated in the delivery of international training. However, another force with a very good pedigree for intelligence-led policing was promoting itself as a global leader. Unbeknown to me, there was an awful lot of politics that had taken place in the background to turn this into a collaborative effort rather than a competition. It made sense for us to work together, but the sensitivities at chief officer level were getting in the way, with bickering about who was running the show. It was my first real exposure to the strategic side of policing. It was another huge challenge and I didn't readily recognise the significance, or how it would assist me in my own personal development.

Course material had to be rewritten and manuals overhauled. Despite there being two of us assigned to the project, I ended up doing 95% of the work. It seemed to be the case that my colleague always had something to do or a course to run. That said, it was a good learning exercise for me and allowed me to digest even more knowledge. Being involved with the project at a national level meant that I would be spending time away from home periodically in various parts of the country. I discussed what would be happening with Emma who seemed comfortable about it. It was infrequent but would then be a week at a time once the course was to be delivered by us for real.

As West Yorkshire Police already had about 75% of the material, we were going to be responsible for training the other trainers in their own force areas so that the three-week course could then be delivered independently in their respective training schools. The first course was scheduled to be delivered in the south of England, much to the disappointment of the West Yorkshire hierarchy. In a nutshell, the head of our training school had been outranked by a chief constable. So, in the middle of dealing with a divorce and navigating my way through a new relationship, I was now responsible for a significant project.

Whilst working on these sorts of tasks cannot in any way be compared to the rigours of operational policing, nevertheless it was hard work, stressful and tiring. In and amongst all of this, I was trying to rebuild a relationship with my children. I had foolishly thought that because they were teenagers, my leaving the marital home would be easier for them to deal with. How wrong I was. I remember the upheaval when my dad left home, but I was much younger. He had ensured that he was in touch with me and my siblings frequently, which had helped. All of us visited him because we wanted to, and it became part of our routine. My two sons were refusing to see me, and I became aware that my youngest was now repeatedly truanting from school. This resulted in more calls from my wife and caused even more tension with Emma who became increasingly unreasonable. In my view, she just did not comprehend that I had parental responsibilities which I was not about to forego. It is only in recent years that I have fully understood the pain this caused them. They are adults now, but even talking about me leaving home is painful to them.

I should make it clear that I now have the benefit of reflecting on my relationship with Emma with a very different set of eyes and for reasons that will become clearer later. At the time, my judgement was clouded. In the initial stages of our relationship, I rarely challenged her behaviour. It was in my nature to placate all parties and try to keep the peace. I was in love and wanted to avoid more tension and stress, so I muddled through as best I could. At work, I portrayed everything to be great. Deep down, my sense was that a lot of people were disappointed in me, including my children, my dad and some of my close friends. I had integrity and was a known professional, yet despite it being very common in the police, I was frowned upon by some for having left my wife and children. Appearances at the divorce courts did nothing to lessen the stress.

It felt that my whole life was under scrutiny by so many people and I got very little support at home. Emma was highly critical of pretty much anything I tried to do. In her mind, I had no responsibility to support my wife. "She can fend for herself and your kids are grown up," was the standard response. I began to feel a growing sense of bitterness and resentment about her attitude. I wanted to resolve matters; the legal bills were beginning to pile up and were putting a burden on our financial position. As part of the process, the courts required me to undergo mediation. This meant sitting in a room with a very angry wife and a mediator trying to agree on a compromise. Suffice to say it didn't work out as my wife's demands were excessive. It ended up back at the courts and dragged on for two years. Anyone who has been through a divorce will know that it is a highly intrusive process because your finances and personal circumstances are subject to intense scrutiny. Emma refused to disclose anything at all about her circumstances, which didn't help me one bit, for I was then the one seen by the courts as being obstructive.

Emma loved to travel, and she rekindled that love in me. For some reason she did not like Christmas, preferring to be overseas. In the time we were together, we travelled all over the world, including many countries in Europe, as well as Borneo, Hong Kong, Mauritius, Russia, The Maldives, Thailand, and North America, with a cruise thrown in for good measure. As soon as we arrived back home, she would be looking at where we could go next. I didn't object as we always shared the costs. I soon became known as a bit of a jet-setter amongst colleagues at work. It also didn't escape the attention of the courts when assessing maintenance. When away from home, it must be said that we had some good times together. When Emma was on form and happy, things were good, but her unpredictability and mood swings always had me on edge. I rarely felt as if I could relax and switch off. One wrong word or mention of the kids and it would set her off.

One afternoon, I was laying some flooring in the bedroom of our newly purchased property. It was laminate and something I had done previously. As far as I was concerned, things were progressing well. I had completed about half of the room when Emma put her head around the door. She took one look at it and said, "You've made a right mess of this!" I looked at her incredulously. I must admit I do not take criticism easily, even less so when I feel it is unwarranted. I asked her why she felt that way, at which point she began to point at gaps between the floor and skirting board. I explained that they were necessary and would be covered by architraves. Her response was something on the lines of, "You're useless. I should have got a real man in to do it."

My reply was less than courteous. "Fuck off and do it yourself then," I said. At this point, Emma took one look at me. Her face was red, she had borne her teeth and was staring at me. This was a look I was accustomed to in the police when dealing with confrontation. In a flash, she launched herself at me with her arms flailing. She had sharp nails which were being aimed at my face and I was trying desperately to avoid being scratched. I had never seen her this angry; she was calling me names and was like a woman possessed. I grabbed both of her arms and held them away from me, at which point she began to use her knees and feet to kick me.

I eventually manage to manoeuvre her into an adjoining bedroom, pin her down and hold her until she ran out of energy. We were both out of breath, red faced and probably in shock. This was like being at the scene of a domestic dispute, but being on the receiving end. I also recognised the precarious position I was in. The narrative with domestic violence is very much about men being the aggressors, but that is not always the case and certainly not what had happened. After what seemed like an eternity, things calmed down. I stood up and then bizarrely she said to me, "Are we having sex now?" To say I was bewildered by this behaviour was an understatement. I left the bedroom, went downstairs and stepped into the garden to get some fresh air. I knew that this was not the way I wanted to live.

This incident was minor in comparison with what would happen in the future though. There were so many incidents over the years that it would be impossible to remember them all but some will always stick in my mind.

One Saturday evening, we were both at home sharing a bottle of wine. As I recall, we both sat on separate sofas. I had a bottle of red wine on the floor next to me and accidentally knocked it over. Emma went ballistic, her response being completely disproportionate to what had just happened, and I told her so. An exchange of words followed as I attempted to clean it up. Arguing with anyone when in drink is not a great idea as I knew from experience. When Emma spat in my face and launched herself at me again, I retaliated and pushed her away. She landed on the sofa she had just sprung from and banged her head against the wall. In the manner I had come to recognise, her face flushed red and she shouted, "Bastard, you are going to pay for that!" The next thing I knew, she was on the phone, calling the police. I then heard her say that I had assaulted her which was nonsense. I knew full well what the outcome was likely to be if she continued to embellish what had happened and how long I had before the police arrived. To make matters worse, we were now living in an area I used to work and knew most of the people at the station. This was a calculated move to embarrass me as much as possible and put her in the driving seat of our relationship.

It was easier to leave, so despite having a few glasses of wine in me, I jumped in the car, went to the local supermarket, purchased some toiletries and checked into a hotel. As I lay there that night in the Premier Inn, I wondered what the hell I had got myself into. I switched my phone off to avoid the onslaught of texts demanding to know where I was.

I went back the following morning to find a very contrite Emma full of apologies, saying she didn't know what had come over her, that she loved me and was sorry. I received a call later that day from the local inspector who requested that I present myself at the police station to discuss the incident.

That afternoon, I found myself in the place I used to work at, being questioned about what had happened. It wasn't a formal interview, there were no injuries, not even a breach of the peace. However, I was a sergeant in a responsible position and this sort of thing was not to be tolerated. I took it on the chin, explained what had happened and after about 45 minutes I left hoping that no one else knew. I was kidding myself; I had worked in a Domestic Violence and Child Protection Unit for God's sake, this would have been all around the nick in no time.

My options were limited, but there was no way I was going back to my wife. My personal life was in tatters already, but still I pretended to myself everything was OK and for a while it was. The situation I found myself in was alien and nebulous. I did not know where to turn. I suspected that Emma had some deep-seated issues, which she refused to acknowledge. She was saying that I didn't understand her situation with my children, that I was stubborn and refused to listen to her.

I wouldn't say my domestic situation led me to fail the next inspector's assessment, but I don't think it helped. I had become very down, felt useless and frustrated, but I was also very aware that I had made my bed and now had to lie in it. By chance, I saw an advertisement in a policing magazine from a nearby force who were looking for inspectors. My sense was that this was a sign. If I was successful, it would put some distance between Emma and my family, would get me to the next rank and now that my reputation had been given a kicking, we could start afresh. With the training project completed, I was now seconded to a team who were reviewing criminal intelligence in the Force. I was given Acting Inspector status and it was a fantastic opportunity. It was providing me with exposure to strategic policing, at the same time as working alongside some rising stars.

My boss at the time was without doubt the best I have ever worked for and to this day we remain good friends. To apply to another police force involved getting permission. My boss knew what was happening in my personal life and having experienced something similar himself, he was supportive and empathetic. He expressed some reservations about me applying to another force as he thought I was running away from the problem. I did listen to him. I also discussed it with Emma and we mulled over the options for a short time. My feelings were that there was a chance that things could improve on several fronts.

I applied, attended an interview where I delivered a presentation, answered some questions, and then awaited the outcome. I wasn't overly hopeful but was blown away when the force concerned telephoned me within 24 hours and offered me the position of DI. I admit to having had reservations about my professional ability, but my overwhelming concern, however, was having the conversation with my children, as I would no longer be so close to them geographically.

Emma was not overly concerned; she knew that she would have to find another job but was confident that her company would help her to relocate. They were a huge employer in the UK and indicated they would easily find a position for her. It took me a while to reconcile myself to the move and I even went to see a senior officer, who by chance was from the same force I was considering moving to.

In a very relaxed meeting, he said to me, "Look, you have given this force numerous opportunities to promote you, and for whatever reason it hasn't happened. You will do well there, go for it." I left buoyed up, accepted the position and put the wheels in motion to move. I knew then that my full term of service would not be completed with my current force.

38. Pastures new

Shortly after receiving the offer of promotion, I managed to get my three children together for lunch to explain to them what I planned to do. It went down like a lead balloon. I think they felt it was a betrayal and that I was abandoning them still further. I promised that would not be the case, that they would be welcome to visit at any time and I would see them at least once a month. It was early December 2001; at work, I was well into the project and wanted to complete it before transferring, hence I negotiated a start date at my new force in February 2002. Before being seconded to the project and whilst at the training school, I made an offhand comment about others in the office getting overseas travel and when would it be my turn. It was said in jest, but the Inspector replied, "Your turn next time."

Some weeks after that, I was informed that I would be visiting the Islamic Republic of Iran to negotiate the delivery of training to their Border Force. Initially I had thought that this was a joke, which it wasn't. However, the events of 9/11 put paid to the trip because of the heightened risk. The prospect of the visit came up again whilst I was on the project. I was asked if I would still be prepared to go. It was intended to occur over the course of a weekend so didn't really impact on the work I was doing. Given world events post the attack on the World Trade Centre, Pentagon and others, I thought it prudent to raise the issue of undertaking a risk assessment with the officer in charge of the Training School. His response was, "If you are scared, I'll get someone else to go."

I had to bite my tongue to prevent a profanity or two coming out my mouth but calmly replied, "I didn't say I was scared. I just think it is wise given what has happened in the world since 9/11, that we know what we are getting into." He conceded and told me that Special Branch would be informed about our visit and provide the relevant advice.

A colleague and I subsequently travelled to Tehran for what proved to be an eventful trip. About 30 minutes before landing, I read an article in the small print of the in-flight magazine suggesting that if Iranian Customs noted in your passport that you had travelled to Israel, then you would be denied entry. Emma and I had been in Eilat, Israel some 12 months earlier and my passport bore the relevant stamps. Whilst this had not been flagged up during the visa approval process, it raised the question about me being turned away the minute we arrived. We decided during the flight that I would go through passport control first. As it happened, my passport did not come under any scrutiny at all. I was waved through, collected my baggage and we got into a waiting taxi.

I will always remember Tehran for the sheer volume of its traffic; it was manic. There was no lane discipline at all, car horns sounded continuously, and it was impossible to conclude journeys quickly. We arrived at the hotel, dropped our bags and went for something to eat, only to see a sheep having its throat cut on the pavement outside. The place was a cultural challenge; as white men, we were most definitely in the minority and attracted some strange glances. There was a deep mistrust of anyone who was obviously not a local.

During our stay, we met with senior representatives of the Border Force and talked through how we could help them with our training. They took us to lunch, treated us like royalty and later that day we returned to our hotel. When I got back to my room, I found a message instructing me to contact the British Embassy. We were to report there the next day. It didn't sound like an invitation, more of an instruction.

The next day was a Sunday. As commanded, we presented ourselves at the Embassy building. We were ushered into a small room and a very well-spoken gentleman arrived shortly afterwards. He introduced himself and produced a business card. It meant nothing to me at the time. I won't quote the details, but the card bore the name of a senior diplomat. Both myself and my colleague were asked a series of questions about why we were in Tehran, whom we had met and who had sanctioned the visit. This struck me as a little odd because I had been assured a full risk assessment had been undertaken. I remember thinking to myself that the process would have involved certain notifications being made. It was many years later when making my own enquiries, which confirmed that the gentleman interviewing us was a member of the security services and not the person named on the business card. What also became evident was that no risk assessment had ever been undertaken. Had it been the case, our visit would never have been authorised. It also came to light that we were at extreme risk simply being in the country, never mind walking around openly, visiting restaurants and sightseeing.

On return to the UK, I finished up on the project, the final outcomes and recommendations being very well received by senior members of the Force with certificates of merits awarded for all those that took part. I learnt an awful lot over those few months about the strategic side of policing and the politics. Those lessons certainly came in handy during the years ahead. I made all the necessary arrangements to leave the Force I had been with for over 20 years. I had many friends, great memories and a lot to be grateful for. I was sad to be leaving my spiritual home, but also excited about what my new role would hold.

I arranged a leaving do. Lots of my friends came along and my boss at the time gave a glowing speech about me, my achievements and wished that I wasn't leaving. Emma was there with me and astonishingly on the way home in the taxi, turned to me and in one of her snidey put-downs, said, "That wasn't you he was talking about, you're crap at what you do, otherwise you would have been promoted here." I did not understand what was going on, so once again we argued when we got home. I was getting the impression that unless she was the centre of attention, then no one else could be.

Our first accommodation in my new police area was a flat above a garden centre. Emma had fallen in love with a brand-new property, although it would not be completed for around six months. She told me that she preferred new things because no one else would have had the opportunity to make them dirty. Property was cheaper than in West Yorkshire and I had benefited from a small pay rise and relocation allowances so we were able to buy a detached house. Given the number of arguments we were having, that was a blessing in disguise. The flat was OK, it wasn't The Ritz by any means, but it would suffice for a few months. I think we were both excited that we were in a different place both physically and emotionally. I sensed that Emma was a little more relaxed. She had found out that her company were only able to offer her what she perceived as a menial job in the area. It was, in fairness, a drop in both status and salary for her. We both agreed that once things had settled, the priority would be to find something more in keeping with her skills.

My first day at the CID office as a new DI was a bewildering one. There had been an influx of transferees into the Force in recent months and I had not immersed myself into the reasons why. I was aware that there had been one or two incidents that had attracted significant criticism, so the drive was on for new blood. The Force was small and was described to me by a very straight-talking senior officer: "The gene pool here is small, we need change." I was overwhelmingly made welcome.

Interestingly, a few of the other inspectors I was introduced to were suspicious of me. One, who I knew from my CID course many years ago, completely ignored me at a meeting, even when I went up to shake his hand. I quickly formed the opinion that some of the home-grown officers saw transferees as a threat to their future advancement. This was amplified still further when the DI I was to work alongside at my new place of work, had three of his Detectives accompany me to headquarters rather than take me there himself. With their line of questioning, it was clear they had been briefed in advance to find out as much as they could about me and my motivations for transferring. As it happened, sometime later I was to become involved with a corruption enquiry involving one of the officers.

The overall boss of the divisional CID, a detective superintendent, was a bit of an enigma. Highly intelligent and not known for his people skills, he preferred to be removed from the day-to-day humdrum of the office. He sat me down very early on and told me what was expected in my role as his 'support' DI. There was a call out rota and I could expect to be called out at night and at weekends. The fact that I had not attended any form of Senior Investigating Officer (SIO) training seemed not to matter, something that I would return to regularly. Working on a serious crime enquiry as a sergeant or constable was a very different matter to managing one, as I was soon to find out. Rather than me working downstairs with my two inspector colleagues, he allocated me an office next to him. I began to wonder if I was to be his personal assistant.

My first week was a gentle introduction to the inner workings of the nick and the various personalities. I must have looked like a rabbit in the headlights. I had only been away from mainstream policing for a few years, but things move along at a pace. The town was extremely busy, yet whilst street robberies were frequent in Leeds and other cities in West Yorkshire, they were not accompanied with the same level of violence. Drugs, burglaries, car crime and assaults were through the roof. The bosses knew I had a background in the implementation of intelligence-led strategies and that was to form part of my new role.

At home, it soon became apparent that Emma was extremely frustrated in her new job. In her view, the role was below her; she became foul-tempered and the mood swings returned. One evening not long after we had moved in, she flew into a rage about something trivial. I recall having to go into one of the bedrooms and lean against the door as she pounded on it, screaming obscenities at me. When I thought she had calmed down and I let her into the room, she launched herself at me again. Thankfully we had no neighbours, because her screaming, kicking and lashing out with her nails was noisy and frightening. My response at the time was to hold her arms high and try to dodge her kicks. The only way I could effectively deal with her was to push her onto the bed and hold her until she tired herself out. It was emotionally and physically draining. I felt completely alone and isolated. I couldn't talk to anyone about the situation at home. I didn't know anyone well enough to do that. I was now in a management position, in a new place and I felt highly vulnerable, given what had happened previously. Frankly, I didn't know what to do. About this time, my daughter told me that she was expecting her first child. This seemed to up the ante, as for some reason Emma felt further threatened by this.

At work I was allocated my first suspicious death enquiry as SIO. It was one of many in a short period of time. I was mentored on the first by a lively and knowledgeable detective superintendent, who guided me through processes and procedures and was there to bounce ideas off. It was a welcome distraction from what was going on at home. The role was full-on pressure, attending meetings, briefing staff, staying on top of what officers were doing, allocating tasks and talking to the media. It is difficult to fully describe to anyone who has not worked on this type of enquiry what it entails. When someone dies, you have an enormous responsibility as SIO to make sure every line of enquiry is pursued, not least a duty to the victim's family to provide them with the answers they need. Any suggestion of failure and you are hauled over the coals during a subsequent trial or enquiry. The media will come after you and I have many examples of colleagues being made scapegoats. This was compounded by being a transferee. Some expected you to fail or be found wanting, but I couldn't let that happen.

My responsibilities at work were ramping up and so was the stress. I began to dread picking Emma up from work, or, god forbid, telling her that I was going to be late. I don't think she ever fully appreciated the role or what it involved. This pressure at work and the lack of support at home was, I believe, a contributory factor in what happened next.

One of the detective sergeants, whom I had become friendly with, gave me a tour of the area one day and pointed out an emergency medical centre near to where we were living. I have no idea why he did that, but I was later very grateful for the advice. One Saturday evening during a weekend off, Emma served me a curry for dinner. My reaction to it was like nothing I had ever experienced before. About 30 minutes after eating, I was doubled up in pain in the lounge. Her response was to tell me to go and lie down in the bedroom as I was disturbing her TV programmes and generally ruining the evening. The pain in my stomach did not abate and I could hardly walk. I recall telephoning the NHS helpline to seek their advice. They advised that I should make my way to the emergency medical facility; the same one pointed out to me earlier that week. I asked Emma if she would drive me there, but she refused point blank, telling me that it was nothing and that I could drive myself. Looking back, I should have called a taxi, but at the time I thought I was suffering some sort of reaction to spicy food. Clutching my stomach and hunched over, I got into my car and set off to make my way to the facility. I managed to make my way to the general area, but by now was sweating profusely and the pain in my stomach was excruciating. I stopped the car and telephoned the medical centre telling them I couldn't find them and didn't think I was in a fit state to drive. Thankfully, they sent someone out to locate me. I had to leave the car where it was on an industrial estate.

A doctor examined me a short time later and said he thought I had appendicitis; his opinion was that I would have to be admitted to hospital immediately. They arranged for me to be taken there. I recall being dropped off at the entrance, walking to reception and collapsing in a heap on the floor. A wheelchair was summoned, whereupon I was taken to a ward and given painkillers. The next thing I knew I was undergoing surgery – the diagnosis had been correct!

Emma arrived the next day in a foul mood, demanding to know why I had left the car in a remote location. Her complaint was that she was forced to retrieve the car and then come to a hospital on a Sunday when she was supposed to be having a day off. I was too tired and drugged up to argue with her. She stayed for a short while and left. I was discharged a couple of days later and much to the disappointment of the detective superintendent, I went onto a period of enforced sick leave. During my service, I had hardly ever taken enforced time off and hated being at home doing nothing. Emma's response to my predicament went from being attentive to seemingly not caring at all. There was no predicting the mood swings. I knew that I had got myself into this situation, so I pretended to myself that everything at home was OK and dug in for the long haul.

My recovery was interrupted some days later by the removal of some problematic wisdom teeth. I have never enjoyed visiting the dentist, and on this occasion I had to have several injections of painkillers. I will never forget the sounds of the deep-rooted teeth at the back of my mouth being ripped out. I was writhing in pain, hoping not to damage the stitches across the lower part of my stomach, held in place with what resembled industrial and transparent Sellotape. Eventually, I returned to work and began to get back into the swing of things. I was getting plenty of exposure to managing serious crime such was the nature of the place.

Domestically, things hadn't changed much. I still look back at my next decision and wonder what the hell I was thinking.

Emma repeatedly told me that the reason why she was so moody was because she felt that time was running out for her to have children. She, of course, knew that I had undergone a vasectomy many years earlier. However, there was a private hospital nearby and she had made her own enquiries about the costs and process of a reversal of the operation. During several tearful discussions, she explained that having a child of our own would make her feel more secure. "I want a boo boo," became one of her favourite sayings. After a consultation, I underwent the operation as an in-patient. My first ever stay in a private hospital. The operation meant I would be away from work for a few more days, attracting further comment from the boss who wasn't a family man.

On my return to the office, I had a slight disagreement with my fellow DI. I had noticed that on Wednesday lunchtime, the CID office was virtually empty. Making my own enquiries, it turned out that one of the DCs had arranged a five-a-side football match each Wednesday at a local sports centre. Everyone who wanted to play, including one or two of the sergeants, effectively abandoned their posts and went off to play sport. Those who had no interest, or didn't want to take part, were left back at the office to do all the work. When you hear your staff telling you how busy they are, but find time to disappear for several hours, it simply does not stack up. The public pay for a service, and as far as I was concerned it was a case of play football in your own time.

I was prepared for the standard excuse of "It's our lunch break"; a lunch break, however, equated to 45 minutes. There was no way on this earth you could get to the sports centre, change, play a game of five-a-side and get back in three quarters of an hour. However, given my role as support DI, the staff were not strictly speaking under my management. I went to speak to the DI, who ran the CID office, to ask him if he knew what was going on. To say it didn't go well was an understatement. I got the impression that he thought I had no right to make enquiries of what he considered to be his area of responsibility. Unbelievably, he saw no problem at all with what was happening. I made it plain that I wasn't happy. My sense was that he then conveyed what I had said to the Detective Sergeant who organised the football session. It set the tone for the rest of my time there. I didn't elevate it further. I could have done, but I have seen how these things play out and how you can easily get ostracised. It was a very different environment to what I was used to, very nepotistic at times and unpicking who was connected to whom and why, was difficult for a newcomer.

Six months after my arrival, our new house was finished and we moved in over the course of a weekend off. Emma immersed herself into making it a home. Around the same time, she got a different job which spoke more to her admin skills. It seemed she was much more settled. Very occasionally, she would accompany me to see the children. My first grandson had arrived, but this seemed to be yet another source of tension.

From a career perspective, things could not have been better for me. I received notification that I had received an award in relation to some training I had been involved with. I became immersed with a partnership project to tackle volume crime and felt I was drawing upon my experience with greater exposure to intelligence work. It wasn't long before someone latched onto this at headquarters. I received a call to say that I would be transferred to the Force Intelligence Bureau. I was over the moon! It was exactly the direction I wanted to take, allowing me to put my skills to good operational use. From that point onwards, and with the help and guidance of thoroughly competent detective superintendent, my career went from strength to strength as I became involved in two significant and linked projects. One was about implementing the National Intelligence Model, the other involving an innovative IT system, set to revolutionise all areas of policing in the Force. There was a lot of work to do, much of it like the task I had completed previously. It involved training staff, introducing new methods of working and reviewing existing ones. I was in my element, because I knew that what I was doing was going to bring about positive change.

39. Strategic policing

With over 20 years policing under my belt, I was now firmly embedded into some heavy-duty projects. I was reporting to senior officers on the command team and operating well above the level of DI.

Some of my cases at divisional CID had now reached the courts and achieved positive results. One notable memory was being sat in the Crown Court whilst a Judge summed up a case. The offender had been found guilty of manslaughter after killing his partner, a disabled woman. Three of us sat in the courtroom: my SIO mentor, the Detective Sergeant who was my deputy on the case, and me. The Judge was very stern, it was his court, and he was known to come down hard on anyone who disrespected the seriousness of the proceedings. Everyone sat in complete silence as he spoke about his views of the case and gave his verdict and opinion about the offender. What happened next broke his flow completely.

A mobile phone began to ring, which was definitely in our vicinity. I always found it easier to switch my device off; at the time it was not quite so simple to put into silent mode as it is now because it involved clicking several buttons. All three of us patted our pockets frantically searching for our phones just in case it was one of ours. Around us, everyone was doing the same. It was well known by all that you absolutely did not piss this Judge off. We then realised it was the DS's phone.

He was desperately trying to silence it, but it continued to ring loudly. The Judge, realising what had happened, boomed out, "Court usher, seize that phone!" The Sergeant sheepishly handed over his device and the Judge looked at him sternly and said, "I will not tolerate phones in my court. Officer, you will be reporting to my chambers later today."

After the initial shock, my mentor and I were now finding it difficult to contain ourselves. Our shoulders were moving up and down and we were both trying not to laugh out loud. We were also painfully aware that if the Judge saw us like this, we would also be in huge trouble. Once outside the courtroom, we all fell about in fits of laughter and poked fun at the DS who knew what was in store for him. The Judge made him wait all day for his mobile phone, and true to his word, made him attend in his chambers to provide a grovelling apology.

There were still occasions even when you achieved rank, that you could have a belly laugh. It was never quite the same as being a carefree constable; as managers, you are expected to set an example. Nonetheless, maintaining a sense of humour was vital for me. It kept me grounded and in touch with my humanity. I never wanted to take myself too seriously or come across as being unapproachable, which was at times a balancing act.

Work was going well. I quickly gained a reputation as 'can do', becoming part of several working groups as well as chairing meetings, something I had no previous experience of. I had been with the Force about 12 months when I was summoned to see the Head of IT, an affable man whom I instantly got on with. He asked me if I would be interested in going to North America in the New Year, as part of a fact-finding mission. He was intent on introducing an all-singing, all-dancing IT system to bring about greater efficiencies across all areas of business. It was a huge undertaking. I became one of a group of six subject matter experts, my contribution being the intelligence portfolio.

We first flew to Chicago, spending time visiting a huge Communications Centre that utilised the system. Staying in a plush hotel close to Lake Erie in the middle of the American winter was something else. It was a world apart from what I had been accustomed to in any of my previous roles. On the way to Ontario in Canada, we were able to visit a frozen Niagara Falls – it really was that cold. Our next call was to the headquarters of the Ontario Provincial Police Department to understand how they ran crime investigation using the system. It was a thoroughly enjoyable experience providing an insight into the strategic side of policing, budgets, change management and working with other agencies. These difference facets of management became very useful skills to draw upon in later years.

Returning home, I began to bring the final part of the dissertation for my degree to a conclusion. This was something else which had been a drain on my time and energy for several years. At an operational level, I became Deputy Authorising Officer for covert policing, was given responsibility for the Witness Protection Unit, and had oversight for the drugs property store. The work pressure was relentless, very different from the cut and thrust of street policing, but still intense.

When it became apparent that the vasectomy reversal had not worked and the novelty of the new house wore off, Emma's mood swings came to the fore once again. I suggested to her that what was happening could be hormonal. Eventually she agreed to go to see our GP, a lovely female doctor who invested a lot of time and effort with her and provided a clinical diagnosis. It would be unfair to disclose that here but it involved the prescription of medication. It all made sense though; the intensity of the mood swings, emotional highs and lows, plus suicidal thoughts. Emma had said to me many times that she 'didn't want to be here'. Now that we both understood things a little better and she started a course of medication, there was an instant lull in the moods and arguments. We both decided that the next step would be to get married. This seemed to give her a purpose in terms of organising the day and the inevitable exotic honeymoon that would follow. Some months later, Emma took the view that she was completely cured, refusing to take the tablets anymore, claiming that the medication caused skin problems. Despite my misgivings, she could not be swayed.

It wasn't long before we were back where we started. The violent outbursts began to escalate again. I had previously always sought not to fight back, often grabbing hold of her arms and retreating. There was a day when during an argument, she spat full on in my face. Spitting was something I could not stand since being in the police. It often happened at football matches and public disorder. There comes a time when attack is the only form of defence and I pushed her away. Something kicked in, the red mist took over, I lost it and fought back.

It turned into a horrible physical fight, something I am ashamed to admit. I have no excuses, but everyone has a breaking point. I had been forced into a corner and was doing my level best to restrain her. I begged her to stop but it continued until we were both physically exhausted.

The violence during these incidents was now beginning to escalate. It would be wrong to say it was all the time. We would go for weeks without any issues at all. The wrong time accompanied by an aggravating set of circumstances would be enough to set things in motion. One Saturday, for example, I was talking to my son on the telephone in the rear garden of the house. It was often easier to take the calls from my children outside. It avoided the sneers and silly remarks from Emma, which would be overheard by the children. Comments like, "How much fucking longer are you going to be?", "Time for them to grow up," etc., etc. On this day, I looked up to an upstairs window of the house to see Emma leaning out and waving a watch of mine from side to side. It was something that she had recently purchased for me and was relatively expensive. Without any warning, she threw it with force out of the window and onto the railway line at the rear of our property; seemingly I had been on the phone for far too long. These sorts of outbursts were now the norm, in my view designed purely to get attention. I lost count of the many household items that were destroyed in her fits of rage. The inevitable argument and fighting followed. There were no winners when it happened; we both ended up sporting bruises and injuries. I had clothes ripped from my back on numerous occasions.

One Monday morning, I recall going into work with a long scratch mark down my neck. Birthday presents from my children went missing, presumably discarded. One Christmas Emma ripped up a card from my eldest son because her name did not appear in it. I simply could not understand why anyone would be so petty, or heartless. It made me angry.

You may read this and be thinking, 'What did either of you do about it? Why didn't you leave her? Why didn't she leave you? Why didn't you get help?' Well, medical treatment as far as she was concerned, was no longer an option. We were still relatively new to the area; we didn't know any people well enough, and our friends and family were nearly 100 miles away. There was no support network. As a male police inspector in a very macho world, it was unwise for me to do anything that may compromise my job. Emma had also said to me on many occasions that if I ever left her, she would ruin me. There were huge reputational ramifications. Work for me was my escape. It was always stressful, but it kept me occupied. I had grown so accustomed to the pressure from work that I needed it to sustain me.

I think we both wanted our situation to be better. There were occasions when things were very good; we had some fabulous times and wonderful holidays. It seemed to be impossible for Emma to cope with the inevitable downsides of life though, always preferring to gaze through rose-tinted spectacles bemoaning what should be. The strange thing was that when we were apart, we would be in touch regularly with loving phone calls, text messages and emails. Our home was always meticulously tidy and clean, and my clothes continued to be chosen and organised by Emma. From the outside, anyone looking in probably thought we were living a perfect life. The reverse was true; it was a toxic and abusive relationship but both of us allowed it to continue, even taking it to the point of marriage and continuing the lie. Now I have the benefit of examining those times with a different set of eyes. The optics were very much around a vicious cycle of argument, apologise, make up and repeat. It seemed never-ending and the frustration for me was just how unpredictable it was.

On the day before our wedding, Emma announced that she didn't think we should get married! By now friends and family were either at the hotel where the ceremony was to be held or were on their way. I had learnt that what seemed to mean much more to her was the organisation, planning and execution of 'something'. That would include holidays, events, city breaks, etc., which were organised like a military operation. When it came to the day, if something wasn't perfect, then all hell could break loose. The multitude of reasons for cancelling something would come from nowhere. The mere act of choosing a restaurant when we were away caused equal levels of angst and uncertainty. It was the case that Emma liked to get her own way all the time. I never quite understood whether this was just another type of controlling behaviour or true anxiety.

The night before the wedding, having received lots of attention from her mother and sister, Emma relented and decided she now wanted the big day to go ahead. My two sons had already declined the invitation to attend, but my daughter wanted to come along and celebrate with us. The wedding ceremony went off without a hitch. For some reason, I have minimal memory of it. What does stick in my mind is what happened to my daughter.

The weather was such that all photographs had to be taken inside the hotel. As a result, it involved switching between certain rooms for different shots. I was being frantically ushered from one location to another as Emma went through her list of planned photos. It wasn't until much later in the day that I spoke to my daughter. She was visibly upset and questioning why she had not been included in any of the photographs. I just hadn't noticed the omission, but it seemed apparent to me that this was not an oversight. Emma had ensured that my daughter was not asked to appear in any of the photo opportunities, deliberately erasing her from what should have been a memorable 'family' occasion. I did not know what to say to her and did my best to assure her it was an oversight. Sometime later in one of our many arguments, Emma proudly admitted she did it on purpose. I know my daughter remains justifiably troubled and hurt by the incident.

Our honeymoon involved a trip to Borneo where we nearly drowned in a boating incident. My sister had trained me some years previously as a scuba diver. Whenever we went away, I tried to get some time on my own for a dive or two. Emma didn't dive, although would sometimes come out on the boat.

On this occasion, we booked a private excursion to an island close to the hotel complex. A local guy, Harry, said he would pilot the boat and organise a private picnic with a couple of dives and some snorkelling thrown in. It was a beautiful day; the sun was shining and everything was going well. Emma sunbathed whilst Harry and I dived. During lunch, the skies began to darken and very quickly. We then began to hear rumbles of thunder in the distance accompanied by crackles of lightning. Harry told us he thought it best that we made our way back. Within minutes of setting off, we were in the throes of a full-blown tropical storm. The sea quickly went from resembling a millpond to something comparable to scenes out of a disaster movie. Sea water was coming over the boat and into our eyes, blinding us temporarily, so much so that the three of us had to don the masks we had been used for diving. The boat was now pitching deeply into the water, rising high and crashing back down.

I had started first by laughing, but when Harry told us to put on life jackets and the sky went black as night, it was no longer funny. We were at the rear of the boat and Harry was now on a raised platform steering the vessel and trying to navigate us safely back to the mainland. The next thing I knew, the tanks of air we had used for the dive were being propelled like missiles in our direction from the front of the boat. These things were heavy enough when strapped on your back. Had they made contact with us, it would have resulted in serious injury. I pushed Emma out of the way and caught them in full flow, doing my best to keep my balance and stop them rolling about further. We were now being pelted with heavy rain. In just our swimming costumes, we began to shiver with the cold. None of this was helped by the constant thunder and lightning.

Several times the boat listed in a way that nearly threw us out. Harry kept yelling, "Hold tight, hold tight!" I was certain we were going overboard but concentrated on trying to reassure Emma, now in floods of tears, that we would be OK.

After what seemed like an eternity, we made it back to dry land. I helped Harry moor the boat in an inland stream and we wandered back to our room in complete shock. Part of me thought it was Mum sending me a rebuke from the heavens for getting married. Of course, I got the blame for taking us out on a day like that and was never allowed to live it down.

40. The green-eyed monster

Once married I somewhat naively expected Emma to feel more secure about us. Nothing could have been further from the truth. Going anywhere together became increasingly stressful. I recall bumping into a female analyst from work in a local department store one Sunday afternoon. I just politely said hello to her. Emma's response was, "So who is ginger minge?" Sometimes this sort of thing would be said in earshot of the person concerned and was a source of much embarrassment. I was repeatedly accused of eyeing up other women, drooling over females on the television or leering at girls who were out running. It was constant, far removed from the truth and began to wear me down.

The opposite sex were invariably a causation factor for our arguments and often with bizarre connotations. I have always enjoyed all genres of music, country being one of my favourites. For example, I enjoy the music of Shania Twain. One evening, even Shania managed to cause a row. It went something like this. "So if Shania Twain turned up outside our door, would you have sex with her?" The question was obtuse and so ridiculous that I burst out laughing. However, when I looked at Emma's face, I knew she didn't think my reaction was funny. It resulted in a furious outburst. Her argument always seemed to be premised on the fact that because we had an affair, I would be prepared to have another one. It was complete nonsense.

Seemingly her part in our relationship had no bearing on anything. It was impossible to get past this irrational thinking and I became increasingly frustrated with it. Believe it or not, within three weeks of getting married we had booked an appointment with the marriage counselling agency Relate. However, because the counsellor was male, Emma decided that it wouldn't work, withdrawing from the programme. We were back to square one; in all honesty, we never moved on from it. I don't think I acknowledged it at the time, men tend not to, but I feared Emma and what she was capable of. She had an inherent ability to go from being charming, to becoming an absolute monster and in record speed. I had tried to placate and calm her previously, but it never worked. If anything, it made things worse.

One weekend, another argument started over something trivial. On this occasion she was screaming at me about how intolerable I was, for reasons I cannot even recall. My response was to walk away, choosing not to rise to the abuse in the hope that it would defuse the situation. Before I knew what was happening, Emma ran into the kitchen and grabbed a carving knife. She turned towards me, her face red and eyes bulging. I flashed back momentarily to that incident in Leeds. It was different then; the knife was never waved at me like this. I was not prepared to try and restrain her with a knife in her hand. I quickly closed the kitchen door, leaving her on the other side, and held onto the handle for dear life. This was frightening; all I could hear was her on the other side saying, "Let me out, open this fucking door!" I fully expected the knife to come through the flimsy interior door, the type that you find in newer houses.

You tend to hugely overestimate time when this type of thing happens. But it seemed to go on forever. I recall asking her to move away from the door and put the knife down. Eventually she told me that she had. I wasn't convinced. I asked her to step away from the door and it went very quiet.

After a time, I gingerly opened the door to see her standing against a worktop in the opposite corner of the kitchen. Her face was red, she was looking down and breathing hard. I still have the image burned into my memory; she looked like a woman possessed.

In a pose of conciliation, I put my hands out, palms facing towards her and said something like, "Look, put the knife down, this is silly, please put the knife down." Emma looked at me, muttered something incomprehensible under her breath, and without warning plunged the knife into her leg, screaming out loud in pain. Thankfully, the blade then fell to the floor. I ran over, kicked it out of the way and looked at the wound. Her tracksuit bottoms had prevented the knife doing more damage, but it had penetrated the skin. After cleaning the wound and bandaging up her leg, I told her that we had to go to the hospital for it to be checked. However, she completely refused to go anywhere near the hospital stating that she would be sectioned. I went to call an ambulance and she pulled the phone off me. I knew that to continue in this manner would only escalate an already tense situation. Eventually I managed to persuade her to lie down and rest. I took a decision to call the NHS helpline for advice and relate what had happened along with her medical history. To my knowledge, there was no further referral. Some years later, for reasons that will become apparent, I was relieved to have made that call. The wound healed, subsequently developing into a small but noticeable scar, a permanent reminder of the incident. In the back of my mind, I was now really on edge and alert to what may happen next.

I was in a no-win situation and did not know where to turn. Medical advice was being ignored, and marriage counselling was flatly refused. I definitely did not want to speak to anyone at work about what had happened. Despite what they say about 'confidentiality', someone somewhere always says something and before you know it, you are the latest gossip. I had seen on many occasions where police officers had been driven out of the job by gossips and rumour. Two women from my previous force had committed suicide after details of their personal lives were made public. My way of dealing with all of this was to put even more of a wall between work and my home life.

I can only recall one work-related function when Emma accompanied me. I preferred not to take her to any social occasions because I knew it would be tense, particularly if I spoke to another woman. On the one occasion I did take her to a formal senior officer's dinner, she was rude to two female colleagues, bad mouthed me to an inspector and locked me out of the hotel bedroom.

It was embarrassing and I found it impossible to relax. I would be accused of flirting, having affairs, fancying other women; the list went on. Being in the company of anyone other than the two of us almost always resulted in a drama. Her explanation was chiefly around the dissatisfaction of not having a baby. The fact that I was unable to have children continued to trouble Emma. Given what had been happening, bringing a child into the world was not a great idea as far as I was concerned. In all honesty, I didn't want any more children. I had three already and now more than ever I really didn't want to start another family. The pressure to try 'something else' was relentless.

Despite everything, I agreed to return to the doctors to find out what could be done. This was the madness of the situation we were in. It would go from all out war and fighting, a lull in hostilities, to being very loving and wanting to make up. I now believe that Emma thought that by becoming parents, it would resolve everything. That if she had a child, then she would no longer be jealous of my children. Perhaps she thought I would be so devoted to our baby that I would never consider leaving her. As for me, I just wanted a peaceful life, free of the emotional turmoil.

The options were eventually set out after referral to a private fertility clinic. It was explained to us that there was a strong likelihood that I was still providing fertile sperm. It was being produced in my testicles, but the tube that carried them to the point of delivery had been 'snipped' during the vasectomy many years ago. There was a procedure available that involved inserting a needle into me and extracting what was required. It sounded painful. Emma also had to undergo IVF treatment, involving injections and taking certain drugs. There was a catch though. It was going to cost several thousand pounds. That was several thousand pounds that we didn't have. The divorce, the wedding, the honeymoon and the new house had all taken their toll on what savings we had between us. We both agreed that taking out a loan was not an option because we were already stretched. I thought on that basis alone, we had put it to bed once and for all.

How wrong I was. It kept on coming up, always being used as an excuse for the mood swings and rows we had.

41. International policing

Work continued to be busy as ever. I was becoming increasingly immersed in both operational intelligence and investigations. Overseeing aspects of covert policing and regularly deputising was good experience and preparation for further advancement. But I was always seeking out other opportunities. Given my military background, I have always had a passing interest in conflict and what was taking place in war zones across the world. In March 2003, I recall watching the TV and witnessing the damage inflicted on Baghdad during bombing raids. The iconic crossed swords of the Victory Arch and the Presidential Palace stuck in my mind. Never in a million years did I think I would see them at first-hand.

Whilst browsing through a police magazine at home one weekend, I saw a tiny advert. There was a need for a police advisor skilled in intelligence and project management to be seconded to the Foreign and Commonwealth Office (FCO) for deployment to Iraq. The role profile suited me down to the ground.

I called the number the following Monday and gathered further information. I was told they needed someone in the country as soon as possible to assist the newly formed government and the police. The task was intended to contribute to the overall objective of nation building, and this specific requirement was for specialist assistance in restructuring criminal intelligence functions. The role would also entail interfacing with multinational military forces. It was made plain it was dangerous. It involved being transported around the country in heavily armoured vehicles, always carrying a firearm and wearing protective equipment. I was attracted to it for a whole host of reasons; it was different, exciting, a rare career development opportunity, but it also attracted tax-free financial remuneration. The successful applicant would receive a temporary promotion to Chief Inspector. Above all, it was a chance to make a difference and revisit my soldiering roots.

Perhaps it wasn't my primary motivation, maybe I wasn't even completely conscious of it, but I could also get away from Emma for a while. I would be overseas six weeks at a time with two weeks at home. It was a means of escaping the tension, the rows and the continual chipping away of my self-esteem that I had grown accustomed to. I sold the idea to her based on it being a means of providing the cash required to try a round of IVF. I added for good measure that we would go away somewhere nice each time I arrived home. Ultimately my plan rested on whether I could get my application approved by the Force Command Team.

My previous boss from West Yorkshire had now also transferred into the Force on promotion. He had always been supportive of me throughout my career. I submitted my application, and it ultimately landed on his desk. Shortly after, he saw me and said, "Don't be so stupid, you'll get yourself killed." However, it was more expletive than that as I recall.

Not to be put off, I arranged to see him in his office, talked him through my reasoning and begged him to reconsider. After about 30 minutes of discussions, he reluctantly supported my application. I was subsequently invited to the FCO in London for an interview where I was successful. Things moved at a pace from then on. I attended a five-day firearms course in Warwickshire where I was the only delegate. I passed the course in three days and spent the rest of the time firing an assortment of weapons and watching police firearms teams performing specialist tactics.

The hostile environment training in Wales came next. This involved several days of understanding the political dynamics in the Middle East, first aid training, convoy drills and exercises. It was all exciting stuff; some of the attendees were diplomats and some were press corps. I was the only police officer; it made a nice change interfacing with professionals from different backgrounds.

I wouldn't say Emma wasn't worried about what might happen when I was away, but she seemed reasonably content and I never really questioned that. She still refused to drive anywhere so my biggest concern was how she would manage the weekly shop. That was soon resolved when we discovered that online shopping and deliveries had just been launched in the area. I visited my children and explained where I was going. My eldest son was the one who expressed the most alarm. I undertook to be in touch with them by email as much as I possibly could and assured them that I would be well away from any danger. The truth was that I had no idea about the latter. The news was awash with attacks on the military and civilian population all over Iraq. Despite that, I was excited to get there. The spirit of adventure washed through me once again, something that had been absent in my life for several years. I was venturing into completely uncharted territory.

In the autumn of 2004, I headed to RAF Brize Norton in a hire car, complete with all manner of equipment: hard hat (blue), body armour (blue), first aid kit, desert boots, blue T-shirts with the Union Jack on the arm, firearms belt, holster and, oddly, a Monadnock police baton. The hire car had been dropped off at my house by a local company used by the Force. There were no instructions about how they were getting their vehicle back. On the way, I called them to advise where it would be after I departed. It seemed that no one had told them it was a one-way journey with the vehicle due to be left in a car park at an RAF base in Oxfordshire. To say they weren't happy was an understatement. It wasn't my problem though and it wasn't going to stop me getting on that plane.

I wasn't far away from Brize Norton. It was early morning, the roads were quiet, the sun was shining and let's just say I was making good time. With the radio at full blast, I was eating up the tarmac. I then spotted what looked like a police motorcyclist in my rear-view mirror. I slowed down without stamping hard on the brakes; I didn't want it to look too obvious that I knew I was speeding. The biker dropping right behind me. Great, I thought, now I am going to have to stick to the speed limit. It took me a minute or two to notice that the motorcycle was not sporting the standard police livery. It looked like a Military Police machine. It took me a little longer to work out what was happening. My brother had joined the RAF Police some years earlier. We were close at the time, he knew where I was going and wanted to wish me well. He had somehow been able to find out my route. He followed me all the way into RAF Brize Norton to see me off! I jumped out of the car at the base, and we laughed, joked, hugged and said our farewells. It was a loving and touching gesture and one I have never forgotten.

Arriving at check-in again reminded me of my time in the military. To an extent, it mirrored what you would find at a normal airport, but rank and position determined how you were going to board and where you sat.

The flight passed without incident, and the next thing I remember was landing in the middle of nowhere. The location was full of large tents and from the surrounding terrain and climate, it was obvious we were in the desert. It was actually an RAF base in Oman, where we remained for a couple of hours before boarding a C-130 Hercules. Looking around, most of the passengers were military but there were also some strange-looking characters sporting copious amounts of facial hair, some very posh chaps and a few females. As I was soon to discover, Iraq was awash with all manner of individuals, contractors, close protection operatives, various government agencies and embedded journalists. They were all part of the cargo.

Our next touchdown was in the early hours of the morning in a nondescript military airfield. Everyone was again ushered out of the aircraft. The building we were escorted to had clearly been taken over in the beginnings of the war. There were smashed windows, a makeshift check-in and everywhere was covered in a layer of desert dust that I would soon become very accustomed to. It was hot, and I was tired, sweaty and had absolutely no idea what was to happen next. No information about when and where we were heading for next was shared. We were given bottled water, told to get our heads down and wait for another order to move. I found a camp bed, laid on it and tried to get some sleep.

Several hours passed by. Early dawn came and a buzz of activity suggested we would shortly board a flight bound for BIAP (Baghdad International Airport). As I clambered onto the aircraft, it was immediately obvious that it was going to be different. We had to wear our hard helmets and body armour and were briefed that the landing into BIAP would be tactical. I had already been warned about this. It was referred to as a 'corkscrew', used by military pilots to combat against the prospect of surface-to-air missiles.

The flight was short and uneventful; the spiralling nature of the C-130 Hercules caused my stomach to churn but not quite to the point of vomiting. Safely on the ground, the rear ramp of the plane was slowly lowered. The heat rushed in; it was like opening an oven door. I started to sweat straight away. "Disembark!" came the command. We all strolled off onto the tarmac of a former civilian airport that had now been completely taken over by the military. Sandbags, blocks of HESCO, military vehicles bristling with weaponry and radio aerials, left you in no doubt as to where you were. This was deadly serious; I distinctly remember thinking to myself, "What have I done?"

After collecting our baggage, we were all ushered to an open but enclosed area. It wasn't long before I was the only one stood there. I was hearing vehicles driving off into the distance and thought, "Just my luck, no one is here, I've been forgotten about." At that point, a bloke's head popped up from the opposite side of a row of HESCO blocks. In a broad Yorkshire accent, he confirmed my identity and came round to help me with my bags. He was one of the many highly professional members of the close protection teams assigned to ensure the safety of those attached to the British Embassy in Baghdad. It transpired that he was from South Yorkshire and we immediately hit it off.

A convoy of three armoured vehicles with a team of about six men had been assigned to ensure my safe passage. Outside, the landscape was bleak. I was informed we were about to enter 'Route Irish', a stretch of about seven miles into the 'Green

Zone'. At the time, this was dubbed the most dangerous road in the world, due to the proliferation of attacks on vehicles. Anything identified as military or forming part of a convoy of armoured civilian vehicles like the one I was now sat in was a high value target for insurgents. Driving on that road was a game of roulette.

I remember asking my escort, "Is it as bad as it is made out to be?" Right at that moment, we pulled up at the first of many American military checkpoints. I'll never forget his response.

"Mate, first and foremost you need to be careful with these guys. They shoot first, ask questions later and they run the show." He was, of course, referring to the US soldiers, and what he said proved to be prophetic.

42. Welcome to Baghdad

My accommodation was located on the ground floor of a single-storey car park within the Green Zone. The concrete car park roof provided the necessary cover from the frequent rocket and mortar attacks.

It was mid-morning; most people were already at work and the place was eerily quiet. There was a female in attendance, dressed in civilian clothes, but a member of the Royal Air Force attached to British Embassy staff. Her responsibilities were for resident welfare and day-to-day running of the place. She gave me a quick tour of what was going to be my home for the next six weeks. The entire floor of the car park was full of white metal shipping containers, several mobile shower blocks and toilets – the type you get at festivals and similar events. I couldn't help but notice a stock of Durex on open display in the toilets, which initially struck me as out of place. I was subsequently shown to my container and got my head down for a few hours. Sleeping in a metal box with no windows was going to be a very strange experience.

Later that day, I met the guy who I was taking over from. I received my handover briefing, and later that evening I was introduced to all the team over a few beers. The bulk of the policing contingent consisted of officers from the Ministry of Defence (MOD) Police and Police Service of Northern Ireland (PSNI), the latter because of their counterterrorism experiences. In the evening, most residents gathered outside around picnic tables to keep cool but situated close enough to the concrete canopy just in case. There was a makeshift bar and little else to do but sit, chat and drink. It was a mixture of people of all ages and backgrounds, including the Foreign Office, DFID (Department for International Development), a representative of the Czech government and some contractors. It was obvious that a lot of money was being ploughed into this operation.

I needed to make a call home to Emma to let her know that I had arrived safe and well. I had been allocated a local mobile phone. The network was controlled at the time by American Forces and was pretty good. However, to get a good signal you had to go onto the top of the car park where there was no cover. At night it gave you a fantastic view of downtown Baghdad. The Green Zone was a heavily fortified area, about four square miles in all. From the roof at night, you could see and hear gunfire, explosions, and occasionally incoming missiles. On one occasion, I had to leave the rooftop quickly as we came under attack. I discovered that flip flops, the standard footwear in the accommodation, did not make for good running shoes. I called Emma every day whilst I was there and kept in touch via email. I was glad of the break though. I was happier coping with the stress of a war zone, compared to what was happening at home.

Later, I was introduced to the guy I was to be sharing my container with. John worked at the Embassy. He was the point of contact when British nationals were missing in the country, a relatively frequent event because of the situation. As such, he would be woken up at all hours by his mobile phone. Inevitably it meant that I got woken up as well. John also liked a drink and would come stumbling into the container in the early hours, on one occasion falling flat onto his face. He was a nice guy, but I enjoyed some quiet time when he was off on his travels or away on leave. In his time there, my incumbent had somehow acquired an American SUV. He told me to hang onto it for as long as I possibly could. It was a great truck for getting around the Green Zone. He reminded me of the importance of checking the vehicle over for IEDs (improvised explosive devices). Just because we were in a fortified area didn't mean that we should be complacent.

Our office was located at what was previously Saddam Hussein's palace. This very grand building had been commandeered by the American Military and CPA (the Coalition Provisional Authority). Getting to 'the palace' from the accommodation was no mean feat. There were several military checkpoints to negotiate. I learnt very quickly to approach them cautiously and only move to the barrier when waved forward. There had been a spate of suicide bombs, so understandably soldiers were wary and taking no chances. The fact that we were wearing an easily distinguishable police uniform sporting Union Jacks on the sleeves held no weight at all. Weapons were levelled at me and my colleagues by so called 'Friendly Forces' on numerous occasions. The sage advice given to me by my escort from the airport proved to be accurate.

On my first journey to work, I took stock of the many buildings that had been bombed. There were fortified compounds everywhere, convoys of military vehicles and the constant hum of helicopters. It reminded me of the first night I spent in Bessbrook. There were threats everywhere. Our SUV had to be parked well away from the main palace building. You had to wear body armour when in the open and always had to have your hard helmet with you. At first it felt strange wearing a pistol on my belt. I soon became accustomed to it though, and it paled into insignificance compared to some of the weaponry that was on display everywhere that I went.

I didn't know what to expect from our office accommodation. Underwhelmed may be the most appropriate description. It was a very small kitchen located at the top of a flight of stairs. Taking stock of what we were responsible for as a police mission, I discovered very quickly that it didn't amount to a great deal. That, I have to say, is not by any means a reflection of the effort and enthusiasm of the UK team. One of the guys, of his own volition, had created a spreadsheet of all known hostage and kidnapping incidents. This proved to be of great interest to the US intelligence agencies who were frequent visitors to our little domain. Beyond that, we were not engaged in very much at all. The attitude displayed by some of the officials in the building made it clear that we were an irritant. Almost everyone was polite, all were fascinated by our accents and stopped to talk to us, but it was obvious that the US military machine was very much in command. It didn't take too long for me to conclude that we were there purely to pay lip service to the commitment of UK PLC to the so-called multinational effort.

One of the projects we did have was to set up a 'tips line', the equivalent of Crimestoppers in the UK. I duly made an appointment to see the US Army Sergeant in charge of logistics about the allocation of some telephony. Our meeting was a short one; he told me in uncompromising terms that we were low priority. When pressed for an estimate of time, he said that it would take at least six months. That would be around the time when my secondment was due to end.

Raising my frustrations with senior British Embassy staff also proved a pointless exercise. 'Don't rock the boat' was the prevailing attitude. Seemingly, most were happy to coast along and just go with it. That didn't sit comfortably with me. We were being paid well for being there and I wanted to deliver something tangible.

Surreal may be the best word to describe living in the Green Zone. Shortly after my arrival, a member of the UK team was due to leave. It was announced that there would be a 'night out' to celebrate. I remember laughing out loud, "A night out?!"

Unbeknown to me, there was in fact a busy social buzz to the place. As a Muslim country, alcohol was mostly banned. However, the Green Zone was no longer under the control of the Iraqi government, so some enterprising Iraqi Christians, probably encouraged by elements of the military, had received liquor licences from the CPA to trade there. There was also an outdoor Chinese restaurant that served beer, which is where we were heading that evening. Grubby white picnic tables and chairs were positioned around a small brick building where the cooking took place. The smell of oriental food drifted around the dusty area where we sat and drank the ice-cold beer in the heat of the early evening.

The next thing I became aware of was the unmistakable thump of helicopter rotors in the distance. Not that it was unusual, I had already become accustomed to them. However, it was their proximity that concerned me. When I looked skywards, I saw two Black Hawk choppers emblazoned with the red cross on their underbelly landing in a compound adjacent to us. When I asked what the compound was, I was told we were right next to the American MASH (Mobile Army Surgical Hospital), which was obscured by an eight foot high brick wall. I couldn't get it out of my head that we were out in the open, drinking beer and eating food, where less than 50 yards away injured and possibly dying troops were being brought in for treatment; the fine line between life and death.

There was also a thriving market for counterfeit DVDs. They were everywhere, in both an outdoor market and in small shops. All shopkeepers were vetted and licensed by the military. You could buy most electronic items. Little thought seemed to have been given to the prospect that these enterprising individuals could be funding terrorism or gathering intelligence. There was also a café, which we were all told not to frequent. As it happened, that also proved to be good advice. It was destroyed after a suicide bomber detonated his deadly cargo, killing one person and injuring many more.

You always had to be on your guard. On numerous occasions, we were forced to take cover as rockets and mortars were launched into the area. Gunfire was frequent both day and night. It was maybe this juxtaposition that led to most of us there having a 'devil may care' attitude; it became all easy to become blasé.

Part of my role involved meeting with senior figures from the newly formed Iraqi Police Service (IPS) and with government ministers. It was easier to arrange visits outside of the Green Zone because of the security processes involved when trying to get anyone into the area. Believe it or not, it was much simpler to arrange a three-vehicle convoy and protection team than arrange a pass. Of course, you had to balance the risks of leaving the relative safety of the Green Zone against the objectives you were attempting to achieve; whether you travelled or not, depended on the threat levels which altered on an hourly basis. We were almost always accompanied by our seconded Iraqi police officer, a young, extremely bright and IT literate man who acted as our interpreter. He was also very brave; having a young family and helping 'the enemy' made him an obvious target for insurgents. Every day, he showed up for work without fail and helped us better understand what we could do to assist. It was doubtless going to be a slow process but after many months of trying, it had proved impossible to set up even the most basic of intelligence units, let alone computer systems.

On one occasion, we travelled to the Ministry of Interior to see the man in charge of the criminal intelligence effort to explore with him how things could be accelerated. We climbed around eight flights of stairs to his office because the lifts were unsafe due to frequent power cuts. On each floor, there were around 10 to 20 men stood around smoking and chatting. When I asked our guide why there were so many people hanging about, he explained that they were friends and relatives of senior figures who were employed for the most part in non-existent jobs. Every single one of those jobs was being funded by the coalition. Unfortunately, nepotism and tribal influence got in the way.

I arrived in the office of the minister whom we were appointed to work alongside. His AK-47 laid across the desk underlined just how dangerous his job was. As was standard, our close protection team waited outside the door to provide security. We slipped off our body armour to take advantage of the air conditioning and cool off after the hot and sweaty walk up the stairs. As was the norm, we drank out of small glasses containing sweet tea and exchanged pleasantries. He seemed a good man. He didn't speak English but made all the right noises.

About 20 minutes into our meeting, the guy in charge of the protection team came into the room with a serious look on his face. He ushered me over and said, "We have to leave, NOW!" Our party rapidly put on our body armour. Outside we could hear the chatter of small arms fire in the distance. The building was coming under attack and we now had eight flights of stairs to negotiate before we could get into the waiting convoy. We vaulted down them as fast as we could and dived into the vehicles. "Get down on the floor, get down!" I was told in a calm but forceful tone by the convoy commander. The vehicles we used were armoured and had darkened windows. However, there had been several incidents where rocket-propelled grenades (RPGs) and IEDs had penetrated or destroyed them, killing the occupants.

We headed off at speed across some wasteland at the rear of the building. The bumpy ride was certainly not the most comfortable I'd ever had, nor was it helped by my helmet banging against the floor. We cleared the area eventually and were able to sit back into our seats.

Fear has a strange way of surfacing; I just recall laughing, joking and generally playing down what had just happened. It wasn't lost on me that we were most likely the targets of that attack. The close protection teams that were employed to look after us were first class. It would not be the only time I had cause to thank them for keeping me safe.

43. The proverbial hits the fan

Whilst I tried my best to keep away from the after-work drinking and social side, it was difficult because there was so little to do. I got to know several of the characters in our compound.

Unfortunately for me, I became a little bit too familiar with one of the girls that worked for a government department. Both of us had too much to drink one evening and the inevitable happened. Melissa (not her real name) had told me she was having problems with her long-term boyfriend. I also shared some of the details of my own relationship issues. We were completely different in terms of personality, yet for some reason we hit it off straight away. She was quite a bit younger than me, a bit off the wall, liked a drink and was sharp-witted. She also held down a very responsible position. I'm not going to try to defend my actions; what we did was wrong. With the daily drip feed of deaths and casualties, maybe we were aware of our own mortality and keen to live a little. It was another stupid affair that lasted much longer than it should have done.

The affair was a causation factor for something that got me into huge trouble, almost sparking an international incident. I had not been in the country long, which made it particularly problematic. Security at the US Embassy had been tightened up for reasons not disclosed to us. Oddly, many of the UK government staff had their access removed, which I found strange. The building was the nexus of activity in the Green Zone and this latest round of bureaucracy stopped them accessing the people and meetings they needed to attend. As UK police, we had a relatively high level of clearance already, and therefore the changes didn't affect any of us directly.

Labor Day is a public holiday in the US and the American Embassy wanted to acknowledge the date despite all the circumstances. A party was to be held that night with the focus being the huge swimming pool and terrace at the rear of the building. That evening a few of us, Melissa, two of her female friends and one of my officers had been at some sort of social event in the Green Zone. I had only consumed one small bottle of beer as I was driving. It was foolish to drink and drive in the Green Zone for any number of reasons. The subject of the Labor Day celebrations came up and somehow it was decided collectively that we should go along.

We approached the security gatehouse manned by the US Military and all showed our passes. The soldier in the gatehouse looked us all over and said something like, "Sir, the males have clearance, but unfortunately the ladies cannot come in." Despite explaining their status, that we could vouch for them, were prepared to sign them in and take responsibility for them, he refused to budge. It wasn't a massive issue for me; I remember suggesting going back to our own bar.

We walked away down the short approach road, whereupon one of our local protection team vehicles was approaching. One of the girls waved at the driver, a friendly guy from New Zealand, who stopped and asked what we were doing. The situation was explained and without further ado, he said, "Well I'm going; hop in, it won't be an issue; just keep a low profile once you are in there."

Instead of declining the offer, I went ahead. Their vehicles had tinted windows and it was rare for them to get more than a cursory inspection. The guy drove up to the checkpoint, flashed his ID and very shortly after we were at the party. Alcohol was flowing but I stuck to having soft drinks. The next thing we knew, Melissa and one of her friends jumped into the swimming pool. This attracted huge cheers from the crowd that were present. It didn't really help us keep a low profile though.

After about an hour, I suggested that we leave by an alternative gatehouse. I wanted to avoid any problems or awkward questions as to how we got inside. I walked through first with my police colleague behind me. We had agreed that the girls would follow a short distance behind. We cleared without any problem. As we reached the exit door, a shout went up from one of the guards. As it turned out, the same soldier who had turned us away earlier. He was raging and said something like, "What the hell did I tell all of you? How did you get in here?!" Trying to reason with him proved to be a complete waste of time, as he said on at least two occasions, "Sir, I have to call my commander." Like naughty children we were all ordered to stand against a wall. The enormity of the situation hit me. I was the most senior, it was going to be me that would have to deal with it.

An officer arrived and asked who was in charge. He took me to one side and asked me to explain what had happened. He was, in fairness, very polite and courteous. At one point, after apologising profusely, I thought I had smoothed things over. That was until he said, "Sir, I need you to hand over your security pass. I am excluding you all from the building and will have to submit a report to my superiors."

We all headed back to the accommodation in total silence. I went to my room, my head spinning. It was a stupid thing to have done but the reaction to it, in my opinion, was a little disproportionate. Every single member of our party was a member of the multinational effort – we were supposed to be working together.

A steady flow of visitors to my room followed. I had already made some good friends and they were all supportive. I was supposed to be heading home in a couple of days on my first stint of leave. Before I left, I was ordered to submit a report to the British Ambassador explaining what had happened. I was informed that during my period of leave, a decision would be taken as to what action would follow. The sense from everyone I spoke to was that I would get a massive bollocking.

I had been in Baghdad for six weeks. I headed home for my two weeks off. There was no way I could share what had happened with Emma. I hadn't told her that there were other women in our accommodation, let alone going out partying with them. I also had to consider the ramifications for my home Force if this all came out.

When travelling home on leave, you were driven to the border with Kuwait to join a scheduled civilian flight the next day. There were normally several people leaving in the standard convoy of three vehicles at the same time. The relatively short journey ended at a hotel in Kuwait used by most foreigners employed in Iraq. As it turned out, Melissa was also going home on leave and we spent the night together in the hotel.

Bidding each other farewell when we arrived in London, I had a connecting flight home and Emma made a surprise appearance at the airport when I landed. I hadn't expected to see her there, but she was really pleased to see me safe and well.

Despite everything that was going on, I somehow managed to separate my two lives. It was as if I was a character in some sort of television drama in Iraq, and difficult to convey or understand. Emma and I headed off for a short break somewhere. I recall being very distracted; it cannot have been pleasant for her. I caught up with my kids, contacted all the family and met up for a massive drink with my boss and some friends. Whilst at home, I was in contact periodically with a few of the guys in Baghdad and the sense was that it was not looking too good for me in terms of the 'incident'.

I returned a couple of weeks later. During that time, a new boss had been installed. I was summoned to see him on my first day back at work. A nice enough chap, but I didn't expect him to fight my corner. He didn't know me and was still trying to get accustomed to life in Baghdad along with the limitations of his post. Despite what he may have been told or even thought, he had limited power or control. We were there to support the American effort, pure and simple.

It seemed that my report had not gone down too well with the UK and US ambassadors. I had admitted being stupid and making an error of judgement, took full responsibility for everyone's actions and was deeply apologetic. The response that came back was that I should be returned to the UK. There was no negotiation to be had as far as anyone was concerned. I was mortified; everyone had expected me to be reprimanded. My boss said it was pointless appealing the decision and that I should start to make plans to leave as my travel around the Green Zone would now be severely restricted.

I was, however, aware of a much smaller British contingent of UK police officers at Al Basra in the south of the country. I had already had some contact with the Police Commander who was running the show down there. He was keen to get someone with investigative experience on the ground for a forensic project that he was struggling to launch. I contacted him via email and asked him what he thought about me being transferred. This decision had absolutely nothing to do with the American Embassy. The British were in charge in Basra and that was the proposal I put to the new boss.

He reluctantly agreed to the suggestion and for a week or so, I remained pretty much confined to the British Embassy. During this short period, I became friendly with a British Army Captain who was embroiled in a biometrics project run by the US Army. It involved the use of innovative and specialist equipment used to capture fingerprints, photographs and images of the eyes. The project's aim was to harvest the biometric data of all Iraqis, a massive undertaking. Over a coffee or two, I persuaded the Captain to give me three units to take to Basra (each unit was worth a significant amount of money). I explained to him that an alternate strategy with biometrics might be to capture the data of criminals or suspects coming into custody there. He saw some value in my thinking, so a few days later I departed on my flight with all my kit and three black heavy-duty plastic boxes full of the equipment. I said my goodbyes to Melissa and all the good friends I had made before embarking on my next little adventure.

44. Basra

Taking stock of the surrounds in Basra was familiar, probably because of my previous military service. The British Army way of doing things was a little different to the US approach in Baghdad. Maybe it reminded me of my army days, but I instantly felt at home.

On previous occasions, I had landed at Basra Airport but had never left the main building, so was completely unaware of the scale of the operation there. It was a large sprawling area, so big that coaches circled the place dropping you off at bus stops dotted around. I stayed overnight and was collected the next morning by a protection team who drove me to the British Consulate. This building was located at a site known locally as the Presidential Palaces. It bounded the Shatt al-Arab waterway and was perilously close to the border with Iran, from where, I was soon to discover, frequent rocket attacks would be launched in our direction.

The operation was a much smaller affair. My new boss, Kevin Hurley, was a seconded Commander from the Metropolitan Police. He introduced me to the guys in the office. The policing team was spread throughout the province in mostly small enclaves. We shared our office with some UK prison service governors. It was a tight-knit, collaborative effort, designed to bring the rule of law to this part of Iraq.

I got on well with my new boss straight away; he was a straight talking, at times outspoken, but highly competent senior officer. He was also an army reservist, so completely understood the optics. He hailed from the south of England, so we had lots in common. He told me in no uncertain terms that I was "a complete ****" for what happened in Baghdad, and I had to agree. He knew though, from his own enquiries, that I was entirely capable for the job he wanted me to deliver on. I was determined to live up to his expectations.

Without further ado, he cracked open a bottle of Champagne, and we had a good drink and got to know each other better. At some point during our conversations, he related to me how he had upset the British Consul because of his views about the poor levels of security around our accommodation. That apparently didn't go down well with the Consulate. It had led to a souring of relationships, but his intentions were the right ones. He always had the best interests of the people who worked with him at heart. I thoroughly enjoyed working for him and we remain in touch to this day.

Over several glasses of Champagne, he decided to present me with what he described as a 'long arm'. I had not heard the term before and was puzzled. It turned out to be a Heckler & Koch MP5 with several magazines of ammunition. Handing it to me, he said, "Whenever you leave here, take this with you. That fucking pea shooter of a pistol they give us won't help you much if the shit hits the fan." The acquisition of that firearm did lead to a small enquiry some months later; however, that is another story.

The IPS in the south had been promised a forensic capability. What they had during the Saddam regime was very basic. One of the big areas for them to move into was crime scene examination, particularly the opportunities for evidence collection following IEDs. The project I was presented with was titled, 'Introduction of a forensic capability'. I approached it with relish; it was something I could finally get my teeth into and do something with. There was a much more 'can do' attitude with the British Armed Forces. As an example, there were around 20 white vans stuck at a port in Iraq, destined for the project but no one could be found to drive them to us. They were intended for allocation to forensic examiners after their programme of training was completed but were needed during the course. I asked for help from the British Army. The reply came back quickly. "It's not easy, but we will do it." The officer in charge of logistics despatched a team and overnight they were brought to a base close to us in Shaibah. It was like a breath of fresh air.

The atmosphere towards me by some of the Consulate staff, however, wasn't so good. It took me a little while to understand the reasons why. I was introduced to the Head of Security, a puffy, arrogant little man who decided that I didn't warrant a particularly high level of clearance. I wasn't overly troubled by it, but his manner was appalling. A guy who ran the armoury in the compound was also standoffish and made one or two sarcastic remarks. It later became apparent that a completely different version of the events in Baghdad had been embellished upon and conveyed to certain individuals. The story was that I had tried to smuggle prostitutes into the US Embassy. I was appalled. Not only was it a blatant lie, but it was also a slur on the girls concerned, all of whom were employees of the British government. I laughed it off in the end, got my head down and worked hard. I concentrated on developing relationships with the people who were there to work and not engage in stupid, petty gossip.

There were two distinct compounds – one British, the other American. With the proper level of clearance, free movement was possible between the two, and it only entailed a short walk. The facilities in the US area were typically much better, and included a well-equipped gym, a bar and a room full of Internet connected computers that we could use to send email. The food in the British sector was awful, a far cry from what I had become accustomed to in Baghdad. Wherever possible, I would either visit the US canteen or make an excuse to go to Basra Air Base. In both places, the food was outstanding.

There was also the opportunity to stock up on food from the NAAFI, or in some cases visit a PX, the US military equivalent. I stopped eating in the canteen at the Consulate for some time because the food was so bad, losing some weight as a result. There were thankfully other ways of getting food as I was to discover on my various trips off site. The US Military had installed several fast-food outlets at some of their bases including a Subway, Pizza Hut and McDonald's. It truly was like an oasis in the desert when you fell across them.

Despite my problems in Baghdad, I was welcomed with open arms by the Americans in Basra and made some great friends, even attending their makeshift Thanksgiving celebrations which were fantastic. It was a place full of numerous colourful characters; many were ex-police officers, diplomats and all manner of contractors. There was also a small number of Danish police officers stationed with us, including a female lawyer who was phenomenally brave and travelled everywhere. Her squad of protection officers bristled with all sorts of weaponry. They were completely fearless. Sometimes the threat levels prevented us from leaving the area, but it never once stopped them.

One of the biggest issues with the project, when I took it over, was how to safely run a course for the IPS in crime scene forensics, and where. Trying to even attempt training within their own facilities was a non-starter because of the risks. Running a course within a military base was a possibility, but not without an element of danger. There had been instances of insurgents infiltrating the classes with the sole intent of murdering the instructors. I was informed by my boss that the Czech Army MPs (Military Police) detachment based at Shaibah had previously expressed a willingness to assist.

At one of the meetings of military and police commanders held at Basra Air Base, I introduced myself to Colonel George. A man mountain sporting a huge moustache, he was as broad as he was tall. He looked me up and down when I asked if I could visit him to discuss the prospect of his staff helping with the running of a course. He simply said, in good English accompanied with that Eastern European twang, "Come over, see me, stay for night, we will talk." His team of MPs were housed within their own compound at Shaibah Air Base, around ten miles away from the Consulate.

A couple of days later, escort organised, I headed there to meet up with him. On arrival at the main entrance to the base, we were held in a queue for a short time. There were always local people and vehicles at the gate, and they had to be checked and searched, so it took us about ten minutes to clear.

I was dropped off at their small headquarters a few minutes later, but as I disembarked the vehicle and bid farewells to my escorts, there was a huge bang in the distance, accompanied by a dark plume of smoke rising into the air. When this happens, I defy anyone not to jump. Your shoulders tend to shoot forward, your head and knees bend as if dodging an imaginary projectile. After that initial shock, we ran and took cover in the buildings nearby until we received the 'all clear'. It soon became apparent that a suicide bomber had attacked the vehicle checkpoint – the very same checkpoint we had driven through minutes earlier. The likelihood was that the attacker had been present when we were there. It was another reminder that you had to be alert all the time. Complacency could get you killed.

I had managed to secure a bottle of duty-free whisky to smooth the wheels with Colonel George. In fairness, it wasn't needed, but nevertheless he was most appreciative. He indicated that all his troops were on an alcohol ban, although from the wink he gave me I am not sure that was strictly enforced. After a few short meetings with his staff and an overnight stay, everything was agreed. His MPs would train the IPS, assisted by one of my guys, a contractor. We first had to audit and allocate all the kit, which was stored at different locations in metal containers across the south. Some of it had been held so long that it was no longer of any use, including 35mm film for cameras, which had melted in the heat.

Our next challenge was selection of the right people to train. I had already been allocated an IPS Captain who was to be my liaison officer. Our first couple of meetings were a little frosty. He was deeply suspicious of the motives of the project, particularly when I showed him the biometrics kit. His view was that this was merely a strategy by the coalition to profile all the Iraqi people. There was some truth to what he said, for that was what the strategy was to be in Baghdad. I told him that my priority was to profile the criminal community and that we would first use the equipment in the prisons to understand who was there. Still, he wasn't convinced. He made much of the fact that he would always be required to visit me at the Consulate, going on to say that I should visit his station to understand the problems he was facing. This to me seemed entirely sensible because I wanted to build trust and a better working relationship. I hadn't appreciated the problems I would encounter getting to where he worked though.

Al Jameat police station and its adjacent prison were out of bounds to our protection team. It was deemed to be far too dangerous. This was the same Al Jameat police station that sparked a huge international incident in 2005 when two UK Special Forces Operators were arrested by the IPS and held there. Only a successful and daring rescue by the British Army secured their escape.

Everyone I spoke to told me that visiting Al Jameat was a non-starter. It didn't seem to matter who I cajoled, no one was prepared to take me there. I spoke to my boss who agreed that it was necessary to show willing, so between us we came up with a plan. We decided to talk to our contacts in the British military who were now frequent visitors to our office. They told me that if I was prepared to "rough it" in an army Land Rover, they were prepared to escort me, which they duly did.

As a result, I earned the respect and trust of my local police liaison officer and got an insight into what he and his colleagues were up against. It was a compound comprising several buildings, and rumour was that the place was a hotbed of corruption and had been infiltrated by anti-coalition forces. My liaison officer showed me to his office where we drank tea and made the small talk which always pre-empted any meeting with locals in Iraq. When I asked where recoveries of ordnance were stored after IEDs were disabled, he took me to the adjoining stairwell. When I saw the mortar shells, mines and all sorts of ammunition laid on the stairs unattended, it opened my eyes to just how much needed to change. Besides the loss of forensic evidence, it would take just one stray round to set the lot off, blowing the building to smithereens and killing everyone in it. Everyone there seemed oblivious of the risks when I questioned it. "Inshallah," (If Allah wills it) came the reply. That summed up the attitude of most of the Iraqi police officers I came across.

With the help of several excellent people, the project was successfully completed. I extended my time in Basra by another month to ensure that all the training was delivered. My enduring memory was watching 20 white vans drive out of the base at Shaibah with a fully trained IPS officer at the wheel. The Military Police were brilliant partners. When I bid my farewells to Colonel George, he said, "You will come to my country for a medal." I thought he had picked up some of my British humour and I forgot all about it. I didn't realise it would later come back to cause me more problems.

Before I departed, I bid my farewells to the Iraqi liaison officer. He had grown to trust me and together we had achieved a lot in a short space of time. He attempted to present me with a handgun as a thank you for everything I had done. I had to politely refuse, informing him that I would get into huge trouble and was unlikely to need a gun when I got home…

45. Home time

My time in Iraq consisted of many highs and lows. It could be a book all on its own, as I couldn't possibly cover everything that happened in a few chapters. It is evident to me only now, that several things happened whilst there that had an impact on me. Hurtling around in helicopters, carrying firearms, living under constant threat in a war zone, dealing with difficult people and having an affair, meant that I was on elevated doses of adrenaline. It became addictive; I enjoyed the exposure to danger and it was a buzz to feel alive. Returning to an unhappy home life and sitting at my desk when I finally returned to work, left me more unsettled than I had ever been. I remained connected to some of the people I worked with and watched with interest on the television as events unfolded, thus it was extremely difficult to switch off and detach myself. I even found myself questioning why I hadn't extended my time there.

My interest was further piqued after receiving two interesting phone calls not long after arriving back home. Both gave me a warm, fuzzy feeling of job well done. One call was from Scotland Yard, the Metropolitan Police HQ. Officers from Scotland Yard had contacted me whilst I was in Basra. They asked if I would be able to assist them in compiling a library of fingerprints of known criminals in the area. With the assistance of my liaison officer, I managed to obtain a huge bundle of hard copy fingerprints from the police. It took me weeks to copy them all. They were then forwarded for input and analysis in London. Sometime later, it resulted in the identification of an insurgent who had applied to be a bodyguard for the incoming President of Iraq. That was the icing on the cake for me as I may well have prevented his assassination.

I also got a telephone call from Colonel George who had lived up to his promise. His detachment of MPs wanted to present me with a medal of service for the work we had completed together on the forensic project. It was a huge deal for them and rightly so. All too often, the news was dominated with the successes of the larger military forces in the country. As a matter of protocol, I telephoned the Foreign Office who bluntly informed me that I was not allowed to attend. To do so would be a breach of protocol extending back to the days of Queen Victoria: "My dogs, my collars" was quoted at me by the man I spoke to. My immediate reaction to that was, 'What a load of bollocks!'

I made an appointment to see my boss. His view on hearing what had happened was equally as uncompromising. "You're going. It would be rude not to and it's great for the Force too." Much to the displeasure of the Foreign Office, I travelled over for a full-blown ceremony in Prague and was once again alongside some of the friends I had made on deployment. The medal was presented by one of their ministers. This episode resulted in me not being invited to the debrief session, conducted by the UK Ministry of Defence, that all returning officers were required to attend, which was yet another petty attitude. My sense was that they had me down as a bit of a rebel and troublemaker. Perhaps they had a point; however, they could not fault my commitment and determination for delivering what I was sent there to do.

Emma and I went on holiday upon my return. For a time, things between us were calm. I was finding it hard to settle down though. I threw myself back into work but, despite getting involved in some interesting intelligence-related work, I struggled to find my feet again. A round of promotion boards were advertised, so I decided to give it a go. I had been appointed to Chief Inspector whilst on secondment and had a wealth of operational experience. I knew competition would be fierce and that meant I would have to get my head down and study hard. To my amazement, I excelled on the board, something which I had always struggled with in the past. Even now I remember getting the phone call at home to say that I had done it. It was a great feeling. I fully expected to get an appointment at one of the divisions as a Crime Manager. With my background, that would have made sense. When I was told I would be remaining at headquarters, I remember that I felt a bit deflated initially. However, when I discovered what I was to be responsible for, that feeling soon slipped away.

The Force had been failing badly. The Police Standards Unit were now involved, and unless significant improvements were made, it did not bode well for our future. Shortly after being promoted, I was put in charge of a Force-wide project designed to improve the investigation of 'volume crime'. As the term suggests, these are the sorts of crimes that occur most frequently: house burglary, car crime and the like. I threw myself into it with gusto. Scrutiny came from not only within the Force, but also from local and central government. Budgets, statistics, performance and ongoing improvements were the order of the day. It was highly strategic. I was working alongside the command team and a Chief Superintendent; it was full-on accountability. I learnt a lot and made more good friends on the way. Sadly, one of those friends took his own life some months after. It wasn't remotely connected to the project we were working on; however, it certainly related to the other pressures he was under at work and how it affected him personally. He was a happy-go-lucky type who had done well for himself in the job, but he rarely switched off and was hyper. You would never have suspected for a minute that he would kill himself. It was a sad moment when I heard the news and asked myself, where was the help for him and why didn't he speak up? Easier said than done.

The Chief Superintendent, with whom I ended up working, remained another good friend and confidante. I shared some, but not all, of what was happening for me at home. This only came to light after yet another incident at home which left me deeply troubled.

The relationship between my youngest son and I had been up and down since I first left the family home. He had gone off the rails at school, partly because he wasn't overly clear about what he wanted to do from a career perspective. Whilst I was away in Iraq, he met a girl of a similar age to him. It later became known to me that they were expecting a child. She was a small, slight, shy girl, whom I had only met face to face once. I recall thinking just how young they looked together.

Early one morning in October 2005, I was at home getting ready for work when the phone rang. It was my daughter, who told me in floods of tears that overnight my youngest son's girlfriend had gone into labour. My daughter's emotional state made no sense, as you would expect a birth to be a joyous occasion. I had to ask her to repeat what she told me, as I thought I had misheard it.

"She's dead, Dad. She died in childbirth." She went on to tell me that both my sons were at the hospital in Leeds.

My immediate response was, "Tell them to wait there. I am on my way."

Emma was close by but had only heard my side of the conversation. It must have been obvious to her from my demeanour that something serious had happened. When I related the full details to her, I was stunned by her response, which was, "What the fuck do you have to go for?"

I looked at her incredulously uttering something like, "Really?" Emma had the ability to detach herself emotionally and be cold, but that comment is one I will never, ever forget. I left the house with my head spinning.

I drove as fast as I could to Leeds. Under normal circumstances, the journey would have taken in the region of less than one hour. On this day, the rain was horrendous, making driving conditions hazardous and seemingly taking forever. I arrived at the hospital in Leeds, where both my sons were standing outside the main doors. I stopped the car, not thinking to park it properly. My youngest was pale and listless; it was apparent he was in shock. I held him tight, kissed his head and promised him that I would look after him. He sobbed and I cried with him. I reached out to my eldest and the three of us embraced before going to the ward.

Unbeknown to anyone, my son's girlfriend had a deficiency in the elasticity of her veins and arteries. The pressure of childbirth caused a blood vessel to burst, leading to massive internal bleeding. On many occasions, my son has recounted being told by a nurse in a blood-soaked gown that his girlfriend had died. It haunts him to this day. Thankfully my granddaughter survived, but many years later she still seems to harbour misplaced feelings of guilt.

Death is an inevitable part of life, but no one expects a young woman to pass away when giving birth. It was hard to stomach. Taking my son to the mortuary and watching him hug the love of his life, sniff her hair and sob uncontrollably was an awful experience for the pair of us.

Later that day, he asked if I would drive him to his flat to pick up some possessions. I had not been there previously. Whilst he was collecting what he needed, I looked around what was intended to be a warm and loving home for their newborn. I walked into the small bedroom which my son had decorated in pink for the impending arrival. There were Disney characters on the wall, a brand-new cot with bedding, soft toys and all the things young couples do together in preparation for the day they bring their child home. It broke my heart seeing it; I had tears streaming down my face.

Arriving home later that day, I never felt more isolated. Emma wasn't interested, shrugging her shoulders and making disparaging remarks. I needed to talk about it, but there was nobody to relate to. Over the coming days, there were people at work with whom I could share this news. It was incomprehensible what had happened, and no real answers have ever emerged from the hospital.

My youngest son still bears the mental scars of that tragic incident. To this day, he has feelings of guilt, has been diagnosed with Post-Traumatic Stress Disorder and 15 years later he still has terrible nightmares. This has created a tumultuous effect on his life and it is fair to say that he struggles. My granddaughter remains troubled and continues to grapple with the loss of the mother whom she never met. It has caused me to reflect about some of the people I met during my time in the police: the drunks, the drug users, the people with mental health issues. We are all too swift to judge;

you rarely know what is going on in people's personal lives behind closed doors.

Back at my home, things were going downhill again. Emma continued to pursue her drive for a baby. Her constant reminders about going to Iraq to save money for IVF were ever present. She never once offered any support about what had happened to my son, she didn't attend the funeral and as far as she was concerned, it never happened. From around that time, she severed all contact with my children. In all honesty, I was content with the arrangement as it was much less stressful to be on my own with them. Unfortunately, I found that strategy proved to be the most effective when dealing with Emma. Keeping her at arm's length was best, for given what had happened with my youngest son I could not risk them being in the same room.

At work, I was several months into the various projects when I had a realisation that I only had around three years' service left before I could retire from the police. I was still relatively young and able to pursue a second career. In a relaxed appraisal interview with my friend, the Chief Superintendent, he told me that I would have no problem making it to the same rank as him. He was at the time the Acting Assistant Chief Constable and would likely be given a permanent appointment in the coming months. He was 'in the know' about the future of the Force and the financial restrictions we were up against. In the same breath, he broke it to me that it would be most unlikely that there would be any promotion boards for at least three years, effectively scuppering any further advancement with the Force.

During my time in Iraq, my boss there shared a lot of career advice during our time together. He told me to aim as high as possible. If not attainable in my home Force, he suggested looking elsewhere for a temporary promotion. That way my pension would be calculated for that rank. Getting to at least Superintendent would see me making up the loss I had suffered during the divorce.

Some weeks later, a recruitment advert arrived in my email inbox. The role had been advertised widely with seemingly little take up. The person who had sent the email was originally from my Force but now worked in London. The job involved working at national level, advising on intelligence systems. It also offered a temporary position of detective superintendent for at least three years. It came complete with a flat in the capital with travel home paid each weekend. The role description looked as if it had been written for me. I applied, and to my surprise was successful.

Before leaving, some senior officer friends pulled me into an office asking if I was sure about what I was doing, saying, "You will be bored out of your head, don't do this." I ignored their advice; I could do three years, no problem. My grand plan was that this could also be good exposure to life outside of the police service.

46. London

The advice I was given about the role sadly turned out to be true. The organisation I was about to join was going through a transition period. The National Policing Improvement Agency (NPIA) was to take over their responsibilities. All new projects had ground to a halt pending the introduction of a streamlined management structure. Whilst I was given some relatively interesting tasks, the truth was that the ACPO (Association of Chief Police Officers) representatives ran their own projects as portfolios of work and were supported by their staff officers. They only ever wanted your input if you could secure them funding or open doors with third-party providers.

I could not complain about the working conditions; they were very good. The work, however, was virtually non-existent, mostly consisting of meetings that achieved very little. It was another glittering example of money being wasted. I saw people sitting at desks most of their working day pretending to be busy. One of my colleagues in the office always arranged meetings on a Thursday near to where he lived in the north of England, the only reason being that he could work from home on a Friday. None of this was ever challenged by management.

I had to keep myself busy; it was not in my nature to sit about. I actively sought out work, I went to various conferences and got myself involved in crime-related projects by volunteering or exploring how I could help. Calling upon my experience with witness protection, Automatic Number Plate Recognition (ANPR), intelligence and forensics, I managed a reasonable workload.

Travelling back home to the North was a bit of a bind and after 12 months, Emma and I decided to up sticks and move to the Midlands. I only had around 18 months left in the police. My forward planning was around being in the centre of the country, giving me greater potential for finding the right job when I left. We spent some time looking in an area close to my dad. We eventually settled on a detached house in a small town not far from a railway station. It made it much easier to travel into London. There were no objections from my home Force, despite it being a considerable distance away, as they did not expect me to return. The sale of our house and the purchase of the new one went through without episode. It was a lovely place, well maintained, with four bedrooms and a large garden. The rise in my salary made it affordable, despite the maintenance I was still paying to my ex-wife. The journey to and from London would also be less demanding.

I didn't think our relationship could get much worse but the move to the Midlands proved to be the death knell for our marriage. There were few weekends when an argument or massive row didn't occur. Emma convinced herself that I was having an affair, which I wasn't. According to her, I was in bed with every woman I was working with. It was a complete nonsense. I can say with hand on heart that it never happened. There was an obsession by her to find something which simply did not exist. One weekend, Emma even managed to disable my work-allocated phone by trying to guess the four-figure PIN. After three failed attempts, it was rendered useless until I got back to the office on the Monday morning. Over several weeks of surreptitiously looking over my shoulder, she worked out the passwords for my laptop and email. I didn't know at the time, but she would get up in the early hours of the morning and go downstairs to access my devices, trying to find evidence about non-existent relationships.

This continual tension at home was relentless. It was always there, simmering under the surface and often resulted in violence. It was the perpetual cycle of accusations, her attacking me, smashing household items, or throwing them at me, that ultimately led to retaliation. On one occasion, she cornered me in the dining room, spat in my face and shouted, "Come on, hit me, I want you to fucking hit me!" I grabbed her by the shoulders and ushered her out of the room, leaning against the door to stop her getting back in, which only resulted in her screaming at the top of her voice. My immediate thoughts were that the police would be called and that accusations would then be levelled against me. The only way to stop her when this type of thing happened was to attempt to restrain her. I was physically stronger, so invariably she came off worse. However, in those types of situations both parties end up being injured – cuts and bruises became a part of life.

Try as I may, leaving the house when this was happening was impossible, because Emma would pin herself against the door knowing that I would have to physically remove her. Wherever I tried to go in the house, she would follow me. It was truly awful and no way for either of us to live. I relished going back to London and lost count of the number of times I left earlier, rather than in the early hours of the Monday morning. As far as Emma was concerned, I was the one with the problems, not her. For months after we moved to the

Midlands, she refused to get a job. In her opinion, I earned more than enough to keep us. Being at home all day only served to allow her mind to run riot and concoct stories about what I was doing.

I am puzzled to this day as to where the anger and rage in Emma originated from. I tried to understand it, I was patient, I comforted her and tried to persuade her to get help. Her behaviour had always been unpredictable, but it was getting much worse. I felt even more on edge with her at any social setting or event. One Sunday in a planned visit to her niece's christening in Leeds, we arrived at the house when without warning she said, "Stop, turn around, we are not going." We had stayed at a hotel the night before. The breakfast hadn't been up to her standards and as a result she was in a foul mood. I tried to reason with her, but it resulted in yet another argument. Travelling southbound on the M1 motorway back to the Midlands and at around 70mph in the centre lane, Emma started to scream at the top of her voice, "I fucking hate you, I want to die!" At this point, she opened the passenger door and began to undo her seat belt. I grabbed hold of her with my left hand, but with the all the pushing and shoving, the car began to swerve between the motorway lanes. Eventually I managed to bring the car safely to halt on the hard shoulder. It was only because there was hardly any traffic around that there was no collision.

On many occasions after that, Emma told me that she didn't want to live anymore, but flatly refused to go to the doctor for professional help. I even discussed the prospect of her coming to live in London with me, which was refused out of hand. The pursuit of IVF did for a while seem to placate her. We embarked upon a course of treatment which gave her a focus and for a time it appeared to give her something to aim toward. Perhaps I believed that her frustrations in life related to the absence of a child, and foolishly thought that filling that void would resolve all our problems. Trying to please her to compensate for my own career pursuits was a flawed strategy. You could describe it as a sticking a plaster to cover a gaping wound. For a host of reasons, the IVF treatment was not successful. There was the potential to repeat it, but there was no money left. I had just over a year before retirement from the police beckoned.

By a quirk of fate, I met up with an old friend from my West Yorkshire days at a conference about organised crime. To cut a long story short, he introduced me to a recently retired senior police officer who had taken over as head of a large private investigation company. His organisation had identified links through their investigative efforts to global serious and organised crime. They had swathes of intelligence but were struggling to pass it to Law Enforcement Agencies (LEAs) across the world. He asked me if I would be interested in joining the company on secondment to examine ways to pass the intelligence to UK police. It was an excellent initiative because partnerships are vital to the fight against crime. If agreed by senior management, the intention was that I would be completely embedded with them at their offices. In addition, as a sweetener they offered to contribute to my salary.

The powers that be agreed to the proposal and before I knew it, I was working in a private company developing working relationships with LEAs and passing good quality, actionable intelligence and evidence packages for enforcement activity. I clearly impressed because very shortly after my secondment commenced, the prospect was broached of me working there full-time, once retired. I could not believe my luck. I had attained a good rank to retire upon and if I continued to perform well, my work future was secure.

At home though, things had worsened, as the failure of the IVF had put Emma into a downward spiral. My workload increased and now included management responsibilities for investigators. I had no complaints about that as I was thoroughly enjoying what I was doing, but it was to the detriment of our marriage. I tried to compensate at home with weekends away at lovely hotels, trips abroad, meals at great restaurants and even purchased a car for her. It worked, but only for a short time.

Next, however, some uncertainty was thrown into the mix from an unexpected quarter. Someone within the National Policing Improvement Agency (NPIA) had raised an objection to my secondment. With about six months left to my retirement, the staff officer for the Head of the NPIA, a chief constable, sent me an email informing me that I was to be returned to my Force. In my opinion, this was a ridiculous decision, and one that I had not been consulted or warned about. I strongly suspected that someone had complained. Who and why is anyone's guess; however, professional jealousy is a thing in the police service and frankly this reeked of it.

I asked to speak to the head of Human Resources, a lady who had been appointed very recently to the post, promising to bring new thinking to the service with 'an effective people strategy'. My request was declined, and no one was prepared to meet, or even speak to me on the phone, about the decision, somewhat flying in the face of the new thinking! The fact that I would have a daily commute of 200 miles to and from my place of work fell on deaf ears. When the police service decided to go after you, they really did go after you. I contacted my home Force, and the response from a senior officer during a telephone call went something like this: "In the nicest possible way, we don't want you back, we don't have a job for you."

Thankfully, the matter was resolved, and it was agreed with my Force that the company would pay my salary for the remaining six months. I lost my provided accommodation and paid travel as a result. I never did get to the bottom of what had happened, but almost certainly someone had taken objection to the fact that I appeared to have been given some preferential treatment. What they failed to recognise was the quality of evidence being passed to forces across the country which enabled cash seizures under the Proceeds of Crime Act (POCA), in turn taking away ill-gotten gains from criminals. Forces were at the time measured in this way and the contribution I was making helped massively so this was an example of small-minded thinking by a chief officer who had little operational understanding of crime fighting.

I retired from the police in the Autumn of 2008. I had a small leaving do with some friends in London and took a few weeks off before being appointed full time in my new job. I had thoroughly enjoyed my time in the service, achieved more than I ever thought possible, and got so many life experiences from it. I knew there was a life beyond it though. I most certainly did not want to give up work and wanted to embrace new challenges.

Before all of that, I arranged to have a weekend away at a Center Parcs facility with members of the family, including my dad, stepmother, children and grandchildren. Emma and I were then to have departed on a holiday to the USA. I had assumed that with my dad and stepmother being present there would be less chance for any conflict with my children. I was wrong, for once again there was more drama. Emma's continued deep-seated dislike for my children, particularly my daughter, which resulted in rows and silly disputes that tarnished the whole weekend. I was caught up in the middle of it all again. On one occasion, Emma took the view that my daughter was freeloading because she had removed a couple of bottles of wine from our fridge. This was despite me saying in front of everyone that all drinks were on me that weekend. It was completely unnecessary and another example of spiteful behaviour. I believe my daughter still feels that I did little to sort things out. However, she was completely unaware of what was happening behind the scenes and the countless arguments and disagreements that went on in private.

After our holiday, I returned to the company as a full-time, civilian employee. The role was the same, but now I was completely free of the bureaucracy associated with public service. It was refreshing not to have to endure so much red tape. My job involved reporting to teams of lawyers and executives. I travelled widely in the UK and abroad, visiting Belgium, Canada, France, Italy, Slovenia and the USA. I was now responsible for all intelligence and investigations functions. We had some very high-profile cases which meant that it was hectic during the week. By the time the weekend arrived, I was worn out.

My first 12 months passed quickly. I learnt a lot about the corporate world in a very short space of time and was enjoying the fresh challenges. On the domestic front, Emma was telling me how lonely she was and how she had put up with me being away from home for too long. The truth was that I was happier when we were not together for too much of the time. The constant accusations of my non-existent philandering and partying were wearing me down. I did go to social functions occasionally. It was a big part of the job because I was expected to represent the company. However, not once did I ever engage in any of the activity I was repeatedly being accused of. It reached a point that when I travelled home at the weekends, I would play the Meatloaf song 'Paradise by the Dashboard Light' at full volume in my car. The words 'Praying for the end of time, so I can end my time with you!' were especially relevant to my situation.

Looking back, I believe I had reached the end of my tether and formed the conclusion that we were over. However, I knew that Emma would not allow things to come to an end. I knew that if I attempted to leave her, she would ruthlessly deliver on her promise to destroy me. Bored with being at home with nothing much to do, she did take one or two agency jobs that kept her occupied. In late Autumn 2009, she took a role at a police station close to where we lived. I have to say that I harboured a nagging doubt about her working there. I suspected that at some point in the future this would lead to trouble. That proved to be something of an understatement. Police stations are notorious for extramarital affairs. Emma had a way about her; she always denied it vehemently, but she knew full well how to get male attention. It wasn't long before that went into overdrive.

In my second Christmas in the job, we had experienced a very successful year in terms of results. The office Christmas party was arranged, a lavish affair held just outside of London. Partners were invited, but Emma refused point blank to attend. Internally I breathed a sigh of relief. We had reached a point where me working away during the week was becoming a huge issue; things were gradually getting worse. I managed a mixed team of men and women. Over a period of time and unbeknown to me, she had started to profile all the females in terms of age and attractiveness. Accessing my email accounts, she somehow extracted names from a staff list, then spent time on the internet gathering further information. Once again, this was a pointless exercise as I was not having any form of affair or relationship. What had happened in Iraq was still firmly etched in my mind. I had learnt my lesson and was not going to get caught up in anything like that again. I now know that Emma continued to interfere with my work phone and laptop on a regular basis.

I attended the Christmas party, had a really good time and stayed the night at a hotel close to the venue, paid for by the company. Arriving home on the Friday evening, I was accused of spending the night with one of the staff members. It was not the case and yet another bizarre, unfounded allegation. I discovered many weeks later that Emma had spent hours on the website of the venue looking for incriminating photographs. There were none to be found, but that did not seem to matter. Wild theories abounded again. As a result, arguments at the weekends leading up to the Christmas break intensified. During one of them, Emma disclosed that she was helping a man in the office come to terms with the loss of his daughter. I found this odd. In all our time together, I had never seen one ounce of empathy towards anyone, in particular my son when he lost his girlfriend. As I anticipated, it turned out there was much more to this story.

47. The beginning of the end

Emma's obsession with my daughter reached dizzying heights in 2009. There had been a minor incident between two of my grandchildren in Leeds. They were both very young and what had happened, whilst unsettling, would only ever have been categorised as 'sexual experimentation' when I worked in Child Protection. I became aware of it, gave advice to my daughter, told her not to make a huge issue of it and just monitor the situation. That should have been the end of it. I made the mistake of talking about the matter to Emma. Before I knew it, she had informed my dad and my stepmother. Not only had she told them about it, but she also appeared to have embellished on the account I had provided her. What happened next completely threw me.

I was in London and about to go into an important meeting when my phone rang. It was my dad. I was shocked when he told me that if I was not prepared to inform social services about the incident, then my stepmother would be. Despite me telling him the matter was in hand, he persisted. With more than a hint of reluctance, I made that call. It set in train a series of events that tarnished the relationship between my dad and daughter forever. I stressed to social services during the call that I was of the opinion what had happened was minor and did not warrant formal intervention. Their subsequent investigations proved that. I felt it only right that I informed my daughter what I had done. I explained that I was acting in the best interests of both my grandchildren. It was not until many years later that I disclosed to her about the call with my dad. In turn, she informed me that social services had disclosed to her that two people had apparently called the offices of social services to 'anonymously' report the incident on the same day.

During the period leading up to Christmas of that year, things at home reached breaking point. Emma admitted that the man that she was meeting as a 'shoulder to cry on' was in fact infatuated with her. She emphatically denied any suggestion that she had encouraged him or that they were involved in an affair. I was unable to fathom whether this was an attention-seeking tactic or that she was covering something up. Needless to say, it affected the Christmas break. We argued continually. She took the decision not to buy me any Christmas presents. We were invited to my stepsister's house for Christmas dinner, along with other members of the family. When the time came, Emma had a huge tantrum and refused to attend. I went alone, but as I left that morning plates were being smashed behind me in the hallway.

I was stressed at home and at work. I was not sleeping well and didn't know what was going to happen next. I would go cycling regularly to get out of the house. I could sense that I was also getting angrier by the day. I spoke to Emma about how I felt; I knew I couldn't go on like this. Her response was that I was the one who should seek professional help. I think our individual perspectives on this were miles apart.

She took the view that I was the problem and not her. I did not know how to deal with her anymore and I openly admit to having been angry, bad tempered and stubborn. In her mind though, she was doing nothing wrong. Her logic always seemed to have its roots in the fact that I had embarked on an affair with her so would do it again.

In January 2010, I seized the initiative and reached out to a counsellor who had an office relatively close to where we lived. It was a life-changing decision on several fronts. I arranged to see Rachael (her real name). I explained why I was there. She explained that she used cognitive behavioural therapy (CBT) and went on to tell me what it entailed. In short, it is used as a method to address thoughts, emotions, and behaviours. During our first session, I must have come across a bit like a wounded animal. I wasn't sure about the whole process; I do recall that I kept asking about confidentiality and trust. My concerns were completely unfounded; Rachael was trustworthy, very good at what she did, and she was warm, kind and a phenomenal listener. I'd learnt how to interview people during my time in the police, but this was a completely different experience, not least because this time I was the subject.

All our sessions were held in a small, quiet room with no distractions. I couldn't fail to notice the box of tissues next to the soft comfy chair allocated to me. My instant reaction was that I wouldn't need them, for I certainly wasn't going to be crying in front of someone I hardly knew. I was wrong about that too. There were several questions that she asked me in those early visits that I still remember vividly.

"What is the worst thing someone could say to you?"

I hesitated for what seemed like an eternity. My lip started to quiver, I took a breath and replied, "That I'm a wanker."

Her calm and measured response was, "Why is that?" Her question triggered something inside me, and I knew within seconds that I was fighting a deep emotional response. I was really struggling to keep this buried; it reminded me of fighting off the tears when Mum died. I swallowed hard as if to keep it from coming out, though I was losing. Before I knew it, tears were streaming down my cheeks. I remember in a mixture of sobs and laughter saying to her, "You're good at this, aren't you!"

That issue of 'being a wanker' appeared to have its origins in childhood, perhaps trying to live up to the expectations of my father, fear of failure, always striving to do better, and so on. I would be asked questions about 'how I felt' about certain things. Initially, my response would be something like, "OK," or, "Not great." Rachael always corrected me, until I finally understood what she was meant. "I'd like you to tell me how you are 'feeling'". She went on to explain what feelings are. Surprisingly enough, that had to be explained to me. Happiness, anger, fear, sadness, joy, excitement, jealousy… I realised I had never really thought about it in that way. Like many of my generation, I had been brought up with the 'big boys don't cry' mantra. That certainly chimed with the 'grin and bear it' mentality of the army and the 'deal with it and move on' doctrine from my time in the police service. I had been conditioned that there was no time or place for emotions.

Initially it was all very alien to me. I had many internal battles with myself but eventually began to look forward to counselling. We discussed things like 'fight or flight' and how the body responds physiologically to threats. We talked about discipline and rigidity, qualities I think we both agreed had massive value given my chosen occupations.

However, the downside was the propensity to be intolerant of others. For me, anyone lacking discipline was lazy and not worthy. It was a good example of one of the many stereotypes that I, and lots of my colleagues in the army and police, had developed over many years. From being around 16 years old, I had been instructed to be five minutes early for a parade. I still maintain it shows respect and lowers the anxiety by avoiding the prospect of being late for a meeting. I haven't changed much on that front, but I do tend to be a little more relaxed about it. As a means of testing my resolve, Rachael suggested eating dessert prior to a main meal. To me, the very thought of that was unthinkable, but a great example of challenging routine. I tried it once. It was strange but liberating.

I had not realised that some of the models I had learnt during my police trainer's course were entirely relevant to my situation, such as the Parent, Adult and Child states that had been discussed back in 1999 in the classroom, when I was being taught how to teach. The psychiatrist Eric Berne developed the idea that people can swiftly move between these 'ego states'. In the context of my situation, I could see that Emma and I were spending far too much time in Parent/ Child states. Very rarely were we communicating as adults.

I had given little consideration to the fact that the jobs I had done involved 'control'. Police officers or former police officers reading this will probably be familiar with what I am about to say. Being a cop means that from time to time you are going to be stopping people or a group of people from doing what they want to do. That could be anything from a criminal out to break into someone's house, football supporters behaving badly, or stopping a member of the public in the street. It involves exercising authority, enforcing the law and exerting power.

One of the things that also struck me from my early days in the police was that we were never wrong. To even acknowledge that would show weakness. My teachers and mentors over the years instilled in me that this was fundamental to doing the job. It was very, very rare for anyone ever to question anyone in supervision or management. As a constable, going against the established norms would lead you to be labelled a troublemaker. As one of my bosses used to say (I must admit, I have used it too!), "I'm afraid it's a case of JFDI," (Just Fucking Do It). There was no doubt in my mind that these aspects of my character were partly to blame for our relationship breakdown. However, something else that Rachael told me about my situation also stuck in my mind. "You are only responsible for 50% of the relationship." I had never considered that either. Knowing what I know now, I would use the term 'gaslighting' to more accurately describe my treatment by Emma. Gaslighting is a form of manipulation that occurs in abusive relationships; it is insidious. It had caused me to continually question my judgement and reality.

The sessions were absolutely draining. I would go home tired but feeling emotionally stronger. I was given homework to do and gradually began to work on more effective coping strategies. When I related to Emma how much better I felt, it wasn't long before she formed the opinion that I was now having an affair with Rachael. It seemed like everything I did was scrutinised from a completely illogical viewpoint. It was emotional abuse, pure and simple. I would relate this back in sessions and on one occasion, Rachael said the following. "There's a story about a man who walks down the road. He sees a manhole cover that is removed and falls down the hole. Each day he keeps walking down the same road and falling into the hole, until he changes his route."

I knew then what I needed and had to do, no matter how painful it was going to be, or the consequences that came from it. Our direction of travel had to change, otherwise one or both of us would end up dead or seriously injured. I had many sessions with Rachael. They were, without a shadow of a doubt, life-changing. A counsellor is not there to make decisions for you. They are, in my humble opinion, there to get you to look at situations from other perspectives and in different ways. Amongst other things that I identified, with some assistance, was that I was a people pleaser. I was used to protecting people. Maybe that had its roots in childhood – I was the oldest of three and often left to take care of my brother and sister.

Ultimately, I concluded that I wasn't happy, I was miserable. I would never make Emma happy and that we were imprisoned in a destructive, toxic relationship. I stopped sharing further details of my counselling with Emma as I suspected I would live to regret it.

48. Separation

In early 2010, Emma told me that another man at the police station was showing an interest in her. I didn't know whether to believe this or not, or if it was yet another strategy to get my attention. I was still aware of the man she was allegedly supporting emotionally. It was even stranger that she disclosed to me that the pair of them had been out for the evening. She wasn't prepared to tell me anymore about him. What she did say was that it was a mistake and that other than a goodnight kiss, nothing else had happened. I wasn't convinced and the investigator in me took over.

I didn't intend going to her place of work and start chucking accusations about. That was not in my nature and in truth I still suspected this latest story had its roots in fantasy, purely because we had discussed separation. Emma was resistant; she did not want us to part, telling me she loved me and wanted me to stay. I continued to work in London and travel home at the weekends. The pressure for me to resign my role and find a job locally continued. This behaviour seemed to be totally in conflict with what she had told me about her and the 'other guy'. If she really was having an affair, then why would she want me to be at home? Nothing made sense. It frequently came up during my sessions with Rachael. I was distracted and didn't know what to do for the best. Thankfully, the sheer volume of work kept me busy during the week.

On Monday 15th February, the day after Valentine's Day, I found a red envelope on my desk at work. It had a postage stamp on it which had been franked. The ink was blurred so I was unable to make out where it had been posted from but was instantly suspicious when my 'anonymous' admirer's writing resembled Emma's. I telephoned her straight away putting it to her that she had sent it. It came as no surprise when she denied having anything to do with it, announcing that this was evidence of an affair. Later that afternoon I started to get text messages from a number I didn't recognise, asking if I had received the card and would I be prepared to meet. I instinctively knew this was Emma and played along. The messages were non-stop and were beginning to make me feel weary. Continual denials from her led me at one point to walking around the office calling the number to see if there was a phone ringing anywhere. My rational mind told me that I was being stupid. There was only ever one person behind this, but the lack of confirmation was preying on my mind.

Through my own enquiries one Friday morning whilst at work, I discovered the identity of the man that Emma was seeing. From the information I gleaned, it was quite clearly more than a passing infatuation. A full-blown affair had been taking place, and for several weeks. It had also led to a huge bust up between the two men who were competing for her attention. I knew what I had to do. I was angry, more so because for long enough I had been accused of playing around.

I arranged to leave early from work on the pretext of a welfare issue and drove home. I'd established the name of the man she was seeing and that he worked in the same building as Emma. On the way home, I called him and introduced myself. He didn't know what to say and could only respond, "I suggest you speak to your wife." I knew exactly who he would be calling next. I also knew I would get home before Emma. I arrived at home, quickly packed some of her clothes up into bin liners and placed them all at the front door. I put keys in both the front and back door and waited for the inevitable knock. It felt strangely liberating, I had known for some time this had to happen. I was not looking forward to the upheaval and shame of another failed marriage, but we simply could not go on like this. Being in the same house together was not a good idea given what had happened before. I did not want any form of confrontation. Deep down, whilst not welcoming the emotional turmoil, I knew that what I was doing was for the good for the pair of us.

There was a knock on the door. I opened it on the door chain and was met with a puzzled look from Emma. Immediately she asked me why I had telephoned her suitor and demanded that I let her in. I stood firm. Replying calmly, I said, "You can go and live with him; you are not getting into this house." I closed the door shut. She knocked and telephoned me for what seemed like an eternity, even telephoning my dad, who in turn called me. I explained what had happened, whereupon he didn't seem to know what to say. I made it plain to him that she was not getting into the house. I knew full well there would be a massive row if she got inside. I would also end up being falsely accused of being the aggressor.

Around 30 minutes later, there was yet another knock at the door. This time a uniformed police officer stood there. We lived in another police area to where Emma worked so I knew there was not going to be any partisan act on his behalf. I explained the situation, adding that if Emma was to enter the house there would be a breach of the peace. The likelihood would be that as the male party, I would be the one to be ejected or arrested and he did not take issue with my argument.

That had been policy across the country for years. Upon his request, I agreed to get Emma some toiletries. He left and all was then quiet. I later got a text message from Emma saying, "You will live to regret what you did today."

I will admit that night was not a pleasant one. I hadn't been in that house for very long on my own at all. I was used to being alone, but reality hit; there was no coming back from this. I had to tell my children, my dad and eventually people at work. I broke down in tears, something I would probably never had done before. The counselling I was having with Rachael helped me understand that crying is OK. Bottling emotions up is not helpful, yet I had been doing it for years. The one emotion I had difficulty containing was anger. I was angry, mostly with myself and for the pain and hurt I had caused my children. I didn't stay sad for long. I entered planning mode, maybe to distract myself.

I had to head back to London the following week. My initial thoughts were that I would change the locks on the house, leave it unoccupied and put it on the market. I didn't want any form of reconciliation. I wanted out and wanted it to happen as quickly as possible. I contacted a solicitor friend who put me in touch with a very down-to-earth and practical divorce specialist.

In the meantime, a member of the same firm told me that I couldn't keep Emma out of the 'marital home' for more than a few days. Prior to leaving for London, I ended up meeting her briefly in a local café and told her that we were separating. Her response, the one I anticipated, was to tell me that I was overreacting, that she was not having an affair and that she loved me. Unfortunately for her, in terms of the affair, I had evidence to the contrary. I had prepared a written agreement that effectively meant I was free to access the house to collect my clothing and personal belongings. I would continue to pay the mortgage, but the house would be sold and divided equally between us. I left and headed back to London. There was a constant flurry of texts and phone calls. Emma was trying hard to persuade me that nothing was going on and wanted me at home. At work ,we were amidst several high-profile investigations with numerous requests from lawyers, so I was able to distract myself.

I had no intention of heading home the following Friday. My eldest son had recently purchased a flat in Leeds so I arranged to stay there for the weekend – as it turned out, on many subsequent weekends. We had always been close; understandably he felt aggrieved when his mum and I parted.

The weekends I subsequently spent with him and his girlfriend (now his wife and my daughter-in-law) were very special. I look back upon them with great fondness. They were both extremely supportive of me and I have never forgotten it. We would go out together in the evenings for meals, to wine bars, clubs and to watch cricket. I was introduced to his circle of friends and despite me being the same age as many of their fathers, they embraced me as one of their gang; it was heartening. Not once did any of them pry into my situation. They knew what had happened and only ever offered support. I came to once again value the love of my children.

I told them all separately what had happened. None of them were judgemental or in the least bit surprised. I think they were quietly happy that it had all broken down. My youngest son came to see me in Leeds and gave me an enormous hug. I couldn't help but shed a tear.

Telling my daughter was probably the most difficult of all. She was bitter because of what had happened over the years.

Once I spoke to her, it felt like a weight had been lifted from my shoulders. I knew it would be some time before everything was over and done with, but I was certain the right decision had been made.

A couple of weekends later, I started to view apartments in both London and Leeds as I was unsure where to have my permanent base. I enjoyed the work I was doing and saw myself there for several years to come. However, I had made the decision to return to Leeds to be close to the children and make up for lost time. I settled on a brand-new two-bedroomed apartment not far from the city centre.

On my way back to Leeds at the weekends, wherever possible I would arrange an appointment with Rachael. We both felt that the sessions needed to continue. In the end, they went on for around 12 months. They proved to be enormously beneficial, and also helped me to cope better with the separation and forthcoming divorce. Emma continued to deny that she was seeing the man from the police station. The temptation to check whilst close by after the sessions often proved too much. On at least one occasion, I did see a strange car on the driveway of the house which I assumed, but never confirmed, was his.

Over time I managed to recover most of my clothes and property by calling into the house whilst Emma was still at work. Arrangements were supposedly in hand for the house to be put on the market but she was dragging her feet. In a telephone call to the local estate agent, I discovered that Emma had visited the offices with a male companion. What became obvious quite quickly was that he had moved into the property, something we had agreed would not happen. I was determined to prove that was the case. As I was paying all the mortgage, I felt strongly that he shouldn't benefit. It was clear to me that it was always the plan for them to have the house for themselves. In my opinion, this was a huge piss take and it gnawed away at me. Whilst I was glad to be away from Emma, I still felt she was playing more games. I had found out about the affair, but I now needed to get evidence for their cohabitation to support my case in the divorce court. The whole thing dragged on for many months. I was making no headway because they were always one step ahead of me.

In the early summer of 2010, I took the decision to leave the company. This was driven primarily by the upcoming divorce. I had a pension from my time in the police and was also receiving a good salary. Emma had reduced her hours at work. On the face of it, this was a plan designed to ensure that I would be forced into paying maintenance for her. There had been an initial hearing attended by my solicitor where the judge had expressed a view that I would be paying for her future upkeep. It was a bizarre decision. I was unable to prove the pair of them were living together, although my solicitor encouraged me to find evidence to support it.

At the same time, I was negotiating the purchase of my apartment in Leeds, buying a new car and setting up my own company. I was completely settled with my own direction of travel and was using the contacts I knew in London to garner business prior to leaving.

One fateful day, I went back to the house on my way to the city for a business meeting the following day. I had some further items I needed to collect but I also thought I may be able to secure evidence that the pair of them were living there together. The plan was then to stay over in London, have the meeting and head back to Leeds. It did not work out quite the way I had intended.

49. Banged up

I arrived at the house shortly after midday to find that the locks had been changed on both the front and rear doors. This was not something that had been agreed. I was still paying all the mortgage and other bills for the house and was allowed access. The garage door, however, was accessible, and this had a connecting door into the house which was normally left unlocked. Given the time, I did not anticipate anyone being at home. I lifted the up-and-over garage door only to find the integral door inside was locked. The garage still contained several of my tools, so I came up with the idea of drilling through one of the wooden door panels and unlocking it from the other side. I began to use a drill and jigsaw to do this.

I remember in the distance hearing sirens. I thought nothing of it all. A few minutes later, a police car pulled up directly outside the garage with blues and twos blazing. The officer came to me and said, "Excuse me, Sir, can you stop what you are doing?" I assumed at that point that someone had called it in thinking I was a burglar. I explained the position and that it was my house. He then proceeded to recite the law about criminal damage. The law in this respect is such that if you are not endangering life, you can damage your own property to your heart's content, I politely pointed that out.

At that point, another police officer arrived. When he came into the garage, I was arrested for assault. I looked at the pair of them completely bemused and asked, "Who exactly have I assaulted?" I did not get a reply and was escorted to one of their vehicles. I then saw one of the officers go to the front door of the house, which opened, and he went inside. I realised someone was in the property; it was odd and had not been obvious. I had fallen foul of a trap. To say I was confused was an understatement. I was also acutely aware of how vulnerable I now was.

This was the revenge that Emma had promised. It was a deliberate attempt to stop me in my tracks, destroy my credibility and every single minute of work I had put in for so many years. The journey to the police station took about 15 minutes; my mind was racing. I was in complete shock. Whilst I knew what to expect in terms of the process, I would now be at the opposite side of the custody counter. My lawyer friend was on holiday in Italy so I knew I would be reliant on a duty solicitor.

During the booking in process, the officer outlined that a detailed statement had been obtained from Emma, detailing historic abuse over several years. My jaw dropped. What made it particularly worrying was that an officer from where Emma worked had obtained the statement. I was then informed that it would be those officers who wanted to interview me. The incidents were alleged to have taken place in our new home; this was located in a completely different police jurisdiction to where Emma worked.

In terms of responsibilities, it was not for them to investigate. I was instantly suspicious; this could not be said to be fair and proper. I asked to speak to the custody officer. I, of course, knew it would make no difference to the process that had to be followed. However, this felt to me like Emma and her boyfriend had exerted some influence on friends at the station where she worked. My objections were listened to, which led to their exclusion from any interviews. As a result, I was detained overnight, spending a very uncomfortable time in the cells. An experience I would not recommend.

It wasn't until the following afternoon that I was interviewed. I had been held close to 20hrs before anyone even spoke to me formally. As it turned out, two female officers from the Domestic Violence Unit, in the area where I was being detained, interviewed me under caution in the presence of a duty solicitor. The officers concerned were very professional, the solicitor was excellent, I answered every single allegation that was made against me, putting forward my explanations and perspective. I was able to provide the additional context and information that was clearly absent from Emma's very one-sided witness statement. I had been painted as the aggressor, being extremely controlling and the sort of person I had investigated and prosecuted for many years. I saw the potential for the case going to court and the shame associated with it in terms of my family and career. I also knew the allegations were false, so would do my utmost to defend myself.

I was released on bail with conditions that I was not to contact Emma. There was a degree of irony in this. Over the weeks prior to my arrest, she had been telephoning, emailing and texting me. Several of those messages asked me to meet her at a local pub for lunch to try and persuade me to come home, hardly in keeping with her statement saying that she was fearful of me. Repeatedly, she told me that she didn't love the guy she was with. This was all about control and coercion, something that Emma was highly proficient at. Having me arrested was part of the game.

Once released from custody, I went to see my dad and spent the night at his house. I explained what had happened. He listened and was supportive but said little. He had never expressed an opinion about Emma, or indeed my first wife. As far as he was concerned, it was none of his business, and I was fine with that.

I didn't sleep well and headed back to Leeds the next day. The enormity of my situation began to sink in. The police service is renowned for gossip. It wouldn't take long before news would reach my former colleagues even though I was now retired. This was horrendous. I was ashamed that it had come to this. Regardless of the truth, the fact that I had been 'locked up' for domestic violence would be all that people remembered.

I had hoped to keep myself busy with my new business but lost all interest. I became very preoccupied with what the outcome might be. I spoke to Rachael and my solicitor friend, both of whom were tremendously helpful and understanding. I tried to spend time with my children as much as possible. My mood became very low. At my new flat I would play computer games, watch TV or talk at length on Skype to my sister in Egypt. When alone in the flat, I became depressed and very down. For the first time in my life, I contemplated suicide. I felt that everyone would be better off without me. The thought of being branded an abuser tore me up inside. The shame associated with a court appearance and possible media attention would be something I could never live down.

I eventually rationalised all that, telling myself I had too much to live for, not least of all my children. I had been at the scene of far too many deaths seeing the mess, anguish and pain people leave behind them. I went to the doctors to seek help. I was prescribed tablets. I took one look at the packet and threw them in the bin.

I decided that what I needed to do was to make a counter-complaint of assault. I telephoned the officer in the case. They did not want to make the time to see me until the CPS had reviewed the case. Not to be put off, I downloaded the necessary witness statement forms from the internet and set about detailing as many incidents as I could remember. It took me several days, but around 50 pages was sent by recorded delivery to the investigating force with the request to record a crime complaint. I only knew it had been received and recorded when Victim Support in Leeds telephoned me to ask if I needed their help. I politely declined; I didn't need that sort of assistance; what I needed was to clear my name.

To her eternal credit, my first wife told me that she would be prepared to provide a statement to say that during our marriage there was never a hint of violence from me towards her. I respected her so much for that. The whole episode had a significant psychological impact on me. If I came home at night to my apartment, I had visions of Emma appearing from a stairwell and stabbing me. Getting a good night's sleep was only possible if I had been drinking. I found it hard getting any business because I didn't want to put myself into the public domain. Despite me being on bail conditions not to contact her, Emma took it upon herself to contact a business prospect to disclose the details about my arrest. There followed an embarrassing Skype call where I had to explain the situation. It was a terrible time. When I wasn't seeing my eldest son at his place, I would sit in my apartment and hardly move from it. I was lonely, isolated and avoided all contact with my previous colleagues.

About six weeks after my arrest, I was in my flat one afternoon when I received a call from the officer who interviewed me. She could not have failed to notice the hesitancy in my voice when I answered. I was still nervous about what was going to happen but was informed that the case had now been reviewed by the CPS who had decided there was no case to answer. For a few seconds I couldn't speak. My voice started to tremble, and she asked me a couple of times if I was OK. I couldn't respond because I had tears running down my face, completely overcome with emotion. All I could say was, "Thank you, thank you." A huge weight had been lifted from my shoulders.

The next person I called was Rachael and then my eldest son. A few days later, I accompanied him and his girlfriend to a wedding reception. I was driving down the private road to the venue when my phone rang. I hadn't been made aware that an officer from the force in which I had been interviewed was assigned to my case. Her name was Penny. The way she spoke to me reminded me of the sorts of caring individuals you find in police units that investigate domestic violence and child abuse; she was lovely. Penny asked me if I had a few minutes. I didn't know what to expect and pulled over to the side of the road. I broke down again after she said to me, "When I read your statement, I was in tears." That was all she needed to say. All I wanted was for someone to believe me, my experiences, the impact on my family and the level of malice and collusion by Emma and her new man. Most of all, I wanted 'my' voice to be heard. I asked if Emma had been arrested. She said that as much as she had wanted to, it had been overridden by her supervisor. The case was now closed as far as they were concerned.

I admit having a little too much to drink at the wedding that day, but I slept the best I had for weeks. I continued to be counselled by Rachael until the end of that year. Her sessions were invaluable; they made me look inwardly, identify my own issues, and see things from different perspectives. Most of all, understanding that we are all individuals, shaped by a host of complex unique experiences. I believe I came out a better man for it. I now have a set of tools and techniques to deal better with what life can throw at me. I also understand there is no shame in acknowledging emotions, who you are and identifying where you can improve.

In the years since, I have, wherever possible, tried to pass on some of those teachings to people who are close to me and struggling. I could never hope to possess Rachael's skills, patience and knowledge; she was amazing. If ever you find yourself struggling, I hope you find the courage to reach out and have the good fortune to find someone like her.

50. New life

The subsequent divorce and financial settlement with Emma made for a long drawn-out affair. Her demands that she should be maintained by me for the rest of her life, despite having moved her boyfriend into the house were, thankfully, dismissed by the Judge. Throughout the proceedings, she refused to instruct any legal representation. This meant that any written communication came back to my solicitor written by someone who was not legally qualified, the net result being that I had to generate additional legal letters at more costs to me.

My eldest son came to the final hearing with me. After what seemed like an eternity, the divorce was granted and a fair settlement agreed. Ultimately, her aim was to get access to my police pension, which she failed to achieve. I gave up the house in return for my freedom, a small price to pay to get away from all the misery and pain.

As we came out of the courtroom, Emma asked if she could speak to me. Initially I refused, but she told me she had something to say. I asked my son to stay outside a nearby private room, being wary of further allegations. It had a panel of glass and he was able to see the pair of us. I was nervous, but I also thought that she should be given a minute or two – after all, we had spent several years together. Perhaps I thought she was going to apologise. I don't suppose I was overly shocked when all she said was, "I never wanted it to come to this!" A small part of me wanted to believe that. I think that from the outset everything had been designed to teach me a lesson, but it all got out of control. However, in the time I had spent apart from Emma, I was reminded about the love for my children and family, something that I had missed for so long. I had become happier, less stressed and felt free.

The damage wasn't over though, for shortly after separating from Emma, I met with her mother in Leeds to update her on the situation. The relationship between the two of them was a strange one. Emma had often blamed her for her own issues, on one occasion apparently being left alone for a week while she went away on holiday with another man. I had always got on with her though and felt she was owed an explanation. Her response was that everything mirrored what had happened in Emma's first marriage. However, when word got back to Emma about the meeting, she arranged to meet my stepmother and proceeded to recount all the allegations she had made against me. This in turn was fed back to my dad. My relationship with him was already strained due to what happened with my daughter.

Approximately three years ago, she reached out to my dad in an effort to build bridges after the incident with my grandson. However, he rejected her out of hand, leading me to step in, try to mediate and make peace. Things escalated to a point where he asked me not to contact him again. I tried several times to sort things out, by sending cards and letters. For a long time, there was no response. Because he is in his mid-eighties, I became resolved to the fact that I would never see him again.

Thankfully, and only very recently, I was able to meet with Dad again; we've moved on and those times are no longer worth discussing.

In my view, all roads lead back to Emma and the emotional damage she seemed to take pleasure in causing. Do I blame her for everything? Of course not – I must take responsibility for my own actions. I regret bitterly the pain that was caused to my children over the years. I harbour guilt that my youngest son damaged his education by truanting from school, in reaction to me leaving home and how that continues to affect him to this day.

For the most part, the outcomes of the divorce from Emma have been overwhelmingly positive. It took me some time to come to terms with the emotional trauma of it all. There was some reputational damage that I had to deal with as a result. Having set up my own business, I was offered work at one of my previous police forces. On the first day, I recall visibly shaking on arrival at reception for fear that someone had knowledge of my arrest. During the time I was there, I saw numerous colleagues, all of whom took the time to speak to me and enquire as to how I was. Nobody made any mention of my arrest, but the police service has its own internal intelligence network. I always suspected that people knew, but never mentioned it. I confided in a very small number of trusted friends about what had happened, often finding myself moved to tears when trying to explain things.

It's over ten years ago now and I have finally put it behind me. Writing this book has been part of a healing process. I have always been an intensely private person but am so much more conscious now about the feelings associated with having your liberty and freedoms removed. It has reinforced my own internal values about fairness, injustice and a realisation of just how easy it can be to have your whole world turned upside down on the word of another human being. I was not without fault in that relationship; we fought, we were verbally abusive to each other, and we hurt each other both emotionally and physically. When I tried to leave for each of our benefits, the backlash was entirely disproportionate. However, I'm no longer angry with Emma. I last saw her at the divorce hearing. I don't know where she is or what she is doing, but sincerely hope she has found some happiness. I have worked hard to build my own business, another ambition I held since being a child. Whilst I enjoyed my time in public service, I don't miss anything other than the camaraderie. I have, through social media, reconnected with friends from my time in the army and the police. Sadly, some have passed, many taken far too early. Doubtless for some, the effects of a life in service, be that the army or police.

Spending over 30 years in public service cannot fail to leave you unaffected. You must be resilient to survive, or you will go under. You get desensitised and you laugh at things others wouldn't. You must fit in and at times you end up compromising your own personal values. All this ends up seeping into your personal life; it makes you very different from the average man or woman in the street. I like to have a social drink, but I no longer drink to excess. Like so many of my former colleagues in the police, I have an inherent dislike of drunks. If I visit a pub or a restaurant, I find it difficult to relax, always watching out for trouble, and I must be able to see the door if I sit down. I still work too hard, but now I do it for me. I get up early, I exercise every day and have a routine. I know I can be a pain in the arse and still have a stubborn streak, but I am honest, hate unfairness and I speak my mind. That trait can occasionally get me into trouble.

After my sessions with Rachael, I didn't get everything right straight away. I jumped back into the relationship game far too quickly and there was some fallout from that. I am much less trusting now. If there is any indication of toxicity with people, I sever ties with them; it's just easier and less stressful.

On a personal front, I regularly tell my children and grandchildren that I love them. I try to see them as often as I can. If I am not able to, I contact them by phone. Sadly, they lost their mum through a terminal disease recently. It was gut-wrenching watching them having to cope with the loss of someone they loved dearly and so early in life. It was reminiscent of when I lost my own mother. I like to think I was much more present for them during that difficult time. I was certainly invested at an emotional level, readily sharing my own experiences and how I came to terms with the death of a loved one.

I've come to accept that life is full of twists and turns and ups and downs. Despite what anyone tells you or what you see on the surface, no one's life is perfect. I look back now, with sixty-plus years on my back, at what I have achieved. I have three great and very different children with a small army of grandchildren. I also have a stepson. We haven't always got on, but that experience has given me a much better appreciation and respect for my own stepfather and what he was up against.

I have several medals from my time in public service. I have numerous letters of appreciation, commendations and awards for my work. Somehow, I even managed to attain a Master of Science degree. I left the police service as a senior officer with experiences in 'the job' that have helped me to build a successful business that has now been in existence for over 10 years. I've worked with, and for, all manner of organisations, including another spell as an undercover operator for a TV documentary. I still like to test myself and undertake challenges accompanied by the odd burst of adventure. I've run a couple of half marathons and recently jumped out of a plane – with a parachute, of course!

I've also now written this book which I hope you've enjoyed. Not too bad for a poor, skinny, cocky, troublesome kid who left school with a smattering of very bland exam results.

In 2013, without any planning on my part, the most amazing woman came along. It is no understatement to say that she transformed me and my life. She is caring, loving, tolerant of my many foibles, and I would be totally lost without her. What's more, my children and grandchildren love her to bits. It was never going to be an easy ride for her given what had happened in the past, but nevertheless she has risen to the challenge with grace, aplomb and patience. Having said I would never marry again, we did exactly that.

I have never been so happy. A smile has returned to my face and I have to pinch myself to check that it is real sometimes. I see my children and grandchildren as often as I want to and there are no restrictions. Do we argue? I'd call it bickering, but it is occasional and never, ever, to the intensity of my second marriage. I have found my soulmate. I am happy, we are happy, my children are happy, and you cannot put a price on that. We live by the sea, have two barmy dogs and are growing older disgracefully together. Life is good.

Glossary

"Appointments" – Handcuffs, truncheon and on night shifts a rubberised Eveready torch that were to be produced at the briefing.

Civvies – Civilians or 'Joe Public'.

Cocker – A term of endearment in Yorkshire. Also, 'old cocker' or 'old cock'.

Communications Centre (ComCen) – A hub where incoming and outgoing messages are handled.

Crown Prosecution Service (CPS) – The agency that handles criminal prosecutions in the UK.

Force Intelligence Unit (FIU) – A police headquarters resource that acted as a focal point for force wide intelligence functions.

'Gated' – Not allowed to leave barracks, confined often because of a failure to reach a standard, such as drill.

Green maggot – A standard army issue sleeping bag.

HESCO – Barriers that are deployed to provide protection against threats.

Major Crime Unit (MCU) – A team of detectives that were deployed to investigate serious and organised crime.

NAAFI – Naval, Army and Air Force Institutes which provide recreational establishments such as bars and shops on service barracks and deployments.

NATO (North Atlantic Treaty Organisation) – A military alliance of countries that collaborate and agree to mutual defence in response to an attack by an external party.

PIRA (Provisional IRA) – The paramilitary wing of the Irish Republican Army who until their ceasefire in 1997 used guerrilla tactics against the British Army and RUC in both rural and urban areas.

QRF (Quick Reaction Force) – A small body of troops that would be on standby as an immediate response to incidents.

Restriction of Privileges, or ROPs – A punishment that could be levied by army commanders for minor acts of insubordination or ill-discipline committed by their troops.

Staff – A localised term for the traditional truncheon, now replaced by more modern batons such as the PR24.

Task Force – A specialist team of police officers who could quickly be deployed to deal with planned or unplanned public order situations, major crime, searches, and other miscellaneous incidents.

'Tick tocks' and gravel bellies – Slang terms for infantry soldiers.

Military and Police Ranks

Army rank structure

<u>Non-commissioned</u>

- Army Apprentice/Apprentice – Tradesman equivalent of Private
- Private
- Lance Corporal
- Corporal
- Sergeant
- Staff Sergeant
- Warrant Officer Class 2 – sometimes appointed as CSM (Company Sergeant Major)
- Warrant Officer Class 1 – sometimes appointed as RSM (Regimental Sergeant Major)

<u>Commissioned</u>

- Second Lieutenant (pronounced 'leftenant')
- Lieutenant
- Captain
- Major

- Lieutenant Colonel

- Colonel

- Brigadier

- Major General

- Lieutenant General

- General

- Field Marshal

Police rank structure

- Police Constable/Detective Constable

- Police Sergeant/Detective Sergeant

- Inspector/Detective Inspector

- Chief Inspector/Detective Chief Inspector

- Superintendent/Detective Superintendent

- Chief Superintendent/Detective Chief Superintendent

- Assistant Chief Constable

- Deputy Chief Constable

- Chief Constable

List of various roles

Military

- Army Apprentice – A boy soldier who attended an army college to undergo trade training, such as the Royal Engineers (RE), Royal Electrical and Mechanical Engineers (REME) and Royal Signals.

- Camp Commandant – The most senior officer with overall responsibility for a services unit.

- Drill Commander – An individual given responsibility for ensuring the quality of drill, deportment and standards of dress is maintained.

- Drill Sergeants – Sergeants in both HM Forces and the Police who instruct staff in drill.

- Duty Officer – In the context of the book, a member of Permanent Staff who was responsible at night for soldiers' welfare and good order of their respective blocks.

- Master at Arms – A ship's senior rating, normally carrying the rank of chief petty officer or warrant officer who oversees security and discipline.

- Officer Commanding (OC) – In the context of the book, an OC tended to be a Major, in charge of a Squadron or Battalion.

- Permanent Staff (abbreviated to PS) – Regular army soldiers who instructed at the Army Apprentice College.

- Quartermaster – In the context of the book, 'Royal Marine Quartermaster', the NCO/SNCO in charge of logistics, supplies and clothing.

- Recruit/Rook/Rookie – An individual new to HM Forces or the Police service.

- Room Corporal – In the context of the book, an Apprentice Lance Corporal or Corporal with responsibility for a room of up to seven boys.

- Senior term – A group of apprentices in their last period of learning at the Army Apprentice College.

- Special Forces (SF) Operator – A soldier who has successfully completed a rigorous selection procedure followed by intense training, SAS (Special Air Service) and SBS (Special Boat Service) or their counterparts in other countries.

Police

- CID – Criminal Investigation Department, staffed by police detectives.

- Community Constables – Designated Police Constables with responsibility for a specific area and local point of contact.

- Custody officer – Police Sergeants who are responsible for managing the custody area and the care and welfare of detained persons.

- Directing Staff (DS) – Not rank specific, those in charge of, for example, training.

- Divisional Detective Inspector (DI) – An individual or small team of Inspectors with day-to-day management responsibility of the CID office and serious crime.

- Divisional Process Sergeant – An individual who had responsibility for ensuring that prosecution files had the 'points to prove' for offences, contained sufficient evidence and were logical and well presented.

- Drill Sergeants – Sergeants in both HM Forces and the Police who instruct staff in drill.

- Office-man – An officer who dealt with 'front of house' at a police station.

- Patrol Sergeant – A Sergeant in charge of uniformed patrol duties, now often called 'response' or 'response policing'.

- Probationary Officers/Probationary Constables – A police officer within their first two years of service and under continual assessment.

- Recruit/Rook/Rookie – An individual new to HM Forces or the Police service.

- Road Traffic Officers – Specialist police officers trained to deal with serious road traffic incidents, patrol motorways and engage in police pursuits.

- Senior Investigating Officer (SIO) – A police officer with overall responsibility for the conduct of an investigation, not rank specific.

- Senior NCOs (Non-Commissioned Officers) – Army ranks above Corporal and up to Warrant Officer.

- Senior Officer – Normally used in police parlance for officers above the rank of Inspector.

- Special Patrol Group or SPG – Similar to 'Task Force', a Metropolitan Police unit who tackled serious public disorder, crime and terrorism that could not be dealt with by local divisions.

Acknowledgements

Without my parents I wouldn't even be here, so they must be at the top of the page. I thank my mum for her DNA that gives me my compassionate and caring side. As to my dad, I credit him for my motivation and drive to do better. They were not together for long but even when parted, they did everything in their power to make me and my siblings good people.

I haven't always got along with my stepfather, but our relationship is a strong one, and only now can I fully appreciate what he took on so many years ago. He is a good man; he adored Mum and made her happy. My stepmother has always made me welcome from being a child; she has brought my dad much happiness and I am grateful for that too.

The list of good people that I have worked with over the years is far too long; the ones that stand out are mentioned in my book. But I do feel that I owe the late Ron Hails, Royal Signals, a special mention. An extremely strict Troop Sergeant but a guide and mentor to me and many other young soldiers, he provided me with the discipline I needed as a troublesome teenager.

There is no stronger bond than that of a family. I have watched my children grow into adults, form their own relationships, and have their own children, my lovely grandchildren. They all continue to make me proud. I always enjoy spending time with them and their partners.

Those two words 'Thank you' cannot possibly convey the gratitude I have for Rachael, my counsellor, who guided me through a very dark time in my life and helped me see the light.

My confidante and proofreader Vivienne helped me transform my early efforts into something more coherent and readable, followed closely by Brenda and the team at Book Brilliance Publishing, who have been fabulous; their support has been outstanding.

Without question, I couldn't have come this far without the support, love and encouragement of my wife and soulmate. Always there when I needed to read out a passage and check that it sounded OK, listening and finding out stuff she didn't know about me. Such is her nature, always asking how 'I' was.

I consider myself to be a very lucky man; thank you all.

About the Author

Colin Tansley is a former soldier and police officer. Now retired from public service, he runs his own business.

As a young man, Colin was trained as an Army Apprentice for two years before being deployed in the UK and overseas, including a tour in Northern Ireland in the late seventies. Subsequently joining the police, he enjoyed roles in uniform, plain clothes, child protection, training and management. During those times, he witnessed at first hand the effects of rioting in the early eighties, the miner's strike of 1984, child abuse, and fighting crime at the 'sharp end'.

Colin has travelled widely in his professional capacity, imparting his skills and knowledge, even volunteering for a spell in post-war Iraq.

A father, stepfather, and grandfather, he has had numerous personal and professional challenges to contend with over the years. Colin is the first to admit he has a stubborn side, something he believes is inherited from his father, and has turned this trait into a positive focus and perseverance towards achieving his goals.

He has been variously described as a people person, tenacious and well-motivated. His passion to investigate, risk manage, protect vulnerable businesses and push back against unfairness is testament to the work he does to this day via his company Intelect.

Keep in touch with the author:

Twitter: @author_colin

https://colintansley.com/

hello@colintansley.com

linkedin.com/in/colintansleyintelect